AGENCY AND ALIENATION

A Theory of Human Presence

Jerome M. Segal

Rowman & Littlefield Publishers, Inc.

ROWMAN & LITTLEFIELD PUBLISHERS, INC.

Published in the United States of America
by Rowman & Littlefield Publishers, Inc.
8705 Bollman Place, Savage, Maryland 20763

British Cataloging in Publication Information Available

Library of Congress Cataloging-in-Publication Data

Segal, Jerome M., 1943-
Agency and alienation : a theory of human presence
/ Jerome M. Segal.
p.   cm.
Includes bibliographical references.
1. Act (Philosophy)   2. Action theory.   3. Agent
(Philosophy)   4. Self.   5. Self (Philosophy)
I. Title.
B105.A35S44   1991
126—dc20   91–11954 CIP

ISBN 0–8476–7628–5 (cloth : alk. paper)

Printed in the United States of America

 ™ The paper used in this publication meets the minimum requirements of
American National Standard for Information Sciences—Permanence of
Paper for Printed Library Materials, ANSI Z39.48–1984.

For Naomi and Max

A Commercial View of the Real Self

"There's a part of me that says 'Just grow old gracefully.'
But then there's the *real* me which says, 'Why?' "

Oil of Olay commercial, Feb. 26, 1990

Contents

Contents

PREFACE

In recent years philosophers and psychologists have increasingly become interested in the self. Among philosophers this has emerged in a variety of contexts. Some authors have been directly concerned with the notion of the self and how it functions within psychological theory. Other philosophers have focused on the question, "What is a person?" and have at times found personhood closely associated with having a concept of oneself, a self-identity, or certain attitudes towards oneself. One prominent philosopher has argued that to be a person it is necessary that one have what he terms "second-order volitions" (i.e., desires with respect to the kinds of desires one acts upon).

For philosophers, interest in the self often emerges out of the problem of free will. An interesting work on the subject has offered an account of freedom in terms of actions emanating from that part of the self with which the individual identifies. Among psychologists, inquiry into the self centers on two questions, "What role does a person's self-concept play in explaining behavior?" and "How is the individual's concept of self achieved?" A leading psychoanalyst has called for a "psychology of self," and in earlier years theorists such as Karen Horney attempted to develop the notion of "the real self" as the key to mental health.

Within these varied discussions it sometimes appears that the participants are not speaking of the same thing—sometimes the self is identified as the person himself, at other times the self is understood as some more limited component of the personality, and at other times simply as one's concept of oneself. Yet these different discussions do reflect a common intellectual thread. That thread is the notion of unity, coherence, integrity, or wholeness—in particular the unity of real human beings. For philosophers this has represented a psychological enrichment of their inquiry. Concern with the self or persons is not limited to the older metaphysical concern with whether or not there needs to be a self or ego or person that "has" mental events. Today the discussion is also concerned with the conditions under which real human beings are or might be constituted into the wholes that we describe as persons. If there is a continuum stretching from the metaphysical notion of a person to the moral notion of a person, philosophers have, then, become more interested in the richer end of the continuum. Thus, in contemporary discussions of utilitarianism, it has been argued that an ethic which requires of individuals that they take an impersonal point of view towards the consequences of their own actions, without giving priority to their own projects, undermines the integrity of the person. And here "integrity" is not being used to mean moral integrity but rather the conditions under which a human being is held together into a specific person—the thought being that part of what it is to be a person is to have projects that are "mine" and to give them a certain priority.

It is not surprising that we find ourselves constantly gravitating towards the issue of coherence or integration of the personality. For several centuries the Western world has been undergoing changes that have threatened the individual's sense of unity. Sociologists have characterized modernity in terms of the breakdown of the traditional meanings that allowed the individual to organize his or her life as a coherent whole. Starting in the 1960s there was a rediscovery of the early manuscripts of Marx in which his central critique of capitalism is articulated in terms of the concept of "alienation"—an alienation that takes its deepest expression in one's alienation from oneself. Building on both Marx and Freud, social critics such as Erich Fromm articulated their critique of modern industrial society in terms of the mental health of the individual, specifically focusing on how modern society blocks the possibility of human coherence.

The theme of wholeness and its possibility emerged explicitly in the existentialist tradition. Sartre located the problem of not-being-fully-whole within the ontological character of consciousness, making it independent of the specifics of history, social organization, and individual biography. Human beings are inherently fragmented into two modes of being—facticity and transcendence. We are forever, so long as we are alive, devoid of a center—at the center there is nothingness, and certainly not the "real self." The anxiety encountered by psychotherapists among patients who have lost their self-connectedness is lifted by Sartre to the ontological level of "angoise."

The existential tradition contributed more than specific theses with respect to the origins and possibilities of human unity; it contributed a particular perspective—the perspective of the individual's own experience of himself or herself in the face of inner fragmentation. It raised the question, "What is authentic self-experience?" For Sartre, to experience oneself as whole, to feel at one with the kind of person one is, is itself a form of bad faith. Authentic experience must be grounded in reality, and if the reality is that the human self is inherently fragmented, then to be authentically human is to live within an awareness of the permanence of this fissure. The implication of this conclusion is a radical challenge to moral and psychological ideals of the person. In particular it suggests an irreconcilable conflict between an ideal of the person that rests upon having overcome inner discord or fragmentation and an ideal that rests on notions of authenticity, self-knowledge, and the absence of self-deception.

Despite the centrality of the idea of a unified self to a wide variety of literatures, there have been relatively few attempts to articulate exactly what it is to be whole. The assumption seems to be that we already know the answer to this question, and thus terms such as "integrity" or "integration" or "coherence" are widely used without further efforts to articulate their meaning. One of the objectives of this book is to give a better account of what it is to be an integrated personality.

The book is divided into two parts. Part One is concerned with human agency, and I offer what might be termed a "presence theory" of agency. This discussion is situated within contemporary analytic action theory. I ask, "What is an action?"; "What is it for one's actions to be one's own?"; "What is it for an act to emerge from oneself"; and ultimately "What is it to have actions that are not one's own?" The theory offered is a new departure. I focus on the notion of "an activity" and treat agency as the presence of the self within one's activity.

There are four chapters in Part One. Chapter 1 considers some of the inadequacies of alternative accounts of human action, in particular, analyses of actions as events with particular kinds of causes (e.g., volitions) and analyses in terms of causation by the agent. Chapter 2 begins the presentation of my theory. It provides an analysis of a molecular activity as a complex unified in a particular manner that I term "indirect perceptual integration." This allows for an independent understanding of activity, devoid of any assumptions about how activities themselves are caused (e.g., by volitions or by agents). Chapter 3 offers an account of the self as an integrated personality, that is, to speak of the self is to speak of a personality that has achieved a certain type and level of integration. The nature of this integration is the central focus of the chapter. Chapter 4 completes the account of agency by addressing the question: What is it for the self to be present in its actions? Two broad forms of presence, immediate presence and indirect presence, are identified and explicated.

The account of agency is designed to elucidate not only the familiar philosophical puzzlement over the nature of action, but our own experience of ourselves as agents—and, when it occurs, our experience of our own lack of agency. The theory moves from a discussion of action to a discussion of the self as the integrated personality and finally to what it is for the self to be present within one's activity.

Part Two is concerned with alienation, including but not limited to being alienated from one's actions. The theoretical discussion contained in Chapter 5 starts by identifying a particular class of experiences; I introduce the term "alienness" to designate these experiences. They are the experiencing of some aspect of oneself (e.g., one's actions, one's emotions, one's values) as not-one's-own, or more precisely, as one's-own-but-not-one's-own. The first task of Part Two is to explain how it is that such experiences are possible. I argue that such experiences are possible only because they occur against a background understanding of what it is for aspects of oneself to be one's own. And it is this that the concept of agency provides with respect to actions.

Part Two focuses on the encounter with one's own incoherence as it is revealed in three central contexts of human life: the search for general understanding of the human condition (the philosophic context), the search for personal self-understanding, and the effort to bring about social transformation.

In Chapter 6, on philosophic inquiry, I seek to show that the most general inquiry into the human condition can generate conclusions with the potential for transforming our self-experience—conclusions which if authentically held may generate a sense of alienness with respect to our own values, beliefs, actions, and even our own sense of identity. The discussion makes contact with the writings of Nietzsche and Sartre. And it includes an examination of Derek Parfit's thesis that a reductionist account of personal identity provides rational grounding for a transformed sense of self. I seek to show that Parfit's views on the nature of personal identity can be fit within a much broader set of philosophical theses that provide grounds for a changed self-experience.

In Chapter 7, on self-understanding, I am concerned with the individual's own inquiry into his or her particular nature. What is it to engage in this authentically? How does alienness differ from self-deception as a way of experiencing oneself? To what extent is there a special authority to the individual's judgments about his or her own identity?

In Chapter 8, on political engagement, I am concerned with the self-experience of the individual who is deeply engaged in a project of large-scale social transformation. I argue that there are features of the political situation that are inherently self-alienating. Yet paradoxically, political action often can emerge as the critical realm for establishing self-identity. I consider three alternative modes of engaging in the political life, three alternative modes of being-political. These are identified respectively with Bentham, Gandhi, and Trotsky. These three psychological styles of political agency are seen as alternative attempts to provide the individual with a sense of integrity in a context that is deeply problematic and a breeding ground of self-deception.

Chapter 9 explores some of the linkages of the preceding chapters to Marx's early writings on alienation and history. It is a fitting place to end. More than any other social philosopher, it was Marx who placed the notion of activity, in particular, labor, at the center of historical change. Marx focused on how human activity is transformed in the course of economic transformation. In *The German Ideology* Marx employed a notion of "self-activity" to put forward a philosophy of history in which a drive for coherence between self and activity is the driving force of political change. If the term "agency" is substituted for "self-activity" in Marx, my analysis of alienation and agency as mutually defining concepts is pre-figured in Marx, and much of my analysis can be viewed as a philosophical psychology that places Marx's early writings on a stronger underpinning. I believe these early writings will remain the lasting legacy of Marxism.

This book is the outcome of work that I began long ago. I wish to extend special thanks to Norbert Hornstein, without whose encouragement and assistance this project would not have reached fruition. I am grateful to Frithjof Bergmann, who was seized with many of the same issues when I was student and he was teacher. Thanks also to Alvin Goldman and William Alston, with whom I studied years ago, to David Luban who helped at a critical moment, and to Ligeia Fontaine.

PART ONE: AGENCY

1

Action Theory

- What is it to be an agent?
- What is it to be passive rather than active?
- What is an action?
- On what basis do we make the distinction between those things we do and those things that just happen to us or within us?

These are the central questions that a theory of action seeks to answer. Every theory is an effort to illuminate some body of information and experience. Theorization may result in our drawing distinctions somewhat differently than we did prior to developing a theory, but every theory takes some set of distinctions as a touchstone for its analysis. Philosophical theories give centrality to our use of language. In the case of a theory of action, for instance, great attention is paid to the fact that we distinguish actions from other occurrences. Hitting a ball is an action, falling down a flight of stairs is not. A theory of action seeks, among other things, to explain the distinctions we make.

A theory of human action should do more than explain linguistic distinctions that we make, a theory should also illuminate our own experience as agents. In what follows I will briefly consider how some of the central questions of action theory have been answered by other writers. I will argue that one of the problems with existing theories is that they fail to illuminate our experience of ourselves as active beings. In the following chapter I will present a new approach to human action, one that I believe has important strengths in just the area where existing theories are weak and that also provides a new approach to the classical dilemmas of action theory.

ANALYTIC ACTION THEORY

Action theory takes as its jumping-off point a question raised by Wittgenstein:

> Let us not forget this: when "I raise my arm," my arm goes up. And the problem arises: what is leftover if I subtract the fact that my arm goes up from the fact that I raised my arm?[1]

Thus, Wittgenstein has pointed out that actions in some sense seem to contain events. In order for it to be true that I raised my hand, it must have been true that my hand went up. But not every instance of my hand's going up is an instance of my having raised my hand; only some of them. In other situations the hand may have gone up as the result of a muscle spasm, or because it was raised by a string connected to my wrist, or because it was buoyed up by the water I was standing in.

Acts

The range of terms such as "acts" or "actions" is so great that it is unlikely there can be a single account of what it is about all actions that constitutes them as actions.Certainly to sell your house is to take an action of major importance. Similarly one does something that one may regret forever if one kills another human being. Yet these actions, selling one's house and killing another person, are such that there are a multiplicity of ways in which they can be done. Moreover, some of the ways in which they can be done seem to involve not doing anything at all.

Some people have special brokerage accounts in which a stock broker is authorized to buy and sell stock for the person. Sometimes the broker actually calls and consults; sometimes he or she is authorized to act on their own. In both cases it remains true that the owner of the account bought and sold certain stocks if all the procedures were exercised correctly.

Imagine that I have an arrangement with my broker such that unless I reject a proposal he will go ahead and execute it. He sends me a telegram or leaves me a message on my answering machine saying that he will buy five hundred shares of IBM at market price. I think it over and conclude that it is a good purchase. Therefore I do nothing; as a result, he executes the order, and I have bought the stock.

From a moral point of view, and from a legal point of view, I have bought the stock. I have done something, and I am responsible for my action. Moreover, in virtue of having bought the stock I may have done a variety of other acts. For instance, I may have kept a promise, I may have proved a point, I may have demonstrated my cleverness, I may have ignored the advice of my wife, I may have risked our life savings, I may have endangered my child's college education, I may have disgraced the family name. In short, I may have done quite a lot that is deserving of either praise or blame. And in our ordinary use of English, it would be quite appropriate, presuming that I was aware and possibly motivated by these implications of my allowing the stock broker to exercise the purchase, to say that I did some or all of these things intentionally. It is a bit odd to say that my intentional doing of these things was not an action. Yet in one sense I have done nothing. Indeed, the agreement with the brokerage house might give the broker full discretion, not even requiring that I be notified. So I can be morally and legally responsible for having purchased stock, lost a fortune, betrayed a trust, and so forth without having even been aware, consciously or unconsciously, that I was performing these actions.

Actions of this sort frequently occur in virtue of complex societal mechanisms and conventions. A good example is the "pocket veto" whereby the president, under certain circumstances, vetoes a bill merely by having not signed it within a specific time period.

Some authors have responded to this feature of action by maintaining that what makes something an action is not something extra that goes along with an event, but rather to view something as an action is to view it as something for which a person is responsible, and to say of someone that he or she performed an action is not to assert the existence of some particular causal relationship, but rather to *ascribe* responsibility.[2] And certainly there is something to this, as seems clear from the example of the stock purchase. Others have said that what makes a piece of behavior an action is that it is embedded within a context of rules and goals. And there seems to be something to that as well.

But for all this, there is a very different kind of problem to which

Wittgenstein's example calls our attention. It is a problem that seems to be sidestepped rather than resolved by viewing actions in these ascriptive or contextual ways. We can define the class of actions so that this problem arises in all instances of actions, or we can simply identify a subset of actions where it occurs. It is not obvious that this makes much difference. The problem, however, is very perplexing, and involves such fundamental issues that it might properly be called metaphysical. It arises most clearly when we focus on a very different kind of example than the stock purchase or the pocket veto.

Consider the following lists:

action	*event*
I raised my hand.	My hand went up.
I opened my mouth.	My mouth opened.
I closed my eyes.	My eyes closed.
I pressed my teeth together.	My teeth pressed together.
I extended my leg.	My leg extended.

Each action is associated with an event. When we are dealing with an action, the relevant event was in some sense *brought about* or *made to happen* by the person. The problem of action is sometimes formulated as the effort to explain what this means; it is the effort to distinguish those cases where an event is embedded in an action from those cases in which we have just a mere event. Alternatively, it could be described as the problem of explaining what it is to have been the agent of an event.

The issue here does not turn on the appropriateness of using "I" as the subject. We might just as well compare:

I winked.	I blinked.
I pressed the bell.	I fell against the bell.
I coughed (intentionally).	I coughed (involuntarily).

Once again, there is some event or behavior that in the first instance I made happen in some direct way that was not so caused in the second set.

Moreover, whether or not this is true is not something that we can automatically tell in virtue of the verb involved. Typically, sweating, growing a hair, and turning red in the face are not things that one does directly—(in an unanalyzed way they are not things that we do "at will"). Rather they are processes that occur, sometimes without our awareness, sometimes because we deliberately do other things that cause them to happen, and sometimes because we do nothing to prevent them from happening. Yet it is completely possible that some people might have the power to simply do these things at will. For instance, some people can directly wiggle their ears; most of us cannot. Intuitively, we know what it would be like for it to be within our power to, at will, make our hair extend from our body—it would be like sticking out one's tongue. We know what it would be like to be able to turn our face red as an action; we would simply make our face red—it would be like deliberately putting on a frown. But exactly what is it we are ascribing to ourselves (or denying) when we say that we can or cannot do these things as direct actions?

What Agency Is Not

Many of us, when we were children, contemplated what it would be like to have extraordinary powers such that we could, at will, cause glasses to rise and chairs to move across the room. Occasionally we see someone with such powers in a movie.

When we played the game, in particular when we tested out whether or not we had such powers, we sometimes looked rather hard at a glass of water and "willed it" to move. It is not clear exactly what if anything it was that we were doing when we willed it to move. Perhaps we gave it an order to move, commanded the glass to move through a directive that we silently said to it in our consciousness. And quite possibly, we tensed certain muscles in the fashion of an isometric exercise, in the effort to make it move. In any event we failed. The glass of water stayed just where it was.

Now imagine that it had moved. And imagine that it soon became clear that we were causing it to move. Certainly moving the glass would be an action that we perform. Moreover, it would be an action with respect to which we might not be able to give any account of how we do it. We might simply say, "I just do it."

This inability to say how we do the things that we do is, in fact, typically the mark of what philosophers have called "basic acts." Examples of basic acts are raising one's hand, making a fist, saying the word "dog," sticking one's tongue out, turning one's head, and so on. Under normal circumstances, these are all instances of things that we just do. We don't do them by doing anything else, and our ability to do them does not depend upon our having any knowledge of how they are done.

On the other hand, an action such as boiling water is not a basic act, because it is done by turning on the heat under a pot of water and our ability to do this depends on a variety of knowings. For instance knowing that the way to turn on the heat is to turn a certain knob. If someone asked us how we turned on the heat, we would say "by turning the knob," but if someone asked us how we turned it, we would probably say little more than that we just turned it. Or perhaps that we squeezed it tight and turned our hand. But with respect to turning our hand or squeezing it, there would be no explaining how we did it. We just did it. Those were basic acts.

Remember again the child's game of trying to get the glass to rise. It might be said that what we were trying to see was whether or not we had over the glass the same power that we have over our limbs. And while it is true that making the glass rise would have been an action if we had been able to do it, and making my arm rise would similarly be an action, "making something happen" is typically not what is involved in basic actions.

It could be. Just as I sat there staring at the glass and willed it to rise, so too, I could stare at my arm and will it to rise; moreover, I could even command it to rise. Interestingly, what I would discover is that even with respect to my hand I don't have the power to cause it to rise by willing it to rise or by commanding it to rise. It just sits there totally inert, until I do something else, until I just lift my hand. And when I do lift my hand, I am not the mere witness of an event I have caused to happen. In some sense I am active throughout the performance.

There is something astonishing and remarkable in all this. We take it quite for granted that we are creatures with these powers to just do things, but it need not be that way at all. In good part the problem of action involves a perplexity in understanding just what this power involves.

Reductionists and Nonreductionists[3]

Broadly speaking there are two schools of thought. There are reductionists and nonreductionists. A reductionist is someone who believes that an action such as my raising my hand consists in nothing other than the occurrence of certain events and the existence of certain relations between those events. For instance, a casual relationship between the arms moving and certain mental events. The reductionist says that this is what constitutes activity, or agency, or an action. There is nothing more to know, no additional fact other than this that is involved.

The nonreductionist believes that an action is not constituted by mere events; it consists in something additional. For instance, a nonreductionist might say that an action occurs when there is some event with respect to which a person is the agent, and that this relationship between the person and the event, which is called agency, is a direct causing of the event by the person. Agency, on this view, is not a matter of some state of the person or some event within the person causing some other event, but is something different, unique and extra.

For instance, Chisholm, at one point writing about agent-causation, said: "The question is not whether there is such a thing as agent causation. But one may ask whether agent causation can be *reduced* to 'event causation'."[4] Nonreductionists have often believed that to view agency as nothing but the holding of a relationship between events is to strip the person of any real activity. It is to actually be passive, to do nothing. Rather, the nonreductionist maintains, to say that a person did something, in this basic act sense of action, is to assert some active role on his or her part. It is to say that he was active or that she moved her hand, and to say this is to affirm the existence of a fact that is not constituted by some events that he or she could just as well have been the witness of. Thus, Richard Taylor has argued,

> If the sequence of changes involving muscular motions, changes within the nervous system, and so on, cannot be traced to some agent as its ultimate cause, then, I have contended, no matter how intimately connected with him these changes may be, none of them represents any act of his. They are instead only the causal consequences of things that happen to him or within him, and things accordingly, with which he has nothing to do.[5]

There is something strongly appealing about nonreductionist accounts. Essentially they appear to conform to aspects of our experience of ourselves when we act. As actors, we experience ourselves as active in the process. We are not mere bystanders who gain a status of having acted even when we do nothing, just because we own the body or the mind within which certain events occur.

And certainly it is not a logical truth about the concept of action that actions conform to some causal pattern. For instance, many, perhaps most, people in the world believe that there are entities that are outside of the normal causal order, gods of one sort or another, and that they simply do things. The notion of doing things predated by thousands and thousands of years the idea of causal relationships between events. Some philosophers have maintained that the direct doing of something by an agent is the origin of our notion of causality, and that the problem is trying to accommodate this age-old intuitive notion with the more modern analysis of causation as a relationship between events.

Now in one sense the nonreductionist is correct. A proposition of the sort:

Event A caused event B

does not entail, and is not entailed by a proposition of the sort:

Person A did action B

Regardless of how one fills in the causal story, ordinary speakers of the language would not be baffled by someone who asserted the first but denied the second, or vice versa. And there is no chain of deduction that does not beg the question that leads one from one type of proposition to another.

Yet the reductionist is not necessarily making a claim about the logical relationships between propositions, rather the reductionist is making a claim about reality. He is simply denying that anything in addition to the reality asserted by statements of the first sort exists; denying that there is anything extra.

For example, suppose that we were talking about a sharp knife. Now certainly the concept of sharpness is connected to the concept of cutting. It is a logical truth that things that are sharp are things that can cut and cut easily. But it is not a logical truth that something that is sharp must be either thin or hard. Nonetheless, if we focus on the property of sharpness, it makes sense to say that this is no extra property but simply is constituted by being thin and hard; that all we do when we make something sharp is that we take something that is hard and we make it thin. If someone asked how its being thin caused it to become sharp and how long that process took, she would be failing to understand that as it becomes thin the hard edge automatically becomes sharp; its ability to cut (i.e., its sharpness) is constituted by its being hard and thin. There is no other additional property of sharpness that it has.

Yet it would remain true that there is no logical contradiction in saying that "this knife edge is hard and thin yet it is very dull." The reductionist with respect to the property sharpness is saying that we will never find any such cases, and the reason we will never find any such cases is that what it is about a knife edge that makes it able to cut is merely that it is hard and thin.

Now someone might respond to this by saying that we can imagine a rather thick-edged knife such that when lubricated with a certain oil results in an instrument that cuts rather easily. And this shows that its sharpness does not consist of its thinness and hardness.

Yet suppose this is true. Does it show that when the knife *is* thin and hard that its sharpness is also something extra? I think not. And this is really all the reductionist needs, because he or she need not be saying that it must be the case that sharpness is constituted by thinness and hardness. Indeed he might say that it is constituted by a variety of other properties, typically thinness and hardness but possibly hardness and something brought about by the oil that compensates for lack of thinness. What he denies is that there is any extra irreducible characteristic of sharpness. He of course is not denying that there is such a thing as sharpness; that would be eliminationism. He is not saying that there can be no sharpness but rather that there is sharpness and this is what it is.

And the reductionist can say that this is all there is to our being active. This is not to say that it is an illusion that people are active, but their activity does not consist in some extra fact beyond facts of this sort.

The nonreductionist rejects this conclusion. Sometimes he introduces a second kind of causality. Chisholm speaks of immanent causality as opposed to the transeunt causality that exists between events. Immanent causality is something about which very little can be said. If there is such a thing, it exists only between agents and the events that they immanently cause. It is the relationship of direct agency; indirect agency being agency that one acquires in virtue of the transeunt causation that exists between the event immanently caused to occur and other subsequent events.

From one perspective the theory sounds outlandish. Agent causality seems like the philosopher's last resort—failing to give an account of what the difference is between the arm that is raised and the arm that merely goes up, she simply asserts that when the arm goes up, its movement is caused by the agent herself. Yet viewed from another perspective, the theory seems to assert something very similar to what it is that we experience when we act. We simply experience ourselves as raising our arm; we do it and we *just* do it, without doing anything else that makes it happen.

The phenomenology of this ability might be well communicated through an animated cartoon in which a dancing figure revels in his freedom of movement. In the dance he exclaims that he is free; he demonstrates his abilities, saying "I can do this and this and that and that and just about anything," whereupon the dancer is confronted by someone who tells him that in fact he is not what he takes himself to be. That in fact he, the dancer, is really a mechanism, a sophisticated robot, and all these movements that he makes are not really done by him but by some intricate machine that he is. The dancer is incredulous at hearing that inside his body there is all this going on. And he says it is impossible, and then says to his challenger, "Here look!" at which he pulls a giant zipper that opens up his body from the tip of his left hand now raised over his head, across his chest and down his right leg, and lo and behold, it is completely empty! There simply is no mechanism in virtue of which he does all that he does. Rather, he just does it. Moreover, he does not do it via some command. His being is suffused throughout the body; he inhabits different parts of it at will, and placing himself in his hand he just moves it (i.e., himself) around, and then like a flash he moves himself into his foot and raises himself up.

These images suggest that although there is very little to be said about what is involved in immanently causing something, it is possible that persons have this unique and irreducible power. And we might, under some circumstances, judge that we have evidence of its existence. For instance, if the event of my hands going up could not be explained in terms of the laws of physics, if through the investigation of events occurring within my body we could not find in nerve impulses and muscle contractions a sufficient condition for the arm to rise, and if this absence was the case when and only when the person raised her hand, we would have evidence of some *different* kind of causal power at work.

But to the best of my knowledge this is not the case. Rather, we do have sufficient explanations of the hand's going up in the events immediately preceding that event.

And in fact, the agent causality approach typically does not assert that the arm's going up is simply made-to-happen by the agent. It recognizes that the arm's going up, even when I raise my arm, is fully caused by prior events in the nerves and muscles and that these events are preceded by certain brain events. What the theory asserts is that one of these prior events is agent-caused, thus setting off a chain of events, each of which is caused in the normal sense, and that terminates in the event: the arm goes up.

Thus Chisholm writes: "The point is, . . . that whenever a man does something A, then (by 'immanent causation') he makes a certain cerebral event happen, and this cerebral event (by 'transeunt causation') makes A happen."[6] And at another point, using the notion of a basic act in much the way I have—as an act that is not done by doing any other act—Chisholm goes on to say that this is not to bring about something directly. What the person brings about directly is an *undertaking* to do the basic act. The undertaking itself is immanently caused, but it is not itself a basic act because basic acts are undertaken and undertakings are not.[7]

There are a multiplicity of problems with the theory.[8] The most central are these. First, it relies on a unique and irreducible type of causality. It is possible that this causal power does exist, but there is no evidence for it in the sense that there are no situations in which we have reached the conclusion that ordinary event causality leaves us with an inability to account for all that occurs.

Second, insofar as the analysis of what it is for someone to be the agent of an event (or of what it is for something to be a basic act) is that it was directly caused by the person, we are not gaining any new insight into agency or action. Rather we are being told that agency is an unanalyzable power of persons to cause events to occur. It may be true that this is the case, but it may not. But it would not make sense to accept this version and thus abandon efforts to provide an analysis before all such analyses were shown to be defective.

Third, insofar as this kind of account meshes with the normal physiological accounts of the arm's going up, and does so by introducing "undertakings" to raise my arm and all other basic acts, it sounds very much like volitions or some similar mental events have been introduced under the name "undertakings." The account is then open to some of the problems faced by such accounts. These will be discussed shortly, but they include the question of whether or not there are such things as "undertakings" or volitions, and second, whether or not any causing of the arm to go up, if originated by an undertaking, is sufficient to make something a basic action. And if not, then just what does make something a basic action is still elusive.

Finally, whether there are events or states or actions that are properly called "undertakings" and occupy a point in a causal chain prior to the arm's rising, the account does require that at some point, in some way, the agent sets off the normal causal chain that results in the arm's going up. The fact that it was the person herself who set off this causal chain does explain why the person should be seen as responsible for her hand's moving. It was she who through her undertaking to move her arm caused it to move. But the account appears to clash with our own experience of ourselves as active in the *movement itself*. For if, as is asserted, her agent-causing occurs at some prior point in time, then if the chain of events were slow enough (or her mind fast enough) she might simply sit back and watch her arm go up. Thus we have an anomaly. We are really the agent-cause of events that we know nothing about (events in our brains). And the events that we do experience as "directly" done by us turn out to be mere causal effects of these brain events. Our sense that somehow we are active in and throughout the raising of the arm is in some sense an *illusion*. If nonreductionist accounts, rather than explaining or at least conforming to the phenomenology of action, instead tend to invalidate it, then they have relatively little to offer. Their great attraction is that by not reducing action to a normal cause-and-effect sequence they initially appear to avoid a reduction of the active to the passive that may appear inherent in all reductionist accounts.

Mental Cause Analyses

Mental cause accounts have in common that they seek to distinguish between actions (e.g., raising my arm) and mere events (e.g., my arm went up, but I didn't raise it) on the basis of the presence of a particular kind of mental cause. When the arm's going up is caused by the appropriate event, or caused by it in the appropriate manner, then and only then is it a case of my raising my arm. Then and only then am I the agent of its going up.

The classic candidate for the appropriate mental event is a volition. If a volition is understood as a kind of mental event, then it would seem that this mental event could occur whether or not the agent made it occur. And if this is so, then the question arises as to what it is that makes the occurrence of these events something of which the person is the agent. If the answer is that they are themselves caused by other volitions, which themselves are actions, then we have an infinite regress.

Alternatively, volition might be understood as some sort of primitive action and not as a mental event at all. On some views volitions are themselves actions rather than the causes that partially constitute actions. This position has been taken by both Pritchard and more recently by Lawrence Davis.[9] Thus, some philosophers have likened volitions to trying and to willing. As such these actions, the actions of trying to raise my arm, are themselves unanalyzable. They are things that we can do, but what it is to do them is not a matter of any relationship between events. Thus, the account can tell us that the difference between my arm's going up and my raising my arm is that in the latter case the arm's going up was caused by my volition to raise my arm. But it is not obvious that this account offers us any insight into human action. Does it tell us anything more than that "I just did it"?

Most volitional accounts fall within the causal analysis group. The term volition can be seen as referring to a very *specific* kind of mental event, one that competes with other candidates in mental cause analyses as the cause of the movements internal to actions, or alternatively "volition" can be viewed as standing for any of a group of mental causes in virtue of which something is an action.

Thus one might view analyses of actions in terms of wants and beliefs as a species of volitional account, or one might view them as an alternative to an account in terms of volitions. Treating volitions as distinct kinds of mental events has unique virtue and deficit in the fact that no one seems to know what a volition is. This is a virtue in that it is rather difficult to deny that something occurs if we don't quite know what it is. The notion of volitions occurs only in the writings of philosophers, and we are lacking any independent way of ascertaining whether or not a volition has or has not occurred. On the other hand this must be judged in the main as a deficit in that it cannot advance our understanding of actions to have them analyzed in terms of events whose nature remains unspecified. If it were possible to provide a satisfactory analysis of actions or agency in terms of familiar, independently detectable mental events, this would clearly be preferable to an account that rested upon volitions.

The problem that arises is that whenever there is clear specification of the events in question it does not appear that their presence is necessary; it seems that we have many instances of action in their absence. One way of viewing the appeal to volitions as mental causes is as the statement of a *program*. It is a way of saying that there must be some mental causation story that is correct, yet each specific one we can offer seems incorrect, so we will introduce the term volition as a place holder for the correct story. So understood, I have some sympathy with the volitional account, but it must be seen as merely pointing the direction to follow in seeking an account of action.

I will now consider in detail a particular mental cause analysis of action that relies not on volitions but on well-known mental events or states, the wants and beliefs of the agent. Many of the objections to this analysis apply to similar analyses that substitute some other mental event as the requisite cause.

Alvin Goldman's *A Theory of Human Action* remains the most complete effort to provide this kind of analysis. I treat it in some detail because I believe that Goldman has carried this line of thought just about as far as it can go.

Goldman and many other writers have spoken of a theory of human action. The term "theory" has many uses, but we should distinguish efforts to say what the causes of human action are from accounts that offer certain causal analyses as an explication of what it is for something to be an action. Goldman's theory is of this latter sort. Whether or not a causal analysis is accepted, it is quite possible that the agent's wants and beliefs are causes of his action. Thus one could view action as constituted by a unique agent-causation relation between the person and certain events, and yet accept that when a person is in certain mental states, they may cause him to agent-cause certain events.

It is quite different, however, to maintain that it is causation by wants and beliefs that is constitutive of action. And it is this latter claim that a philosophical theory of action is concerned with.

In somewhat simplified form, Goldman's view is that the difference between an action and a mere occurrence or happening is that the former is caused in a certain characteristic way by the person's occurrent wants and occurrent beliefs (when it is done in order to do some higher level act). The central features of this account are:

1. The necessity of the causal relationship (event causation)

2. The specification of the causes as occurrent wants and beliefs (events in consciousness at the time of the action)

3. The inclusion of the phrase "caused in the characteristic way"

The analysis can be criticized as failing to provide either a necessary condition or a sufficient condition for action.

With respect to the former, the central problem is that in requiring causation by occurrent wants and beliefs as a general feature of all action, the analysis insists on a degree of premeditation that is present in only certain specific contexts. The account fits very poorly, for instance, with actions that involve spontaneity and creativity. Consider the use of language that involves novelty, whether it is the creative writings of an author or just relatively spontaneous conversation. In such contexts we don't have occurrent wants and beliefs about what we are about to say or write, as we don't even know what we are about to say or write except in general terms.

Suppose the explanation of my saying to someone, "I saw that suit on sale for forty-five dollars in K-Mart," is that I sought to hurt his feelings. The analysis maintains that prior to uttering this sentence, I had some occurrent belief about it. Yet surely this is mistaken. What is true is that I have some general ability to produce novel utterances, and that I have some background understanding about what kinds of statements would cause embarrassment, and these factors may play a causal role. But they are not occurrent beliefs, and are enormously general, covering thousands of possible things not said or written. Nor is it the case that I had any occurrent desire to say just this sentence. Of course, sometimes I may deliberate and consciously choose in advance from among various options, but just this kind of deliberation is what is not present in the normal spontaneity of everyday life.

Moreover, spontaneous action cannot properly occupy a place on the edge of the realm of activity. When we feel most creatively alive, it is typically the case that we express ourselves in ways not formulated in advance. When we are in a vibrant conversation, it is not merely that this is the first time that the beliefs were expressed out loud. They were not silently said to oneself either. Indeed, it seems more accurate to say that these beliefs were formulated in the course of the conversation.

Goldman is not committed to saying that all action must be preceded by a prior belief or want to do just that which was done. Certainly there are things that we do or say accidentally. For instance, when we just blurt out a secret, or when we say something and thereby unintentionally hurt someone's feelings. (It was unintentional because we did not realize that saying such a thing would cause that impact.) But these situations are quite different from normal spontaneous action. In normal speech there is no prior belief about what we are about to say, and yet our speaking is neither accidental nor the unintentional performance of a higher-level act. It is simply that our intense sense of activity in creative, spontaneous speech is not a matter of acting in accord with an action plan.

To say this is not to deny that there are beliefs that are causally operative even in spontaneous conversation. We do not just say anything. What we say is guided by our sense of relevance, our awareness of who we are speaking to, by our broad sense of ourselves and even the impression that we might want to make. But it needn't be more specific than that.

Consider someone with a quick wit. In so characterizing the person we are saying that she has the ability to spontaneously come up with clever remarks. This is not something that occurs at random. What is or is not clever in a given situation is a rather complex matter. Thus the witty individual is quite far from being devoid of causally operative wants and beliefs. But they are not beliefs about the very remark she will utter, and these beliefs serve as background conditions within which she acts. They are not themselves the mental causes of her saying such and such.

The spontaneity we find in lively conversation is not a special feature of speech. Most action occurs without being prefigured in consciousness by a want to do that act, or a belief that by doing that act certain other actions would be accomplished.

Consider what it is like to sail a small boat. I am out on the lake, just for the pleasure of it. I have no plans or purpose to speak of; I am there for the pure pleasure and excitement. I am in a partnership with the wind. One hand works the tiller, and the other works the rope connected to the sail. True, by moving my hand I move the rudder and keep the boat on course. But I am not thinking about my hands, or the rudder, or the sail. I am not thinking at all. I am looking at a point on the land and watching it come forward at good speed. Because I know how to sail, I don't have specific beliefs about my movements. I just make them; my hands "take care of themselves." My consciousness is filled with the rush of the land.

Consider the fencer. John lunges forward to touch his opponent with his sword tip. His opponent steps back and lunges himself. John sees the move and parries. Did he have any beliefs about his own actions? Did he even have a prior belief of the sort, "To avoid that, I must do such and such"? Or did he have any occurrent wants? True, there is a general want that he had, which was not to lose the match, and a belief that you loose the match by getting tagged by the other fencer. But these were not occurrent events, and they play a loose casual role in explaining the actions he takes. Part of what it is to be a practiced fencer is to be able to avoid being tagged through almost automatic responses, and to almost automatically take advantage of openings. Most skills manifest themselves in this way.

Finally, consider actions that are expressive of some emotion. A child is playing in the kitchen and accidentally knocks over a pot from the stove. He is not badly scalded, but he is terrified and cries hysterically. His mother rushes in from the next room. She tries to comfort him. She reaches down and picks him up. She hugs him tightly to herself and says comforting words; gently she strokes his head. Her actions are a spontaneous outpouring of feeling. Her stroking his head is neither accidental nor unintentional; it is highly expressive of her concern, of her total being. But she is not even aware of the fact that she is doing it. It has a naturalness that is constituted by the very fact that it was not caused by an occurrent belief that if she were to stroke his head then she would be expressing her love and that to do so would be comforting to him. It is not that she believes the opposite. And if she did believe the opposite, then she would not be doing what she does. But it is only in this negative way that her beliefs are part of the causal matrix within which her actions occur. Her action is instinctive; her responses are automatic. But she is anything but an automaton in so acting.

If I am correct, as I believe these examples show, it is not a necessary condition of action or agency that our behavior be caused by occurrent wants and beliefs. Now it may be that this is because of the great diversity that is covered up by words such as "action." It may be that the mental cause account is adequate to a limited range of actions, but not all. Further, it might be suggested that in the cases we have cited, the problem was that the analysis required occurrent wants and beliefs where there were none, but that this can be accommodated by insisting only on occurrent wants, which operate in conjunction with a rich set of background beliefs.

While I do not find this convincing, the examples I have given probably would not be viewed as decisive by someone who puts forward a theory of this sort. For instance, it might be maintained that in each of the circumstances cited there would be an occurrent want of some sort and a more general background belief. So, for instance, in the case of the fencer it might be maintained that occurrent wants can occur almost instantaneously. Similarly in the case of the mother and her child and with the man on the sailboat. And perhaps in defense of the theory it could be maintained that spontaneous conversation is a rather unique area of activity in which we are not fully active since we have only a general sense of what we are going to say prior to actually saying it. Thus, the power of counterexamples of the sort I have introduced, though perhaps persuasive, is limited. In defense of the theory it is possible to deny that there are clearcut counterexamples. The theorist may accept that the examples raised place the theory under some strain and stress; he may accept that the casuation by occurrent wants analysis doesn't fit the facts as gracefully as one might like, but with a bit of pulling and squeezing, it can still be maintained. (And of course, if volitions are posited instead of wants, who's to say that they are not present, since no one knows exactly what they are.)

What should be clear, however, is that except for the fact that the analysis might require such wants (or volitions), there is nothing problematic about the idea that there are actions not preceded by these mental events. We can readily accept the story presented, that in each of these cases the person just acts without the requisite occurrent wants and/or beliefs.

The only reason we would accept the claim that such events are present and indeed the cause of the behavior in question, would be if we had a prior commitment to the analysis. For instance, if causation by wants and beliefs were to be sufficient to establish agency, and if nothing else that was sufficient emerged, then we would be led to conclude that even where not obviously so, all cases of action must have these mental causes. Thus, the question of what it is that is sufficient to constitute something as an action or someone as an agent is the more basic question.

Is Causation by Mental Events Sufficient for Action?

On Goldman's account, it is not. He insists that the causation must be "in a characteristic manner." It should be clear why Goldman has introduced the phrase "in a characteristic manner." As Goldman points out, it may be the case that a behavior that is clearly not an action (e.g., my grimacing, my coughing involuntarily, my sweating) might be caused by the very fact that under certain circumstances I wanted it to be the case that such behavior occur, and that because I had this want I became so anxious that these behaviors came about involuntarily (i.e., without me doing them).

A different kind of case is also problematic. Suppose that my leg is paralyzed, but that I am attended by a doctor who has a device that tells him when I want to move my leg. Whenever he sees that I have this occurrent want, he moves my leg in exactly the correct way. Here there is causation by an occurrent want, but it is not the case that I raised my leg.

Any mental cause account that did not in some critical manner restrict the kind of causal chain that it asserts to be sufficient for action or agency would thus be open to very powerful counterexamples. These kind of cases have been referred to as "wayward causal chains."[10] And in order to distinguish between those situations in which there is action or agency from those in which there is not, Goldman suggested that in the cases of action the mental causes caused the behavior in a certain appropriate manner that is not present in the wayward examples.

It is certainly an empirical question as to whether or not there is a single characteristic causal pathway that holds in the cases of actions and is not present in the cases of behaviors that were similarly caused by the mental events. But let it be assumed that there is a unique causal path and that it is specified. If this causal pathway is such that whenever there is behavior that is caused by a want and is not a case of action, the causal pathway was not used, then it follows that whenever there is a behavior that is caused by a want and the pathway is used, then it is a case of an action. So in an extensional sense we would have come up with a sufficient condition for action.

Now it might be maintained that there is something circular in this, that we have essentially added to the fact that the behavior is caused by a want, a second condition, to the effect that the behavior is caused through a pathway that is sufficient for actions when it is triggered by a want. But this is not a fair criticism. True, we would need to have some other way of identifying actions from mere behavior than on the basis of that causal pathway, or else we would never be able to know that some pathway is the one that occurs only in cases of actions. But in general we do have this ability. Science isn't frustrated by an inability to know which movements are involuntary and which are embedded in actions. It is philosophy that is frustrated in its ability to say exactly what actions are.

And since scientists can separate the different cases, there is no reason to think that they will not be able to identify some causal pathway that is only involved in the case of actions. Once this is identified, say as the use of pathway-2, which is spelled out in purely physiological terms, there would be nothing circular in saying that whenever something is caused by a want operating through pathway-2 it is an action.

True, it could be pointed out that this does not provide a logically sufficient condition for actions, but the reductionist, as I noted earlier, is not committed to providing a logically sufficient condition. Though admittedly it would be nice to have one, the reductionist seeks to tell us what actions really are. And he or she might say actions are nothing more than movements caused in this particular way.

What is unsatisfying about this is not the fact that it fails to provide a logically sufficient condition for action, but rather that what is provided simply isn't informative relative to the perplexity that motivates the inquiry. It doesn't provide any insight into the philosophic puzzlement. The example of explaining sharpness by reference to being hard and thin also does not provide a logically suffcient condition for sharpness, but hardness and thinness do offer an understanding of sharpness in that when hardness and thinness are understood we can understand why objects that are hard and thin can cut easily, and why making something thinner increases this ability.[11]

Thus, what we need is a reductionist account of action that gives us an understanding of why causation of just that sort is constitutive of action or agency. To provide this illumination, however, it does not suffice to know the physiological specification of the causal pattern in question (Goldman's "characteristic way"); we would have to understand why something that conforms to this pattern has and must have the various attributes of actions. This is not provided by merely having a unique physiological specification of the way in which all movements (embedded in actions) are caused that is not open to any actual counterexamples. We should still be in search of an answer to why it is that when a movement is so caused it has the various attributes of actions (e.g., that I feel active in the doing of them, that I am not astonished by their occurrence, that they will not occur if I am trying to prevent them). Judged against this standard, the analysis presented by Goldman falls well short of what we are after, and there is no strong reason to believe that a causal story that starts, as Goldman's does, with occurrent wants that move through a unique physiological pathway, is in fact the correct causal story.

As I noted earlier, some philosophers have objected to the very possibility that any causal account of actions could be correct. They have put forward what are general arguments against a reductionist position, when in fact their objections are telling only against certain specific causal stories.

Consider the following statement by Melden:

> But let the causal explanations of my behavior be given in terms of my volitions, desires, interests, etc. . . . and equally well it seems to follow that I am a victim of all that transpires within and without me! For what I willed both when I accepted the drink proffered by my friend and when I drove my car turns out on this picture of what transpired, not something I really willed and did, but something that was made to happen by antecedent conditions, my mental condition, my inclinations, my desires, motives and so on. If these are the causal factors and if these are subject to causal explanation in terms of antecedent psychological factors, then whatever happens is none of my doing but of these very psychological factors themselves. I am not any one of these factors, nor all of them; they may be 'mine' in some proprietary sense, but they, not I, do what they do since they, not I, are the psychological levers and pulleys that issue in whatever it is that does get done in the form of overt behavior. It is then a vulgar mode of speech fostered by superstition or some incredibly obscure notion of personal agency that leads people to say that a person does anything at all.¹²

Melden's position is much stronger than a rejection of the mental cause *analysis* of action or agency. What he is saying is that agency is incompatible with the mental causation story. The key premise in this argument is that if some behavior is fully caused by my mental states it is *they not I* that have brought it about. He is maintaining that if the mental event accounts were correct, then *our entire experience of ourselves as agents would be in error.* We would not be agents at all, merely passive entities that witness the occurrence of things that we want to have happen.

Because Melden accepts this premise, he is able to reason that since our experience of ourselves is not delusionary, it follows that mental events do not cause our behavior in the instances we typically identify as actions.

But is Melden correct in saying that if the behavior was so caused it would not be an action? And that we would not be agents? Why couldn't a reductionist maintain that what it is for a person to bring something about is nothing other than the fact that the event was caused by the person's being in certain mental states? Why can't the reductionist maintain a person's experience of herself as active is in fact correct, because her being active is nothing other than the holding of certain causal connections between her states and her behavior?

A good deal depends on exactly what the causal story is. Melden's view has some credibility when advanced against the view that a given piece of behavior was caused by a discrete mental event. Goldman's view is one example of this kind of causal story. Typically it involves some critical single event, be it called desire, intention, volition, or act of will. If the mental event causes the arm to rise, then it must do so by setting off a particular causal chain. But if this is so then there is a minute time delay between the mental event and the arm's going up. This time delay is critical. As was pointed out above, if there were more time we could passively await our arm's going up as the effect of our having been in the appropriate causal state. The fact that we do not experience ourselves as the passive witness is simply a function of the brevity of the causal chain. Our experience of ourselves as an active presence in the very movement would be an illusion, similar to the way in which in viewing motion pictures we experience ourselves as witnessing continuous movements, when in fact we are seeing a series of discrete photographic frames, each one being only minutely different from the next. We do not see continuous motion when viewing a film, but the discrete episodes are below our threshold of discrimination.

Moreover, this possibility of our being the passive observers of our own behavior is only a matter of the speed at which nerve impulses travel. But this is something that can be changed. Live radio programs often operate with a five-second delay mechanism that allows someone to monitor what is being said to weed out obscene remarks. The listener is of course unaware of this, but if one is listening to the radio in the broadcast station and watching the person "on the air" from behind a glass, one hears them saying things that one saw them say five seconds earlier.

A similar device could be introduced into the nervous system adding an extra second or two to the time it would take for the mental event to cause the bodily movement. And this possibility, if all that is involved in our agency is that a mental event set off the causal chain, would reveal that our experience of being active in the action itself is an illusion, one that would become apparent by simply slowing down the speed along the causal pathway, or by speeding up our mental processes.

This problem also exists for volitional accounts that treat volitions as internal actions, the effects of which are bodily movements. Of course, it could be the case that the movements internal to actions are merely the consequences of inner actions, consequences of the real points at which we are agents—but certainly this is not what it seems like to be an agent. Rather, this would assimilate actions to certain kinds of other phenomena—for instance, lowering one's hand would be like allowing it to fall of its own weight. The downward movement would not be something within which we are active, but would just be the consequence of a decision that we made to let it fall. Similarly there are some bodily processes (e.g., urination, excretion) that happen of their own accord, but with respect to which we are agents in the sense that we either allow them to occur or inhibit their occurrence. A model of agency that locates agency in a command mechanism in advance of the actual movement is internally consistent, but it simply isn't adequate to the experience of human agency. As humans we are *lived* bodies, and we are active in and throughout the movements that are internal to actions. If there is an adequate causal analysis of human action, it must be true to these features of our being.

This problem is not a general feature of *any* theory that maintains that the movements internal to actions are caused by mental events. *The challenge is to provide a causal theory in which the agent is present during the actual behavior, a reductionist account that does not invalidate the phenomenology of action.* In the next three chapters I will offer such an account. I call it "the presence theory of agency."

SUMMARY

Despite an outpouring of writing during the last few decades, the notions of action and agency remain perplexing. The accounts that have been given are deeply unsatisfying. Taken in their own terms they have failed to adequately answer Wittgenstein's question in a way that is faithful to our ordinary experience of ourselves as an active presence in our own actions. What is needed is a new account of human activity, one that is built upon closer observation of the subject matter and that is sensitive to the phenomenology of agency.

2

Activity

In this and the two chapters to follow, I will offer a new theory of human agency, the presence theory. The touchstone of the approach I take is a person's experience of himself or herself as active or present within his or her own actions. The concern with our experience of ourselves as agents is the larger reference point of this inquiry, and in Part Two I will draw on the theory of agency to explore the experience of oneself as not being the agent of one's own actions (i.e., alienness).

Briefly put, the theory of agency that I will offer contains the following elements:

1. A distinction is made between two questions, "What is agency?" and "What is an action?" In general, the entire field of action theory has assimilated these two questions into one. Thus, the agent causality approach invokes agent causation at one and the same time to say what it is to be an agent and to specify what an act is (to be an agent is to have agent-caused something to occur; an action is an event that is brought about through agent causation). Similarly, on mental cause theories, to be the agent of an event (my arm's going up) is for that event to have been caused by my wants and beliefs (or volition) and it is this that constitutes action.

2. Rather than treating "acts" or "actions" as the primary concept of action theory, I will instead build the theory on the concept of "activity." I will offer an account of what an activity is that does not require that a person be the agent of that activity. This account of

activity, however, will be offered as an answer to the fundamental question of action theory, as posed by Wittgenstein. Broadly speaking, my analysis will be within the reductionist camp, but it will not be a matter of a mental cause that triggers a chain of events that results in a movement. Instead activity will be analyzed as a complex causally interactive process whose exact character will be specified in the analysis.

3. Having distinguished the questions of agency and action, I will explicate agency as the presence of the self within its actions. This will require an explication of the notions of self and presence. By distinguishing the two questions it is possible to develop a notion of agency that builds on all the rich connections between self and action, and at the same time it allows for the development of a theory of action that can distinguish actions from mere happenings on a much more limited basis.

THE ACTIVITY MATRIX

Consider the answer to a very simple question, "What did you do today?"

- Got up
- Got dressed
- Went downstairs
- Ate breakfast
- Worked on the car
- Ate lunch
- Worked on the car some more
- Worked on my book
- Had dinner
- Worked some more on my book
- Called my sister

The person can be pressed for more of the details: "Exactly what did you do in working on the car?"

- Went outside
- Spread the tools out
- Took off the rust
- Mixed the crack filler

- Filled the cracks
- Painted the fillings

"Tell me exactly what you did in mixing the filler."

- Picked up the can
- Read the instructions
- Picked up the screwdriver
- Pried open the can

"Exactly what did you do in prying open the can?"

- Grasped the can in my left hand
- Inserted the tip of the screwdriver into the groove on the lid
- Pressed down on the screwdriver
- Put the screwdriver down
- Lifted the lid off

If we were to ask if this was exactly the way it happened we might be told, "to the best of my knowledge it happened that way." But if we focus on the pressing down with the screwdriver and ask, "Did you press down once or several times?" we may learn that there was a sequence of these pressings down. At this point the agent may not be able to tell us anything further. He may be aware of little more than of working the screwdriver around the lid, prying up as he goes. Nevertheless, there is more to it than that. There is an extraordinary richness to our simplest actions, and action theory must start with an awareness of this.

Ask someone to open a small paint can and watch what he does. Carefully observe him as he works the screwdriver around the groove. He moves his entire body. He does not simply hold the can rigidly in one hand and move the other around the can. This would put him in a position from which it would be impossible to exert any pressure on the can. Instead he rotates the can through a half circle, all the while keeping the screwdriver in roughly the same place, allowing the can to rotate past the screwdriver in much the way a record rotates past the needle. As he rotates the can in a half circle, he moves the screwdriver through a small arc of about a tenth of a circle in the opposite direction. From time to time he stops these two rotations and pries up on the lid by pressing down on the screwdriver. This he does five or six times. Each time he presses down he does so with measured force, so as to avoid bending the groove a good deal in any one spot. How does he rotate the can? Using his left hand, he pushes it along with his thumb and middle finger and guides it with the ring and index finger; occasionally the pinky helps guide the can.

And what is the other hand doing while the can is rotating? Is it merely lying in wait for its turn to press down on the screwdriver? No, the thumb is halfway up the can, the fingers are in contact near the lower edge. The screwdriver helps in the steadying process by exerting a slight pressure against the side of the groove. Is this pressure constant? I do not know. I doubt it. Probably there are many tiny motions of adjustment that escape even the keenest observer.

And the rest of the body? Is it rigidly in place? No, there is a good deal of shoulder and arm movement as the hands move. The torso moves through an arc of about a twentieth of a circle and there are slight movements of the legs and feet. He tends to "lean into" the can a bit, pressing down on the ground with his left foot, going up slightly on the ball of his right foot. His head bends over the can and moves in various ways as he rotates the can, as do his eyes and eyelids. His mouth holds to a slightly stiff position, expressing a slight tension.

This does not complete the description of "prying open the can," but I will stop here and take stock starting with the original question, "What did you do today?"

1. The response to this question was a list of several activities, each of which endured over some period of time

2. It was possible to subdivide each of these activities into a temporally ordered series of other activities until we reached "prying open the can," which was marked by numerous cotemporal goings on

3. At some point the agent's ability to enumerate what he was doing was exhausted

4. Yet we could see that he was doing a number of things that he was not aware of

5. These doings were nonetheless crucial parts of what he was aware of himself as doing

6. Many of these cotemporal goings on were coordinated with each other

7. Only because of this coordination was he able to accomplish his goal

8. It is generally clear to what activity a given subactivity belongs. For example, taking the food out of the refrigerator is part of eating lunch and not part of fixing the car

9. The activities are not mere collections or conjunctions of their parts. To agent and observer alike, they occur as, are perceivable as, and are experienced as, organic wholes

10. These organic wholes occur on various levels. We may recognize a complex called "working on the car," a complex called "mixing the crack filler," a complex called "opening the can." The individual movements of each hand, each leg, each eye, are *parts* of these organic wholes

I will now focus on the most unified level, which I shall call "the activity molecule." Above this level there are also activities, but below it there are only elements of the activity molecule. In the above example the activity molecule was "opening the can." Consider the activity molecule a bit more thoroughly.

Point 1: *The activity molecule is made up of various elements of various sorts.*

a. Sequences of movements of some part of the body that play a primary role (e.g., the movements of the left hand)

b. Sequences of movements of some part of the body that play a secondary role (e.g., the movements of the legs)

c. Sequences of movements of some tool manipulated by the person

d. Changes in some situation being effected by the above (e.g., the gradual lifting of the lid)

e. Movements of the body that allow the person to be aware of what is happening (e.g., eye movements)

f. Perceptions of and sensations arising from these various goings on

Point 2: *Activity molecules are internally integrated collections of elements.* Through various modes of integration the elements are interconnected with one another. There are other events that occur at the same time as the activity and in the same general area, but these are not part of the activity. An activity is not just any sequences of events. If we consider two sequences of movements, say moving one's foot up and down and moving one's arm up and down, they may or may not belong to the same activity even though they are cotemporal. When one is shifting gears on a standard transmission car, the movements of one's arm and the movements of one's foot are both elements of a single activity. When one is keeping time to the music and waving to a friend the movements are elements in two distinct activities. In determining if two elements belong to the same activity molecule, we do not look to see if there is one volition that causes the two or a volition for each. It is a matter of the relationship between the elements. Are they integrated with each other?

Point 3: *Some elements of an activity molecule may be changes in the world.* Typically an activity involves some interaction between a person and some changes that he or she is causing (at least in part). In the example of prying open the can, there is the series of movements of the lid of the can as it opens. These are not to be understood as consequences of the activity, but rather as elements of the activity. In playing tennis we have the movements of the ball, including those caused by the other player. These movements are not causal consequences of two activities; we do not have each player engaged in separate instances of tennis playing. Rather, both players are engaged in a single instance of the activity: playing tennis.

Point 4: *Not all of the consequences of the elements of a given activity molecule are parts of that activity molecule.* Whether or not a given causal consequence of some element is itself an element of the activity depends upon how it is integrated with the other elements. If it is part of an interacting sequence such as the motions of the ball in handball then it is part of the activity. If it is tied to the elements only by virtue of the single causal connection then it is a consequence of the activity but not part of it. For example, the disturbance of the air caused by my hitting the ball is not part of the activity.

Point 5: *The key to the integration is the level of awareness.* Insofar as we are dealing with activities that contain sequences of events and sequences of bodily movements that produce these events, the level of awareness is not on the level of each successive bodily movement. Rather it is on the level of outcome. The sequences are integrated via this awareness of outcome. Thus, the musician's awareness is not concentrated on the blowing of air across the flute mouth. The series of events of air blowing take care of themselves. His experience is on the level of the integrated consequences of the air blowing, the music itself. An experienced driver is aware of the road; her arms move, her feet press, pedals go in and out. But these are *to her* as though they were goings on inside her body.

Point 6: *Activity molecules are not merely integrated bundles; they have flow or internal harmony.* Consider a conversation. One does not merely offer a sequence of sentences. One *carries on* a conversation. One point tends to follow another, or if the topic shifts there is a certain harmony that is maintained. Perhaps the conversants were really just trying to get to know one another; the emotional melody flows forward over various topics. When this rhythm is truly broken, the activity ends. Two friends stop *talking politics* and turn to an exchange of intimacies. To do this is to do something else. They are not unified parts of a single activity molecule of conversing. Each series of events has its own flow and internal logic. Because of this, activities appear as wholes. Phenomenologically, we do not construct them out of their elements; they are there already. This may or may not be seen by a given observer; that depends upon his or her ability to perceive the meanings that are integrated.

With this general account, it is crucial to identify the particular kind of integration that makes something an activity molecule.

THE STRUCTURE OF MOLECULAR ACTIVITIES

The activity molecule is a set of causally integrated events. In the most familiar cases the types of events consist of three sorts: movements, outcomes, and an awareness of these outcomes as they occur. If these events are related to each other in a particular manner, then they constitute an activity molecule. I use the term "indirect perceptual integration" to characterize that causal relationship that is constitutive of activity on the molecular level.

The activity molecule is represented in Figure 2.1. The diagram shows only a fraction of the activity complex. P is the ongoing perceptual awareness of the outcomes O^1, O^2, . . . O^{12}. The perceptual assessment P causes these outcomes to conform to some standard or form. This is represented by the circle that runs through the O's; it stands for the harmony that is produced in the outcomes. The route of

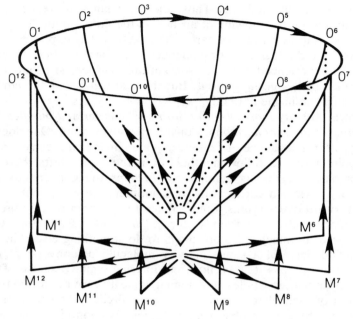

Figure 2.1

causation is indirect. The outcomes, which might be the appearance of certain colors or shapes on a canvas, are caused via the movement of the arm and the paint brush. These movements are M^1, M^2, ... M^{12}. While the curves running from P indicate the object of the awareness P, the straight lines running to and from the M's represents the causal chain. Each movement produces some shift in outcome and this is perceived and in turn results in some adjustment of movement. P is thought of as continuous throughout the activity; and in a harmonious flowing activity, the number of movements and outcomes may be considered to be infinite. The duration of the activity is the length of time required by the completion of the series of movements, or alternatively, the series of outcomes.

It may be maintained that for some activities the intended outcomes never occur and hence there are no outcomes to serve as the object of awareness. First, it should be realized that there is a sense of "outcome" that is not relevant. Thus, I may be playing the guitar hoping to produce the "outcome" of impressing a listener; yet, the listener may fail to be impressed. In this case, however, impressing the listener is not the outcome necessitated by my analysis. The outcome that is the object of the ongoing awareness is the production of the music. The event that does not occur—the listener's coming to have a favorable impression—is an intended causal consequence of the molecular activity, playing the guitar. The absence of this consequence is not relevant to the analysis of molecular activity. Sometimes, of course, it happens that someone tries to play the guitar and fails to produce the musical sounds. Here, there is no molecular activity of the type "playing the guitar." Of course, "trying to play the guitar" and "learning to play the guitar" are activities even if there is no molecular activity "playing the guitar." Trying to play the guitar may be a compound activity made up of a series of molecular activities such as plucking the first string, pressing the second string against a fret, and plucking the second string. When someone who is unable to play the guitar tries to play the guitar, he or she may succeed in performing these activity tokens. The fact that the relevant outcomes have shifted from "producing music" to "holding the string firmly" and "plucking the first string" is to be expected. *It is just this shift in objects of awareness that reflects the difference between those who can and those who cannot play the guitar.* Becoming accomplished at an activity such as playing the guitar is the process whereby a new molecular activity (type) enters one's repertoire. For the person who knows how, playing the guitar is not composed of a set of more basic molecular activities such as plucking the string or pressing the fret, even though it is true that he or she does pluck the string and press the fret when playing. These have now become internalized within the structure of his or her basic activity molecule.

With the above in mind, I offer the following definition of the key relationship (indirect perceptual integration):

A set of elements is indirectly perceptually integrated if and only if it contains a series of events, a subset of the causal consequences of those events (the outcomes), and an ongoing perceptual assessment of the outcomes such that this perceptual assessment causes the series to produce an outcome that satisfies or approaches the standard implicit in the perceptual assessment.

By "perceptual assessment" I mean a form of seeing-as. The outcomes are not experienced in a phenomenologically neutral manner. They are seen critically, with some standard implicit in the perception. In the following illustrations, coffee is seen as shaking-too-much, the handwriting as not-being-clear-enough, the truck as being-too-close. In the next section I will provide a fuller discussion of these perceptual assessments and discuss their relation to wants and beliefs.

Illustration 1: I am carrying the coffee to the table; my eyes are focused on the surface of the coffee inside the cups; the coffee is seen as shaking-too-much. This perception causes my pace to slow down and my hands to grip the saucers more tightly, which causes the coffee to become more steady.

Illustration 2: I am writing a letter and perceive that my writing is illegible. This perception causes my hands to move more slowly, which causes the writing to be legible-enough.

Illustration 3: I am riding my bike through city streets. I perceive myself as too close to a moving truck; this causes my feet to move less quickly and my hands to squeeze the brakes lightly, all of which causes me to be further away from the truck.

In objection to my claim that indirect perceptual integration is sufficient for some complex to be an activity, it might be pointed out that I have not specified *how* the perceptual awareness causes the events to produce an outcome in conformity to the implicit standard. Thus, a painter with a paralyzed arm to which a brush is attached may find his arm moving the brush in conformity to his perceptual assessment of the painting being produced. A machine (or another person) may be producing the motion of the painter's arm. The machine is caused to do so by the perceptual assessments of the painter. Here we would not want to say that *the painter* was moving his arm. Thus, the account may appear vulnerable to the so-called "wayward chains" that plague accounts of action in terms of causation by a mental event.

But the above example does not constitute a problem on the analysis I have offered. I have severed the question of *agency* from that of *activity*. My claim is only that the painting of the picture is an activity. The wayward causal chain may defeat the claim that the person with the paralyzed arm is the agent, but not the claim that there is picture painting activity. In standard action theory approaches, this distinction is not made.

Similarly, if it is sufficient that there be indirect perceptual integration, then my account commits one to saying that something is an activity even if the person doing it finds that this process is occurring even against his or her will. I accept this implication because this bears not on the question of activity, but rather on the question of agency.

Similarly, someone may be hypnotically or electrically caused to perform an activity. She may not be an agent, but so long as the outcomes are indirectly caused by a perceptual assessment to conform to a standard implicit in her ongoing perception, it is an activity. If, however, she is hypnotically or electrically caused to make certain movements that by chance happen to conform to the perceptual assessment, but are not *caused by* the perceptual assessment to conform to the standard, then we do not have genuine activity. In short, if the external cause cuts in prior to the ongoing perceptual perception, then what has been caused is an activity. If it cuts in after and short-circuits the perceptual integration, then what is caused is mere behavior, not activity.

Is indirect perceptual integration also a necessary condition for action? Are there actions where indirect perceptual integration is lacking? Consider someone who is blind. Surely he performs actions, yet he does not have the perceptual awareness that people with vision have. This is correct, but it doesn't undermine the analysis. What typically happens is that some other sensory awareness becomes more acute and meaningful, whether it is auditory or tactile awareness. One can develop the skill of doing things with one's eyes closed, but one develops this skill by learning to depend more on other forms of awareness. It is just this problem of learning how to rely upon other senses that makes it so difficult to do without the senses that typically provide the indirect perceptual awareness.

Indirect perceptual integration is a particular kind of feedback process in which the perceptual awareness carries the standard against which feedback information is evaluated. The broader question is whether or not ongoing feedback is a necessary feature of action. Suppose that someone is totally anesthetized, and deprived of any sensory awareness of what she is doing. She is asked to pick up her violin and play it. And suppose that she does so. There is no ongoing perceptual awareness, indeed, no feedback at all, but there is the complex behavior of violin playing. Is this an action? Suppose that the person is participating in an experiment of some sort, and agrees to respond to a variety of commands to perform this or that activity. And suppose that she does behave accordingly despite the absence of any perceptual feedback. We might be surprised that this occurs given that the individual has no awareness of the activity as it is occurring, but certainly it is possible. How are such situations to be characterized?

I would not find it very problematic to say that such instances would be complex behavioral compounds that are not themselves actions. This is not to say that they are mere happenings, akin to processes that occur whether we want them to or not. Given that the behavior occurrences are the result of directives that the person wants to obey, in such a situation the person is making them happen. He or she is the agent of these physical processes in much the way that we can be the agent of involuntary bodily processes that once begun occur of their own accord. But *agency* is a different question than that of *action*; on my account we may or may not be the agent of our activities, and in principle we could be the agent of processes that are not actions.

It may be wondered whether or not we have indirect perceptual integration in relatively simple and brief actions such as raising one's hand or moving one's finger. First, it should be noted that such movements are most frequently parts of an activity molecule, and in those instances we would not look for indirect perceptual integration within the hand raising but between it and other elements. Still, even if only infrequently, these movements can stand alone. I may for instance raise my hand to signal someone, or to ask a question, or to give a salute.

Is there indirect perceptual integration in these cases? I think that typically there is. A hand can be raised in many different ways. The German salute we see in movies of World War II is not the same as merely lifting one's hand. The ballet dancer who raises her hand does something that is measured and graceful. At the very least when we raise our hand there is always some determination of how fast to do it and how far to extend it. In short, even something as simple as a hand raising occurs within a temporal interval during which there is perceptual feedback and adjustment.

Suppose that there are behavioral elements that are so simple and so short that there is no feedback, but simply a one-way command mechanism. These would not be molecular activities, but they would be things that we make happen and of which we would have a perceptual awareness, but no adjustment mechanism. We would be the agents of these events and in virtue of having made them happen we might perform numerous other higher level acts. And if one wished one could say that the making happen of these simple occurrences is an action. What is striking, however, is that actions of this sort, if they do occur, would operate on the margins of a theory of action, whereas classical mental cause theories have treated them as the paradigm instances of action. The activity molecule, held together through indirect perceptual integration, can serve as a relatively solid central concept for a theory of action.

Rather than stipulating that indirect perceptual integration is or is not a necessary feature of human action, it is, I think, more revealing to say that there is a spectrum of more and less active complexes of elements. What is of interest is to consider what such a spectrum of activeness might look like and what the criteria would be that determine the position of a given instance.

It is possible to distinguish between four major categories of molecular activities: bodily motions producing some change in an external object; bodily motions resulting in some effect but not in or via an external object; bodily motions in themselves; activities where no bodily movement is necessary. Associated with each of these categories are numerous *manners of performance*. These manners of performance are not necessarily restricted to one and only one category. The categories (with examples) and some performance modes are presented in the following list.[1]

I. Bodily motions producing some change in an external object

   A. Some examples
      1. Painting a fence
      2. Driving a car
      3. Playing a violin
      4. Drawing a picture
      5. Opening a can

   B. Some typical modes of performance
      1. Attentively
      2. Mechanically
      3. Spontaneously
      4. Relaxedly

II. Bodily motions resulting in some effect but not in or via an external object

   A. Some examples
      1. Speaking
      2. Singing
      3. Scratching an itch

   B. Modes of performance
      1. Haltingly
      2. Ferociously
      3. Softly

III. Bodily motions in themselves

    A. Some examples

       1. Exercising
       2. Dancing
       3. Swimming
       4. Diving

    B. Some typical modes of performance

       1. In form (gracefully, properly)
       2. Mindlessly
       3. Rigidly

IV. No bodily movement necessary

    A. Some examples

       1. Thinking
       2. Reading
       3. Listening to music
       4. Watching a sunset

    B. Some typical modes of performance

       1. Intently
       2. Carefully
       3. Perfunctorily

For any activity there are many manners in which it can be performed. This is not something peripheral to its being an activity. It seems that it is an essential feature of an activity that it can be performed in various manners. However, it is not the case that all instances of a type of activity performed in various manners are equally instances of activity. *The manner itself reflects the extent of the activity of the performance.* There might be performances so mechanical as to lack any ongoing awareness at all. Where this is truly the case we are not dealing with an activity, but merely a set of movements. And if an activity is done haltingly or spasmodically we are not dealing with a single molecular activity, but rather a series of molecular activities.

The most fully active performances are marked by indirect perceptual integration. Our best examples come from category I (bodily motions producing some change in an external object) when they are done attentively, as well as instances of category II such as speaking and singing when these are done with care. If we consider activities in category III (bodily motions in themselves) to be subject to certain norms of form, such that the outcome is, say, a graceful movement of the entire body, then we can find good instances of indirect perceptual integration when these activities are done in good form. In the last category (no necessary bodily motion) it may be difficult to find instances of indirect perceptual integration. While it is true that we may read a book critically, or watch a movie attentively, what is viewed critically is the book read or the movie seen. The book and the movie may be the objects of attention, but they are not the outcomes of the activity. The outcomes are the gradual unfolding of the plot to the reader, the perception of the sun as it sets, the hearing of the music. However, we are aware of these outcomes as they occur and this awareness affects their occurrence. If we are not understanding the book, we slow down. If the music is not being heard, there is a focusing of consciousness. Thus even here we may find examples of indirect perceptual integration, though not as clearly as in the other categories. Insofar as these outcomes are out of our control, or not subject to modification as they occur, they are not activities. This finding fits well with our preanalytic uncertainty as to whether or not examples from this category are activities.

If activity is a matter of degree, the extent to which a performance is an activity depends upon three factors: the degree to which the outcome is capable of modification; the range of causally operative criteria within the perceptual assessment; and the fineness of the discriminations of each of the causally operative criteria.

Some types of activities are susceptible to greater modification than others. If there is little way in which the outcomes can be different, then the type offers less potential for activity, or activeness. The more it can be different, the greater the opportunity the type provides for activity.

In a sense, this is like judging diving—certain dives, according to their type, are given higher multiples for difficulty. Here we are not concerned with difficulty but with *degree of modifiability*. Thus, filling in pictures in a coloring book is subject to less modifiability than drawing a picture on a blank page. The replacement of script by type restricted, in certain dimensions, the modifiability of writing. There is more variability between different performances of playing a violin than there is between different performances of opening a can.

When we speak of modifiability, we are concerned with a property of the activity type and not of the activity token (instance) except insofar as it was a token of a type with a certain degree of modifiability. Modifiability may be thought of as a property that reflects the variability of the possible instances that would count as instances of the type in question (e.g., there are a vast number of ways of making a sketch of a particular tree).

To some extent this distinction corresponds to that between skilled and unskilled labor. And we may understand something of the distinction between tools and machines along these lines. A farmer with a hoe uses the hoe as a tool to communicate to the outcome her vision of it. If anything, the tool enhances her ability to transmit her vision, to implement her perceptual assessments. It functions like an artist's brush. We can contrast this with machines. Consider someone working with a hand stapler. This is not a passive or partially passive performance as with an automatic can opener where the machine takes over the task. Here there is a sensory awareness that is carried through the activity to the end; there are a variety of ways the activity can turn out; there are good jobs and bad jobs. Nonetheless, the stapler permits relatively little communication of vision. There is little in the way of possible ongoing correction, adjustment, and extension of outcome, as the outcome is being produced.

While the first index to the activity of a performance dealt with the type of the activity, the second and the third deal with the actual performance.The ongoing performance includes a perceptual assessment. Within the perceptual assessment there are criteria that specify some standard or form or bench mark against which the activity's outcomes are perceived. These criteria may range over a number of dimensions of the outcome or may be restricted to just one. Thus, an individual may or may not perceive the aesthetic dimensions of the outcome. One person may be concerned only to get the job done; for him it is enough to get the message across. The range of values in his awareness is restricted. For another, matters of style may be important: economy of resources, avoiding sloppiness, pleasing appearance. These dimensions, which are present in *his* awareness of the outcome, were missing from the first person's awareness. But it is not enough that they be present in the perception—they must be causally operative. The artist must learn not only to perceive (to have criteria); he must learn control, craft (how to make his criteria operative). Furthermore, it is not enough that the person has the perception and the ability; the activity of the actual performance is determined by those criteria that have emerged in the outcome. Thus sometimes we are faced with an activity token that might have been performed with great attentiveness, elegance, or grace, but is in fact sloppy and gross. The complex is crude and grotesque; it barely hangs together. Here there was no necessary lack of critical perception or ability. The criteria were rendered inoperative, suspended. We may say of the agent, "he didn't care how it turned out."

Finally, there is for each operative criteria within the perceptual assessment a matter of the fineness of the discriminations. Two craftswomen may both be concerned that a surface be smooth, but one is able to perceive more finely the differences in degree. Whereas the first craftswoman quickly reaches a point at which she is no longer able to tell if she is making the surface smoother or not, the second craftswoman can still evaluate the outcomes she is producing. The first craftswoman soon reaches a point at which the edge is as straight as she can make it. The second craftswoman is able to do better because she can perceive more acutely. Two singers may both care about the rhythm and pitch of their performances. But one has far greater discrimination than the other. He hears more accurately any variation from the ideal. Here too, the finely discriminated perception must be operative.

Each molecular token must be separately appraised to determine the extent to which it is activity. If it is a clear case of indirect perceptual integration, then it is a clear case of activity. Insofar as this is not the case, we may speak of it as more or less active. As there is less modifiability of outcome, and more impoverishment of operative perception, there is a movement away from the active. As there is greater modifiability and richer operative perception we move towards the artistic. Cast in these terms this appraising may sound intellectual and arduous—in fact it is perceptual and immediate. It constitutes the *aesthetic dimension of everyday life*. It is something we *feel* in our own activity and *see* in the activity of others.

Perceptual Assessments

A key term in the definition of indirect perceptual integration, and thus in the analysis of activity, has been "perceptual assessment." I have characterized perceptual assessment as a form of seeing-as where what is experienced is perceived in terms of a standard. By "standard" I do not mean a value and certainly not a moral value. All I have in mind is a bench mark, something that allows us to see something as not-being-such-and-such or as conforming-more-and-more-to-such-and-such.

These hyphenated expressions indicate that we are talking about a feature of the awareness itself.

This richness of perception is commonplace. Consider the following: I have just returned to my apartment. I look it over to see if everything is in order. I see it as in-order or as not-in-order. I do not first see it and then *judge* that there is a low probability that something has been disturbed in my absence.

Sometimes, of course, we do experience in this reduced way, but it is a phenomenologically different experience. Indeed, the neutralization of experience, the elimination of standards otherwise implicit in perception, is one of the characteristics of certain forms of alienation.

It might be suggested that perceptual assessments can be equated with the mental elements offered in classical accounts of action (e.g., volitions) or in their recent variants (e.g., wants, intentions, beliefs). I wish to reject any such suggestions.

First, let us dismiss the notion that perceptual assessments are beliefs. That they are closely related cannot be doubted. If I see the cup of coffee as shaking-too-much then it is typically the case that I believe that it is shaking too much. Of course, I could believe this and not have the experience of seeing it, but could I see it this way and not believe it? The answer to this question is yes. Though it is not typically the case, there are many circumstances in which we know that things are not really the way we see them to be. We have our perceptual experience but we do not accept it as veridical. Perceptual assessments, typically, are the expression of beliefs—because I believe that that amount of shaking is too-much, I see it as shaking-too-much. Typically, seeing it in this fashion emerges from beliefs that I have. But this need not always be the case. And because it need not be the case and sometimes is not, we know that perceptual assessments are not the beliefs themselves, they are simply phenomenological episodes.

Thus we can see the diagram ⊠ successively as:

a. An elevator shaft seen from above
b. The top of the Washington Monument
c. An "x" in a box

Each perception is a distinct seeing-as but we need not have any beliefs that the diagram really is, or really represents, any of these possibilities.

But might they be wants or desires?—the desire that it not shake any more than a certain amount, the desire that the boat sail straight for the island it is heading for, and so on? Here again, it is the case that perceptual assessments do typically express and reflect wants and desires. Typically it is only because I *want* it to shake less that I see it as shaking-too-much; and because I want the boat to go towards the island, I see it as going-just-right. But again, this typical interpenetration of wants into the perceptual assessments does not mean that the assessments are wants. Indeed, they may occur even when the person does not have the appropriate desire at all.

Consider the following case. Mr. Percoti is a furniture maker, a fine craftsman who because of economic circumstances has been forced to seek employment in a furniture factory. Previously, he carved his furniture with great care; now he works on the assembly line. His job is to make left front legs for bridge chairs. He works for pay and must complete seven legs each hour. His lifelong perceptual discrimination does not vanish. He knows that he is working too quickly. He sees the inadequacy of every piece he completes; they are all perceived as ill-formed. Nonetheless, it does not follow that he wants these legs to be well-formed. He may not care one way or the other. The product belongs to the boss, not to him. His only concern is that he gets seven legs finished each hour. Indeed, he may even take satisfaction in the fact that the legs are not up to his standards.

In the above example, the person has perceptual assessments of the outcome of his activity. He sees the table leg as too-fat, but he does not want it to be less fat. He might, of course, but not in this case. And since there is no desire that it be less fat, the perceptual assessment of it as too-fat is merely a perceptual assessment, it neither expresses nor is the desire that it be less fat. In this example, these are free-standing perceptual assessments; they are not causing his movements to create an outcome in conformity with their standard, rather they are "over-ridden" by a much more minimal standard.

It might be maintained that the situation is different when the assessments *do* enter into the activity, when they do cause the outcomes to conform to the standard implicit in the perception. It may be said that such assessments are wants or the expression of a desire that the outcomes conform to the implicit standard. This fits well with the dominant rational picture of human behavior. One might ask, "If he didn't want the outcome to conform, then why did he make it conform?"

Let us again consider the alienated craftsman. We may find that, in fact, his work is of superior quality. When we ask him why he puts so

much into someone else's product, he may himself be surprised that
this is so. He may remark, "That's the only way I know how to do it,"
or "after a lifetime of fine carving it would take an effort to *not* do it
right, yet I don't give a damn about these table legs!" Here the indirect
perceptual integration has a life of its own. The craftsman continues to
perceive with his trained critical eye, and his hands respond as they
have always responded despite the fact that he is *indifferent* to the
quality of the outcome.

Indeed, the perceptual assessment may be operative even in *direct
conflict* with the craftsman's wants. We can imagine him in a shop
where his skill is causing problems for the other workers. He may be
under great pressure to not work so ably. He may *want* to produce
shoddy legs; he may want the outcomes of his activity to *not* conform
to the standards of craft that are imbedded in his perceptions. Nonetheless, in a relaxed moment he may find himself doing work that
meets his perceptual standards, despite his desire not to!

In the last example we have a normal individual operating in a
marred social world, but the problem is manifest a thousand times in
the life of the compulsive. She has standards that are not hers and that
she may even recognize as not-hers. Nonetheless, they enter into her
behavior. She tells us, and we may believe her, that she does not value
her excessive neatness or cleanliness, that she does not want everything she does to be so perfect. Indeed, she may correctly regard her
acute perceptions and stringent perceptual standards as parental intro-
jects. She may wish that she did not always do everything "to perfection." In spite of herself, she is always seeing and correcting her
imperfections. Now if one wishes, one may insist that she feels a need
to do it that way, or that she wants to have it be perfect, or that her
general desire to not be perfect is momentarily overcome by an
overpowering occurrent desire to perfection, but the compulsive may
not sense any such need, or feel any such desire. She just finds herself
acting contrary to her desire. The existence of an overpowering need
or desire are inferred by the *theorist* who insists that they must be
there because the model admits of no alternatives.

On the account I have offered, the activity stands as activity even if
it is divorced from any network of wants and beliefs. Naturally this is
not the case with healthy individuals engaged in self-expressive activity. But we should not take this perhaps rare situation as the model for
all activity. The link between perceptual assessments and the wants
and values of the individual is one of the ways that the self achieves
presence in its activities. It is not always the case.

The upshot of this discussion is to avoid any general identification of causally operative perceptual assessments with wants or beliefs. Similarly, they cannot be said to be the expressions of wants and beliefs. The main significance of this account is that it allows for an *internal* analysis of activities. They are what they are because of their internal structure and not because there exists a set of wants and beliefs that causes them or some of their elements (e.g., bodily movements) to occur.[2]

Acts and Activities

Before proceeding to the discussion of agency, a word must be said about how activities are related to other actions. Philosophers have frequently noted that some things are done by doing other things. Thus, by moving my hand in a certain way, within a specific context, I may do all of the following:

- Wave good-bye to a friend
- Alert a third party
- Betray a trust
- Violate the law
- Break a promise
- Embarrass my friend
- Undermine a relationship

Actions have been separated into those that are basic and those that are not, basic acts being those that are not done in virtue of our doing some other act. Thus, my waving my hand might be viewed as basic, the breaking of my promise (e.g., the promise to not call attention to the fact that we know each other) as nonbasic. While my account does not view (typically) movements such a moving a finger as an act, and therefore not as a basic act, my account is compatible with the basic/nonbasic distinction. In my account, the molecular activity functions as basic. The doing of the molecular activity typically "generates" many nonbasic acts, and it is often the case that the explanation of the person's performing some molecular activity is to be found by understanding what nonbasic acts are thereby generated (e.g., a person's hand movements are understood as the signing of a contract).

In what follows I will use the term "action" to cover both activities and acts that are generated through the performance of activities. Having given an internal analysis of activity in terms of which the mere existence of activity does not imply agency, the outstanding question is: "What is it to be the agent of an activity?"

3

The Self as Integrated Personality

The account of activity that I have given does not involve any notion of agency. It need not be the case that we are agents with respect to all of our activities. In the previous chapter we considered imaginary cases in which through hypnotic or physiological intervention someone causes us to perform a given activity. In some instance it may be something that occurs without our wanting to do it, in another case it may be that the desire to perform the activity is itself artificially induced and thus is not really mine.

In situations of these sorts, it would be natural to say something like, "Yes, he performed a certain activity, but he didn't really do it," or "He wasn't really the agent of those activities." It is this kind of distinction between those activities in relation to which we are agents and those activities in which we are not that I wish to develop.

Examples that rely upon highly artificial circumstances such as hypnosis or chemical or electrical interventions barely scratch the surface with respect to what it is for an action to occur and not really be one's own. If the distinction arose only in cases of this sort, it would hardly be the case that these issues stand at the center of human experience.

Most visions of human nature have made important distinctions within the personality, distinguishing that which is one's true essence from that which is not. There are a multiplicity of ways of marking such distinctions. Sometimes there is a distinction between the person and his or her true self or real self. Sometimes there is a distinction between the person and the self. Sometimes the term "free" is used to characterize actions that have their source in some particular part of the psyche.

The account of agency I am offering maintains that we are agents of our actions when and only when we (our self) are present in these actions. This can be restated as:

A person is an agent of his actions when and only when his self is present in them.

This generates two questions:

1. What is *the self* that is or is not present?

2. What is it for the self *to be present* in an action?

In this chapter I focus on the first of these. The second question is dealt with in the following chapter.

A WORD ON PHILOSOPHIC DISCUSSIONS OF THE SELF

Philosophers have long been concerned with the questions, "What is the self?" or "What is a person?" And most often these are treated as the same question. In the account that I will offer, I make a distinction between the person and the self. Briefly stated I view the self as a highly integrated structure of personality that typically exists only partially formed within a person. I view persons as also being integrated complexes but ones that are much more loosely integrated and disharmonious.

It is possible with respect to a given human being for the person and the self to coincide. This is an ideal state, and with far less air of mystery it can be characterized by saying that the person has achieved full selfhood. What is meant by this is that there are no longer any parts of the person that are foreign to the self and that his or her entire personality conforms to the kind of integration that is requisite for the self.

Parfit has distinguished between reductionist and nonreductionist accounts of persons. An example of a nonreductionist view of persons is that we are Cartesian egos. On reductionist accounts, the existence of a person is similar to that of a nation. Its existence is constituted by the existence of other things standing in certain relations to one another, but there is no extra fact in addition to those facts about other things and their relations.

The analogy of a radio should help in this regard. That radios exist, no one disagrees. And no one would maintain that a radio is any single part of a radio. Yet the radio is not something that lurks behind its parts and "has" them—it is simply constituted by the parts, but only when they are properly assembled. Take a radio completely apart and put the parts in a sack and there is no radio, just a bundle of parts. So a radio is not just any bundling of its constituent parts, it is a very specific kind of bundling.

Reductionist views of persons view the existence of persons in a similar way. And with respect to their continued existence through time, it is thought to consist in certain relations of connectedness and continuity between the bundles at two points in time. But it is not thought to consist in the continued existence of some extra thing through time. This of course is quite different from believing that a person is an immutable soul or ego that cannot be so analyzed and simply exists through time.

In distinguishing between persons and selves, I am distinguishing between certain kinds of integrated bundles. I hold reductionist views both with respect to persons and selves. But for the account of agency that I am putting forward, it does not really matter whether the person is viewed in reductionist or nonreductionist terms. For the person is not the self, and even if persons are thought of as Cartesian egos or souls, they are not selves unless they have attained selfhood. Even on a Cartesian view of persons, we can understand selfhood as a particular condition of the personality, and we can say that the self does not fully exist until the person is such that the elements of his or her personality stand in a specified manner of integration.

Most of this chapter concerns itself with the exact nature of that integration. This is not really the subject matter of metaphysics but rather falls somewhere within or between theory construction in psychology and ethics.

ALTERNATIVE CONCEPTIONS OF THE SELF

Different traditions, religions, philosophies, and cultures maintain different visions of the self and selfhood.

In the Yoga Sutras we find:

A mind free from attachment to perceptible enjoyments such as women, foods, drinks, and power, and having no thirst for scriptural enjoyables, such as heaven and the attainment of the states of the Videha and the Parkritilaya, has, when it comes into contact with such divine and worldly objects, a consciousness of its supremacy, due to an understanding of the defects of the objects, brought about by virtue of intellectual illumination. This consciousness of power is the same as the consciousness of indifference to their enjoyment, and is devoid of all desirable and undesirable objects as such. This mental state is desirelessness.[1]

Desirelessness is but the highest perfection of spiritual knowledge; and absolute independence (kaivalya) is nothing else.[2]

The Higher desirelessness is but a form for the Cloud of Virtue.[3]

The cognition of pleasure under these circumstances is Nescience. Similar is the cognition of the self in the not-self. The external accessories, whether sentient or not sentient, the body which is the vehicle for enjoyments, the mind which is only a vehicle for the Purusa, are all manifestations of the not-self. The notion that any one of these is the self is Nescience.[4]

A man who has become a Dharma-Megha—a Cloud of Holiness, is above all afflictions and Karmas, his mind is free from all taints, . . . this is Kaivalya, this is Self-realization—the state of true Freedom, though full of highest activity.[5]

In *The Republic* Plato divides the soul into three types of elements, the rational, the appetitive, and the passionate. Recognizing the possibility of conflict between these elements, he does not treat them as equal. He writes:

And it will be the business of reason to rule with wisdom and forethought on behalf of the entire soul, while the spirited element ought to act as its subordinate and ally. . . . They must be set in command over the appetites, which form the greater part of each man's soul and are by nature insatiably covetous. They must keep watch lest this part, by fattening on the pleasures that are called bodily, should grow so great and powerful that it will no longer keep to its own work, but will try to enslave the others, and usurp a dominion to which it has no right. . . .[6]

Only when he has linked these parts together in a well-tempered harmony and has made himself one man instead of many will he be ready to go about whatever he may have to do. . . .[7]

A similar outlook may be found in Plotinus. In the following selection, the identification of the self with only one aspect of the conflicted soul is clearly brought out:

But when our Soul holds to its Reason-Principle, to the guide, pure and detached and native to itself, only then can we speak of personal operation, of voluntary act. Things so done may truly be described as our doing, for they have no other source; they are the issue of the unmingled Soul, a Principle that is a First, a leader, a sovereign not subject to the errors of ignorance, not to be overthrown by the tyranny of the desires which, where they can break in drive and drag, so as to allow of no act of ours, but mere answer to stimulus.[8]

Nietzsche represents an almost total reversal:

Behind your thoughts and feelings, my brother, there stands a mighty ruler, an unknown sage—whose name is self. In your body he dwells; he is your body.

There is more reason in your body than in your best wisdom. And who knows why your body needs precisely your best wisdom?

Your self laughs at your ego and at its bold leaps. "What are these leaps and flights of thoughts to me?" it says to itself.[9]

The moral values of the individual are singled out by Nietzsche as that which typically intervenes between the individual and the self. One must go through a process of stripping away this barrier. In the passage entitled "On the Three Metamorphoses" he writes:

Of three metamorphoses of the spirit I tell you; how the spirit becomes a camel, and the camel, a lion; and the lion, finally, a child. . . .

To create new values—that even the lion cannot do; but the creation of freedom for oneself for new creation—that is within the power of the lion. The creation of freedom for oneself and a sacred "No" even to duty—for that, my brothers the lion is needed. . . .

The child is innocence and forgetting, a new beginning, a game, a self-propelled wheel, a first moment, a sacred "Yes." For the game of creation, my brothers, a sacred "Yes" is needed: the spirit now wills his own will, and he who had been lost to the world now conquers his own world.[10]

In these passages we get not only a sense of what Nietzsche regards as representing the non-self (i.e., moral attitudes, concepts of duty) but also why: they do not express one's own will. For Nietzsche, expressing one's own will is not a matter of doing anything one wants to do. Only some of these wants are truly one's own. To get to one's own will one must strip off that which comes from others; much of Nietzsche's concern is with the processes whereby this is accom-

plished. In particular, that which is one's own is marked by spontaneity and joyfulness.

D. H. Lawrence presents a similar perspective:

> By idealism we understand the motivizing of the great affective sources
> by means of ideas mentally derived. . . . This motivizing of the passional
> sphere from the ideal is the final peril of human consciousness. It is the
> death of all spontaneous, creative life, and the substituting of the mechan-
> ical principle.
>
> It is obvious that the ideal becomes a mechanical principle if it be
> applied to the affective soul as a fixed motive. An ideal established in
> control of the passionate soul is no more and no less than a supreme
> machine principle. . . . For there we are, all of us, trapped in a corner
> where we cannot and simply do not know how to fulfill our own natures,
> passionately. We don't know in which way fulfillment lies. . . .
>
> We have actually to go back to our own unconscious. But not to the
> unconscious which is the inverted reflection of our ideal consciousness.
> We must discover if we can, the true unconscious, first bubbling life in
> us, which is innocent of any mental alteration, this is the unconscious. It
> is pristine, not in any way ideal. It is the spontaneous origin from which
> it behooves us to live.[11]
>
> By the unconscious we wish to indicate that essential unique nature of
> every individual creature . . . soul would be a better word.[12]
>
> . . . then at last we can begin to live from the spontaneous initial
> prompting, instead of from the dead machine principles of ideas and
> ideals.[13]

Sometimes the opposition to the rational and ideal aspects of the self
emerges an as enhanced emphasis on emotions. In the short story
"The Desire to be a Man," by Villiers de l'Isle-Adam, the protagonist
proclaims:

> Here it is nearly a half a century that I have been impersonating, that I
> have been play-acting the passions of others, without ever feeling them
> myself—for deep down, I myself have never felt anything. It's a joke to
> think I'm anything like those others! Am I then only a shadow? Passions!
> Feelings! Real acts! REAL ONES! That's it, that's what constitutes a
> MAN in the true sense of the word![14]

These differences are profound. So profound that they hardly ever
emerge as arguments between different outlooks. When Charles Stevenson was developing an emotivist vision of ethical disagreement, he
distinguished between disagreements of fact and disagreements of

attitude, and he maintained that while much ethical disagreement was about factual matters, it was often the case that arguments turned on the definitions of key terms. These definitions he named "persuasive definitions," and he saw them as expressive of alternative ethical outlooks, but not themselves subject to any decisive mode of rational evaluation.

How are we to conceive of the differences between these different conceptions of the self? Are they rooted in some differences in fact that could in principle be adjudicated? Are they, rather, arbitrary specifications? Are they, as used to be said of ethical terms, devoid of descriptive meaning?

Though these alternative conceptions of the self are typically deeply embedded in diverse cultural outlooks with long historical traditions, it may be useful to think of the issue as if we were engaged in a de novo exercise in theory construction. The key theoretical term to be introduced is "the self" and we have a variety of alternative ways of conceiving it. Viewed from this perspective, two points emerge.

1. The adequacy of a specific conception of the self cannot be assessed without some prior conception of the kind of theorizing in which we are engaged. Is it scientific theory or moral theory? Or is it something different from both of these? What do we intend to do with a concept of the self? Against what purposes are we to appraise alternatives? Are we interested primarily in predicting human behavior? Are we seeking a conception to guide a therapeutic endeavor? Are we constructing a moral theory?

2. Even within a specific enterprise (e.g., development of moral theory) we cannot assess the adequacy of a specific theoretical conception of the self independently of the adequacy of the broader theory (e.g., utilitarianism) of which it is a part.

Seen from this point of view, it is not surprising that concepts of the self have typically emerged as part of some normative enterprise. The theorizing in question almost always goes beyond mere prediction and explanation of behavior. The normative context may involve the development of a specific moral outlook, or may be an attack on morality as part of a larger Lawrencian or Nietzschean effort to articulate non-moral ideals for human and cultural development; it may involve the development of specific views on desirable social change ranging from questions of schooling to the basic structures of social organization (Marx); it may be in the context of one-on-one therapeutic endeavors typically in the psychoanalytic tradition (Karen Horney, Kohut); or it may be within metaphysical and religious speculations that carry with them a view of authentic life and self-experience (Augustine, Sartre).

The nature of the self is intimately connected to all normative enterprises that engage the issue of human transformation (morality, education, religion, therapy, social development, political and economic theory and revolution). The ideals in question may range beyond ethical ideals in a narrow sense. The basis for a specific view of the self may ultimately rest on a largely aesthetic notion, a vision of a certain kind of creature that exhibits behaviors and responses that one endorses or rejects on what is ultimately an aesthetic level. For instance, the celebration of the unfettered expressiveness of the small child, or of the vibrant animal that lacks a concept of shame may be of the nature of ultimate preferences.

Alternatively, a view of the self may be supported by specific empirical beliefs with respect to the sources of human pathology (where what is viewed as "pathology" is not unique to the theoretical outlook). Thus, when Karen Horney locates the real-self in much the same place that Nietzsche did (in the spontaneous, in the pre-moral realms of desire), she is more explicit in her view that a personality that is in touch with and organized around these sources of energy will be free from the troubles that bring people to the psychiatrist's office. Yet even in Nietzsche there is the implicit claim that cultural greatness is vitiated by the moral and that individual pathology (essentially lack of a vibrant will) is covered up by the rule-governed personality structure.

The account of the self that I will present is accommodating with respect to these various conceptions, but probably not fully neutral. It is in a sense a schema that can accommodate a multiplicity of specific conceptions. And it can be expected then that the account of agency that follows will also be general enough to not rule out specific visions of the self.

Before proceeding directly to my analysis, I want to briefly consider one parallel attempt to do something of this sort. In his book, *On Being Free,* Frithjof Bergmann is concerned with alternative conceptions of freedom.[15] Bergmann calls attention to the fact that there is tremendous diversity with respect to what kind of act is viewed as a free act. For instance, he examines the outlook of the Underground Man in Dostoyevsky's *Notes from the Underground* and finds that the Underground Man experiences himself as free only insofar as he acts for no reason whatsoever; he experiences acting for a reason, even his own self-interest, as the antithesis of freedom. Alternatively, Bergmann points to Aristotle as one who identified the free act with the rational act.

Faced with this kind of diversity, Bergmann asks what would an individual's self-experience have to be in order that he or she experience himself or herself as free in one case as opposed to another. Bergmann's answer is that the individual would have to view the self as having its true locus in one or another place, in our rational faculties, in our emotions, in our desires, or in the case of the Underground Man—in a pinpoint of reflection or action that is estranged from all else.

Thus, Bergmann maintains that at bottom it is alternative approaches to the self that lie behind different conceptions of freedom. There is more than an analogy between what he is saying about freedom and the approach to agency that I have been developing. It might be suggested that my notion of agency is equivalent to a notion of free action or free agency. This will be discussed more fully in the next chapter.

It is Bergmann's approach to the self that is my present concern. Bergmann does not put forward his own conception, which specifies wherein the locus of the true self lies. Rather, he seeks to pull back to a level that allows him to offer a schema that can accommodate these various outlooks on the locus of the self. And in this regard, his project is similar to what I am seeking to do in the present chapter.

Bergmann's answer is not totally straightforward, so I will let him speak for himself.

> . . . nothing less than an act committed by my own self can be free.[16]
> The critical requirement is still that of identification: only if I identify with the making of a choice is it free; if I do not identify with it, then it is not. [17]
> It is not just a "thinking" that constitutes the self: it is the act that we from the outset called *identification*. It is crucial to understand that the self is literally "constituted" through this act of identification. There is no self apart from or prior to it. The self—if we may put it so—has its being only in the fact that something is given that significance. [18]
> The absence of any inherent self and the fact that it arises only when that significance is attached to some parts of an otherwise neutral experience lead us to speak of its "self constitutiveness," but this does not mean that the self (or an identification) exists only in the thoughts we have about it, that it comes into being only through reflection, or that it is as we think or imagine it to be. The genesis of the self involves a rearranging of experience and that reorganization exists and is real

whether we are aware of it or not. . . . We can be mistaken about our own identifications. [19]

There are three aspects of Bergmann's view of the self to which I want to call attention:

1. The self is not inherent. It is something that emerges in the life of a person

2. The self is self-constitutive. It is the person himself or herself who brings the self into existence

3. The self is brought into existence through "acts" of identification

In the account that I will offer, each of these three claims is reflected, but they are held in a weaker form. The self is not some inherent inner part of the psyche, and a person does play an active role in the creation of his or her own self, and a person's own understanding of what is and is not really oneself does play a major role in the development of the self. Yet none of this should be overstated. I see identifications as something less than fully self-constitutive of the self, and I envision the self as something that can exist in the absence of or in opposition to identifications. Or to put it differently, I see the self as a *structure of personality*. It is brought into being through a variety of factors. Bergmann is quite correct about the person's own role in creating this structure and that "acts" of identification play a key role in building the structure. But in the end, I want to maintain that the self is the structure, and not the building of it. And it is a clearer picture of that structure that I seek to provide.

THE INTEGRATED PERSONALITY

In a classic article, written over fifty years ago, McDougall put forward a very specific vision of the kind of integration of personality that is required for what he called "volition in the full and higher sense."

> Development of integrated character consists in the growth of a *harmonious system of the sentiments,* a hierarchical system in which the working of the sentiments for the more concrete objects is regulated and controlled by the sentiments for more general and more abstract and ideal

objects, such as devotion to the family, the clan, the occupational or civic group, the nation, or mankind, the love of justice, humanity, liberty, equality, fraternity; and by hatred for cruelty, for injustice, for oppression, for slavery. And *volition in the full and higher sense* implies that this hierarchy of sentiments culminates in and is presided over by a sentiment of self-regard which, by incorporating in its system these higher abstract sentiments has become an ideal of self, an ideal of character, and of conduct to which our daily actions must conform, and with which our long-range motivations, our ambitions and personal loyalties must harmonize.[20]

Here McDougall is spelling out the notion of integration as unity in terms of some ideal. Ultimately the individual has some ideal of self—and the personality is unified insofar as it fits this ideal. McDougall does not tell us what it is for a motive or an emotion or an action to "harmonize" with the self-ideal. However, it is a value system in which judgments about virtues (e.g., ideals with respect to selves and their character) plays a central role. Around this central structure will be a harmonized set of sentiments, actions, ambitions, motivations, and loyalties. McDougall is offering an account of how the parts have to be wired or assembled for character to exist, for the individual to be able in the "true" sense to exercise volition. On the account I am offering, the phrase "to truly be an agent" might substitute for McDougall's reference to volition.

What is parallel to my account is that McDougall envisions true volition (agency) as requiring that there be an integrated structure of personality out of which the person acts. I am using the term "self" for this integrated structure. Such a formulation leads to a variety of questions: (1) What are the parts of the integrated complex we call the self? (2) How must these parts be related to one another? (3) And if the parts must be related in a manner that allows the whole to function in a certain way, what are those modes of functioning?

Philosophers have tended to approach these types of questions with a focus on the minimum, asking what relationship between what elements would be the minimum necessary in order for there to be a self—or as the question is sometimes asked—in order that a living being be a person.

The approach that I take is somewhat different. Instead of focusing on the minimum for the existence of a person, I am concerned with the other end of the continuum, with full selfhood or the fully constituted self. A person may be thought of as a more loosely organized complex than the self, or perhaps as a more chaotically organized complex. Within this complex there may be a variety of subcomplexes that are not fully organized with each other. On some views such as those just considered, one or another of these subcomplexes may be viewed as the central locus of the self, as its core. But a person would be said to have attained full selfhood only when the self complex comes to encompass all that is the person.

Marcus Aurelius described the perfected soul as having achieved a perfectly rounded form. It is perfect when it becomes "a totally rounded orb, rejoicing in its own rotundity."[21] Achieving selfhood may be a task that persons engage in throughout their lives. The pursuit of selfhood might be the central project of human life and one that is never fully achieved. Thus becoming a self (attaining selfhood) may be thought of as an ideal towards which a person may move (of fall away from). So thought of, the quality of agency, which depends upon the existence and presence of a self within activity, may also be viewed as a quality to be possessed only more or less completely. In this way it may be like the quality of being beautiful as opposed to the quality of being the color yellow or green. A person may become more and more beautiful without ever fully exhausting the human potential to exemplify beauty. But a block of wood painted yellow can be as fully yellow as is possible.

From Plato through Freud the notions of unity and disunity, of harmony and conflict, of integration and discord, have been central to theories of the human personality. Despite the centrality of this image, the history of psychology offers surprisingly few straightforward answers to the first two questions I am concerned with: What are the parts of the integrated personality? What are the relations between them in virtue of which they constitute a unified whole?

Most psychologists proceed as if they have an adequate grasp of what they mean by "integrated" or "integrated personality." It is not unusual to find entire books with titles such as *The Integrity of the Personality*[22] or *The Integration of the Personality*,[23] which make no direct effort to define or explicate the notion of integration or to say what it is that is integrated with what. This is not to say that psychologists have not addressed these issues, but they have typically done so indirectly and with limited scope.

One way to develop a general picture of what it is for the personality to be fully integrated is to consider specific instances of conflict and disintegration that are detailed in the literature on psychopathology.

Harold Searles's *Collected Papers on Schizophrenia and Related Subjects* are rich and subtle.[24] Searles writes:

> I have found repeatedly that the individual with paranoid schizophrenia, initially so unwavering about everything, and never doubting that his own views are his very own, reaches, after years of psychotherapy, a point where it becomes clear not only to the therapist, but to himself also, that nearly everything he has been saying is in actuality but an ill understood hodge-podge of the parroted—though unwittingly caricatured and otherwise distorted—utterances of his parents and other significant persons from his childhood. He comes to reveal, at long last, precisely the confusion of a small child who has been exposed to a bewildering cacophony of parental statements and who has not heretofore found anyone sufficiently trustworthy and patient to help him out of his confusion. Two among the patients who have reached this point, in our work together, have come to say, quite simply and seriously and trustingly, "I don't know anything."[25]

This passage is of interest in that it describes a change from an unwavering certainty to a total sense of unsureness. Yet, the certainty itself was a disguise for internal confusion. The patient had interjected parental statements without having integrated them. Thus, the patient reaches the conclusion that he doesn't *know* anything. Searles speaks of the patient's coming to see that everything he has been saying is "ill understood" and "parroted." The contrast that is suggested is that when the individual does "understand" his own views they are not parroted, but more fully his own. Thus the question of reasoning or of having or seeing reasons for what one believes appears somehow powerfully connected to wholeness. And the patient's remark that "he doesn't know anything" suggests that somehow having knowledge is a part of what it is to have a unified personality. This link between knowledge and psychological unity needs to be drawn out—it is a crucial connection, and I will pick up on it subsequently.

Searles goes on to describe certain "fragmentations" he has witnessed: "Markedly varying moods, and widely disparate levels of ego-organization may appear in a rapidly changing and random sequence."[26]

He describes a patient's fragmentation:

> She would bellow at one moment that we criminals should kill her and thus end her torture, and at the next moment would be laughing warmly; would at one moment be a monumentally arrogant woman, and the next moment a touchingly childlike creature.[27]

Here the lack of integration is between elements of the same kind over time. Moment to moment there is a radical shift as one mood replaces another. From our point of view the apparent randomness of these shifts is as important as their dramatic nature. This example is also important because it illustrates that having a coherent personality is not merely a matter of an integration at a particular point in time, but something that exists over a period of time. Or if we want to explicate a concept of having a coherent personality at time *t,* this would include having dispositions at *t* to have certain responses at *t* + 1.

Speaking of the paranoid, Searles says, "His inability to differentiate important from trivial . . . ingredients around him may account for some of his well known suspicion. He may be suspicious . . . because his suspicion provokes his only mode of processing, of sifting out, the data from a world which is bewilderingly complex."[28]

Searles goes on to speak of the way in which some schizophrenic patients are unable to recognize certain expressions as mere figures of speech. What he is calling attention to is the fact that the paranoid personality tends to experience things as meaningful in ways that are different from those of the healthy person. Sometimes the paranoid reads far more meaning into a situation than is really there, sometimes less, and sometimes quite differently. This illustrates a tremendously important fact. In trying to specify what we mean by the integrated personality, the term "integrated" is much too crude. What is of concern is not integration per se, but certain kinds of integrations and not others. If we think of the personality as similar to a radio in that it can exist only if the parts are wired together in certain very specific ways, then what we are after is a map that lays out how to wire the parts correctly, not merely all the different possible ways in which wires might link one part to another. The paranoid might not lack integration; rather he may be integrated (wired, assembled) in ways that are different than those of the normal individual. Indeed, he may have *more* integration. For instance it may be that his perceptions themselves tend to be formed in ways that conform to very powerful beliefs and fears, whereas the healthy individual might have perceptions that emerge relatively independently and thus are *allowed to conflict,* contradict, and not harmonize with prior beliefs. In short, the healthy individual may be such that his perceptions are only loosely connected to prior beliefs. And this gives rise to his openness and flexibility in the face of new experience—he is capable of changing his mind.

In a discussion of ambivalence, Searles brings out a number of features that are not present in the integrated personality.

> A hebephrenic woman . . . managed to convey to me . . . that she wanted to subscribe to her home town newspaper. . . . But no sooner had I said that I would bring it up with her doctor than she proceeded to make it clear that she felt, on the other hand, that were she to start receiving that newspaper, it would be a great burden to her.[29]

Having mixed feelings about something is, of course, an appropriate response to complex realities. However, ambivalence may take different forms. Thus, the schizophrenic may waver between an intense fear of something and an intense desire for it, without forming any single attitude that is a balance of the two. At any given moment only one aspect of the situation is responded to, and thus only one attitude is manifest. Searles describes:

> . . . verbal communications in which there is a split between content and vocal feeling-tone. . . . On still another occasion she said, "You're such a darling!" with a peculiarly hostile vocal tone such that I felt that, despite the complimentary words themselves, she was cutting off my head.[30]

The relationship between the integrated person's verbal content and her feeling tone is a complex and interesting matter. It is not simple. After all, one can be sarcastic. The integrated person, however, is aware of the split and aware of what she is feeling and what she is expressing. The lack of awareness, attributed to the schizophrenic, reflects some deeper lack of integration. I will come back to this in considering what it is for the self to be present in one's activity.

One way of systematizing these insights is to start with a listing of the various elements that might enter into the compound that we are calling the self, or integrated personality. Once these elements are listed, we can then ask what forms of integration (or alternatively, what forms of incoherence) might exist between such elements and other elements of a same or different type? Thus, consider Figure 3.1.

Imagine that the grid lists horizontally and vertically all possible component elements of the self. The intersections specify the varieties of integration that are possible between elements of these various sorts (e.g., beliefs and perceptions, memories and beliefs, values and desires, desires and desires). For each of these possible combinations it would be necessary to spell out what constitutes an integrated relation-

	beliefs	values	emotions	desires	intentions	moods	projects	attitudes	tastes	memories
beliefs										
values										
emotions										
desires										
intentions										
moods										
projects										
attitudes										
tastes										
memories										

Figure 3.1

ship between the relevant elements. Having done that one could add a third dimension and then go on to consider what is involved in the integration of any groupings of three types of elements (e.g., a belief, a value, and an intention). By working through some such enormous task, one could in principle give an exhaustive account of the different kinds of integration that might exist between the elements of the self. One would then have at hand the raw materials from which a variety of *different* notions of the self could be constructed. The theorist could specify a particular conception of the self by specifying types of elements and modes of integration that constituted wholeness on that particular notion of self.

I will not undertake anything so grandiose. Instead I will offer some thoughts, first about specific kinds of elements of particular centrality to the self, and then about certain modes of integration that seem of particular importance on any conception of the self.

Elements

First let me say a word about the elements I have listed. In explicating the notion of an integrated personality, it seems reasonable to emphasize the dispositional rather than the occurrent modes of mental states. For instance, consider a conflict between one's belief that it is wrong to do something and one's desire to do it. If we are talking about a specific occurrent desire, that is, a phenomenological occurrence of a certain sort, this lack of integration would hardly represent a significant challenge to the wholeness of the self. But if what we were postulating was not a mere momentary occurrence, but rather a standing disposition, the situation is quite different. If the elements in question are central enough (e.g., the belief that incest is wrong, and a long-standing desire to sleep with one's mother) then when they conflict, we are dealing with a rather fundamental fissure in the personality.

One way of proceeding is to view the component parts of the self as all being dispositions (one aspect of which would be the disposition to have certain mental events) and to say that when there is conflict between these dispositions, there will also typically be occurrent states that conflict with one or another disposition or with other occurrent states. But the occurrent states are not themselves the component parts. So, rather than viewing the self as a bundle of ideas, we are viewing it as a bundle of dispositions. But which dispositions should we consider? And are there any that are more critical than others?

Within some theoretical orientations (e.g., psychoanalytic theory) the personality is conceptualized in terms of certain subsystems (e.g., id, ego, and super-ego) and an ideal of integration can be specified in terms of the unification of these subsystems or within specific subsystems. As I wish to give an account of the self that is not dependent upon the adequacy of any specific psychological theory, I will restrict myself to those aspects of the psyche that form our commonsense understanding of persons. The most important ones are listed on the illustrative grid. I have left out thoughts, perceptions, and actions, viewing them as occurrent events or processes rather than dispositions. While they may be integrated with the elements that make up the self, they are not themselves constitutive elements of the self. On the other hand one might include thoughts in a dispositional sense, as well as tendencies to perceive in a certain way, and projects. While my performing a specific action is itself an event, projects are things that one has. Having the project of writing a book is a complex dispositional state that one is in over a long period of time, and is distinct from the actions that might constitute carrying out that project.

The body

How is the body related to the self? The human body is itself an integrated system. Moreover, it is an integrated system of integrated subsystems. The relationship between the body and the self is complex and elusive. Conceptually, the body is separable from both the person and the self. There is no contradiction in affirming that a person may survive even if his or her body is destroyed. Moreover, it is logically possible for more than one person to occupy the same body.

Yet all known human persons have in fact not only had bodies, they were embodied. The only way certain kinds of things can happen to a person is in virtue of their having happened to the body. Thus, if it is true that person X was hit by a car then this is true in virtue of the fact that his body was hit by a car. We are physical beings in virtue of being living bodies.

I will treat the living human body as a component element of the human self. We can think of the human self as existing when there exists a living human body that has certain dispositions that are integrated in certain ways.

The sense of identity

On certain views of the nature of the self (or of persons) specific kinds of elements have been identified as necessary. Thus for instance it might be maintained that there cannot be a self or person unless there are beliefs, indeed, unless there are beliefs of a specific sort (e.g., beliefs about oneself). Or it might be maintained that for there to be a self there must be desires and, indeed, certain kinds of desires (e.g., Harry Frankfurt attaches tremendous importance to having desires about which desires one will act upon). But the element that plays the most central role in accounts of the self is a person's sense of identity. So central is this to conceptions of the self that some writers have simply identified the self with the person's concept of himself or herself. This, of course, gives rise to the problem of what it is that has a concept of itself. I will treat a person's sense of identity as one particular element of the personality; as one of the component elements of the self.

But what is the sense of identity? First a distinction should be made between a person's identity and his or her sense of identity or self-identity (or self-concept). On some theoretical orientations these are the same, but this is not always the case. For instance, as will be discussed in a subsequent chapter, Marxist theory suggests a distinction between objective identity and subjective identity. Objective identity is a matter of who you really are. Subjective identity is a matter of who you identify yourself to yourself as being. It is subjective identity that I am referring to with the terms "sense of identity" and "self-identity."

From some theoretical perspectives, such as the psychologist's efforts to explain an individual's emotional responses, there may be no use or need for a distinction between subjective and objective identity. Thus, it is not surprising that many writers have not seen the distinction, and have used the phrase "a person's identity" to mean "a person's self-identity." The distinction between subjective identity and objective identity is not a matter of what a person thinks his or her self-identity is and what his or her self-identity really is. This latter distinction can also be made, and it is possible that we do not always know what our self-identity is—but that is yet another distinction.

To have a self-identity is to have a certain view about who you are. So, an entity that has a self-identity is first of all an entity that has beliefs. Secondly it is an entity that has beliefs about itself. Moreover, these beliefs about itself are not merely extensionally about itself— they are not beliefs of the sort "Harry is six feet tall" when it turns out that the believer is Harry. Rather, they are beliefs of the sort "I am six feet tall"—they carry with them the recognition of their reflexive character.

It is possible to treat having a self-identity in a minimalistic manner that would be satisfied by merely having some self-referential beliefs. Were we to stop at this point, we would be at the metaphysical end of the continuum between the metaphysical notion of the self and the moral/psychological notion of the self. Descartes's cogito ("I think") was of this sort, and from the existence of this thought, he passed to the existence of a minimal self. But in the present context, a person's having a self-identity should be seen as more than a matter of merely having a belief about oneself of the sort "I am such and such"—only certain self-ascriptive beliefs are constitutive of a person's sense of identity.

Self-ascriptive beliefs ascribe to oneself particular properties. For instance, a person believes of himself that he has the properties of being male, young, Jewish, a lover of music, a good craftsman, and so forth. But the properties one ascribes to oneself may also be far more trivial, the properties of being in front of the bookcase, having brown hair, having thirty-two teeth, and so on. Only some of these ascriptions of properties embody the person's self-identity. Of those properties that we believe ourselves to have, the ones that constitute our self-identity ("being p" is part of X's self-identity) can be recognized by the following:

- the belief that he is p causes him to feel pride or shame
- the belief that he is p plays a role in a wide variety of choices that he makes
- to come to believe that he was not p would be highly unsettling
- he believes that he is known only to those people who believe that he is p
- he seeks to communicate to people (or hide from them) the "fact" that he is p

To speak of a person's self-identity is to say that the person has certain beliefs and certain dispositions that relate those beliefs in complex ways to certain specific kinds of emotions (e.g., pride and shame) and certain kinds of actions. Thus the very existence of this particular element (a self-identity or self-concept) presupposes the existence of other elements and certain forms of integration.

One reason why the self-concept is seen as central to the self is that the plausibility of the beliefs that constitute the self-concept may be either supported or undermined by much that the person does, and it appears that people typically are strongly motivated to act in ways that support these beliefs. Thus, having a particular self-concept plays a central role in determining the individual's behavior, and in particular in those actions that add to the further integration of the self. Thus, many of the components of the self can be seen to be organized around the self-concept. Lecky's motive towards self-consistency and Mc-Dougall's view that the self is organized around an ideal of self can be seen as variants of this primacy of the sense of identity; however, it is an error to restrict the properties that may be constitutive of a person's self-identity to ones that the person views positively. It is equally possible to have a negative self-identity.[31]

Integration Between Elements

Beliefs and beliefs

In looking for elements that are absolutely central to any view of the self, it is hard to find a firmer starting point than beliefs. Can we imagine the existence of a person or self that has no beliefs? Perhaps the newborn infant has no beliefs, but then is the infant a person or a self? We could perhaps imagine a normal adult who is suddenly struck by an amnesia so powerful that not only does he have no memories of the past, he has no beliefs about it at all; but could we imagine that there was such a person and he had no beliefs about the present or the future? A person who is asleep or unconscious still has beliefs. It appears that having beliefs is very much at the core of what it is for a person to exist.

The fuller notion of the self, however, requires coherence between a person's beliefs. But what is it for one belief to cohere with or be integrated with one or more other beliefs? To have a belief is to believe of a certain proposition that it is true. When we speak of the coherence between someone's beliefs we are speaking about a coherence between the embedded propositions. And since the relationships between propositions is a matter of formal and informal logics, the pattern that we are calling integration within the self must be a mirroring of a pattern between propositions. In the simplest instance, two propositions are in conflict with each other if one is the negation of the other. And thus, two beliefs are in conflict with each other when one is the belief that p and the other is the belief that not-p This is not, however, to say that the conflict between belief elements will be experienced as conflict. For two contradictory beliefs to be experienced as conflicting, the person must be aware of "tension" between the two propositions. The proposition $123/7 + 13 \times 2\frac{1}{8} = 50$ contains a contradiction, but there is no conflict for people who believe this proposition so long as they do not realize that it is contradictory.

In general terms we can express the varieties of coherence between beliefs as expressions of the *reasonableness* of beliefs, either the reasonableness of holding certain beliefs in view of others, or of holding them with certain attitudes (e.g., certainty) in the face of other beliefs also held. Or to put it differently, we can articulate rationality in terms of the relationships between beliefs such that in its complete absence the very existence of the self would be hard to understand. The irrationality that we encounter among human beings, or at least those that we conceive of as persons, is never complete.

If persons exist only in virtue of having certain beliefs, and if the fuller existence of the self requires a coherence between beliefs, which consists in their being reasonable in relation to each other, it is tempting to take the next step and identify the self with reason or with its rational capacities and functions. From the Greeks onward many have made this move.

In calling attention to the link between selfhood and rationality, I am not embracing a view that humans are inherently rational, nor am I affirming a vision of the self that treats the rational faculties as the central locus of the self. Rather I am saying that all notions of a self as an integrated compound involve some commitment to a minimal rationality, even those conceptions that emphasize the nonrational.

The fundamental character of some minimal structure of rationality can be seen by reflecting upon how some rationality is presupposed in explaining irrationality. For instance consider the preconditions for the mechanisms of repression, and of the psyche's *need* for an unconscious. If repression is to be understood as a defense against that which is threatening, then there must be a capacity to perceive something as threatening. In particular, if some information about oneself is to be perceived as threatening, for instance threatening to one's self-identity, then there must be a *capacity to perceive that certain propositions undermine the credibility of others*. Were there no such capacity, which is to say, no mechanism that embodies even some limited notion of rationality, then there would be no psychological difficulty in accepting, as true, information that totally undermined the very dearest beliefs that we entertain about ourselves. Thus, while it may be an idiosyncrasy of Western civilization, or Socratic culture, that it so heavily identifies with Reason, no notion of selfhood can fully abandon rationality. In Chapter 6, I return to this feature of selves when I consider the way in which reflection, in particular philosophic reflection, which calls into question the very possibility of rational beliefs, can threaten a disintegration of the personality.

The norms of reasonableness with respect to beliefs can be thought of both in terms of integration between beliefs at a given moment in time, and also as integration between beliefs at different moments in time. At any moment in time we may ask a variety of questions about the reasonableness of the set of beliefs. Are they logically consistent with each other? Relative to the other members of the set, is each individual belief at least as probable as its negation? (Or more broadly, is it reasonable for a given person to believe *p* in the face of the evidence she has?) Is the degree of certainty with which she holds a particular belief in proportion to the evidence she has for it? (More broadly, is her degree of certainty reasonable?)

With respect to each of these questions, as noted earlier, there will be no psychic tension so long as the individual does not operate with some internalized norm of rationality. To say that we have internalized norms of rationality, however, is not to say that our beliefs fully conform to such norms. Most of us have some contradictory beliefs; we all believe certain things in spite of the evidence that we have for the greater likelihood of an alternative, and we all hold many beliefs with a degree of certainty that bears little measure to the evidence we have for their accuracy. The norms of rationality define idealized versions of what it would be for a belief system to be fully integrated. Selfhood, on any conception, requires some conformity to these ideals. But there is considerable leeway with respect to how much.

Finally, I should say a word about these "norms of rationality." The philosophic project of explicating the notions of "reasonable belief" and "reasonable attitude of certainty" is itself a task that is not complete and will no doubt undergo considerable rethinking and trans-formation. I am not suggesting that an ultimately defensible version of such norms can presently be articulated. However, I do believe that there is some central notion of norms of rationality that would be part of the minimal rationality that is inherent in any notion of the self. Insofar as the actual articulation of such norms awaits the completion of a project in philosophy of science or epistemology, it follows that the fuller specification of what the self is awaits the completion of that project. Thus philosophy remains a central part of the attempt to discover who we are.

To say that a person's belief structure conforms to a norm of rationality is not to say that he or she explicitly holds such a norm. But for many persons, a norm of rationality is not merely something that we may or may not conform to; it also exists as a somewhat explicit view about what constitutes a reason for believing or not believing something.

Charles Peirce, in his classic essay "The Fixation of Belief," spoke of "the method of authority" as one of the ways in which human beings come to have or not have certain beliefs. But the method of authority is more than a mere *habit* of believing what one is told by certain authorities; rather it involves the designation of certain institutions or individuals as authoritative in the sense that it is viewed as rational for one to believe what they assert. Thus, if one has internalized specific norms of rationality in line with the method of authority, not only is there a question of the coherence of first-level beliefs with each other, but also of the coherence between the norm and the beliefs (i.e., between the belief that *p* and the belief that the authorities believe or assert *p*). To internalize a norm of rationality is to build into one's functioning a mechanism for the fixation of belief—and also a mechanism for the unfixing of belief. It is a structure that determines how beliefs get added to the system and how they get changed. Among individuals there is a great deal of difference with respect to both what such internalized norms are, and their scope and power.

Beliefs may also fail to be integrated over time. The simplest notion of integration over time is that of constancy of beliefs, and the most striking lack of integration would be the discrete substitution of one set of beliefs by their negation at a subsequent point in time. Having a coherent structure of beliefs over some interval of time cannot be a mere matter of having an integrated set at any given moment during that time, nor, however, could it be restricted to having the same integrated set throughout that time period. Moreover, whatever requirements of constancy or continuity are introduced, they are not equally applicable to all beliefs. The constancy of some beliefs is certainly more central to the existence of the self than are other beliefs. Thus, there is very little problem if I keep changing my mind with respect to a certain isolated matter of fact (e.g., whether or not Helen of Troy really existed). But if we were to focus on the set of beliefs that are central to a person's sense of identity (e.g., the belief that he is male, American, a parent, born of Jewish parents), and if these beliefs were simply replaced by the negative every other day, we would lack the coherence needed for selfhood. But even if we consider beliefs that are not as central to the personality as those that constitute the sense of self, the norms of rationality include norms of rational change. In some rough sense, selfhood requires that our changing set of beliefs itself exhibit both some conformity to such norms and also a degree of substantive continuity.

Beliefs and other mental states

The term "reasonableness" covers a variety of relationships of integration between beliefs, but it can be applied to mental elements other than beliefs, and in each case signals some particular mode of integration. Thus, we can speak of projects, desires, emotions, attitudes, intentions, and values as rational or irrational. As with integration among beliefs, the integration of beliefs and other elements points to a relationship between rationality and selfhood:

1. There is a minimal notion of coherence/rationality that is part of any notion of an integrated self (e.g., one cannot have selfhood where the emotions are totally irrational).

2. Norms of rationality with respect to these elements may themselves be component elements of a particular self. Thus, someone may hold a norm in addition to merely conforming to it. When norms of rationality are held by a person, they represent commitments to not hold elements that do not conform to those norms. This makes possible new kinds of coherence and conflict (e.g., for some persons the having of irrational desires may represent a far greater fracture of the self than for others for whom norms of rationality have a more limited role).

3. There is the unfinished and changing project of articulating just what it means for such elements to be rational, and thus to some extent the articulation of the concept of self is dependent and parasitic upon future philosophic inquiry.

The key to an analysis of the rationality of elements such as desires, emotions, values, and intentions lies in a recognition of *the way in which these elements of self are penetrated by and partially constituted by beliefs.* Consider, for example, a particular emotional state John ascribes to himself: "I am afraid that my sister will die of her disease before I see her." How is such a state connected to the following beliefs that John has?

- the belief that he has a sister
- the belief that his sister has a disease
- the belief that the disease is life threatening
- the belief that she may die of the disease

There is no single term that captures the relationship between the emotion and these beliefs; we can speak of beliefs as "presupposed," "implied," or "expressed" by emotions. We have no adequate way of capturing the varieties of intimacy. With respect to the first of these, the belief that he has a sister, we would be hard pressed to understand what it was for John to fear that his sister might die (not that x, who turns out to be his sister, might die, but someone who is for him his sister) if he also had the belief that he had no sister.

This strong relationship is not present with respect to the last belief on the list: the belief that his sister may die—we could understand someone who said, "I don't really believe that she will die, it's just that I keep having this fear that she will." Indeed, we and the person himself might say that it is a quite understandable fear, even if irrational. Here what is meant by "irrational" is that in one's emotional reaction (e.g., the intense fear that she will die) one is responding as if one believed what one doesn't (e.g., as if one believed it probable that she will die when one knows that it is highly unlikely). In characterizing the response as irrational, there is presupposed some notion of "proper fit" between the intensity of the fear and the probability one ascribes to the feared event.

But the most I can say about this notion of "appropriateness" is the direction of the relationship. The more probable the feared event is believed to be, the more reasonable is the intense fear. Beyond this, however, it is not obvious how to proceed. What level of intensity of fear that she will die is appropriate to a belief that there is a 10 percent probability of death? I don't see any way of determining that any particular absolute level of intensity is more appropriate than other alternatives, given some specified level of subjective probability of the feared event.

The issue of proportionality arises not just in relation to the believed probability of the event's occurrence, but also in relation to one's judgment of its seriousness or importance. Our emotions are sometimes irrational in that we are tremendously agitated (angry, jealous, petrified, terrified) by what we ourselves view as little things. And some people are simply more emotional than others in that the strength of all their reactions appears more intense. We can understand irrationality internally for each person, but there is no standard for saying that an entire emotional make-up that has internal proportionality is either too strong or too weak. Entire cultures differ one from another along these dimensions. Stereotypes aside, the English look a certain way to the Italians, and the Italians look a certain way to the English. It may be that these differences reflect importantly different internal structures, that to produce one sort of emotionality requires repression or internal conflict that is not present in the other case. But it also may be the case that nothing of this sort is true, and that all we are left with are aesthetic preferences—some people prefer it when the sound is turned up, others prefer a quieter rendition.

Given that certain beliefs are constitutive elements of emotions, and given that such beliefs may either cohere or fail to cohere with other beliefs, the emotion is thereby drawn into relationship with a broader circle of beliefs external to it. For instance, one could talk about the relationship between the emotion and beliefs that should give rise to the conclusion that one's sister who is ill is not facing any serious danger. Thus, one might have read (and accepted as true) that such illnesses are never fatal in adults over thirty, one may believe that one's sister is over thirty, and yet still have the fear that she will die. Here the lack of integration is between certain beliefs that are totally separate from the emotion (e.g., she is forty years old) and other beliefs that are embedded in the emotion (e.g., she may die from the disease). Thus, starting from the fact that certain beliefs are inherent, embedded, or presupposed by certain emotional states, and through those beliefs and a prior notion of integration between beliefs, a second class of beliefs is reached that may or may not be integrated with the emotion.

The presence of beliefs within complex mental elements is not unique to emotions; it occurs with respect to almost all of the other mental elements that make up the self. Consider someone with the project of "being elected president of the United States." The following set of beliefs, or something quite similar, is partially constitutive of his having that project.

- The belief that there is something called the United States
- The belief that the United States has a presidency
- The belief that it is possible for him to run for the presidency
- The belief that it is possible that he may be elected president

It borders on the unintelligible to say of someone that he does not believe that the United States has or ever will have a prime minister, but that his project is to get himself elected as its prime minister. And because these beliefs are part of what it is to have such a project, having the project can fail to be integrated with other beliefs that render *these* beliefs irrational. For instance, if the person had abundant evidence that there was no likelihood whatsoever that he could be elected president (and thus his continued belief in the possibility was irrational) then his having that project would fail to be integrated with many of his other beliefs. It would function as an independent element, impervious to evidence that the project could not be achieved, a rigidity within the personality. Depending on how evident it was (in terms of the individual's own norms of evidence) that the project was impossible, we might view the person as quite mad—for instance, a person whose project was to fly to the moon by flapping his arms. It is similar for the other mental elements. In general, the cognitive content of mental elements sets up the possibility for rational linkages between them and a wide variety of beliefs.

Much of what people desire is not desired for its own sake, but rather because it is a means to some other end. And typically, in a complex society, this other end is itself not desired for its own sake but also because it too is seen as a means to something else. Thus, parents desire that their children attain good grades in school because they desire that their children be able to attend superior colleges because they desire that their children have superior job opportunities because they desire that their children have money or status or more happiness. The fact that desires are supported by lengthy chains of belief—the example could be stretched out much further to all that is desired because it is believed to contribute to good grades—has nothing to do with the strength of desire. Indeed, one may be quite intense with respect to desires that are only made rational in virtue of extraordinarily long chains of inference. For the integrated personality, desires for objects not experienced as inherently desirable must be linked via beliefs to those that are. If in fact the individual does not have the beliefs that would make these secondary desires rational, but nonetheless has the desires, they are functioning in a detached manner, and an awareness of their detached status can call the most central projects into question, thus unraveling the unity around which the everyday has been organized.

Values and beliefs

In Figure 3.1, "values" were listed as a separate element. An inquiry into a person's values might be concerned with one of two very different subject matters, a person's "explicit values" or alternatively her "embodied values." They differ in the extent to which the individual's beliefs are engaged.

The explicit values are those values that the person explicitly affirms or would affirm if asked. Here we are essentially dealing with a particular kind of belief. This is evidenced by the expression, "What does she *believe* in?"—an expression used typically to ascertain what a person's values are. The shorthand answer to such a question might be: "She believes in her country, the family, and education." But what is it to believe "in" the family or "in" one's country or "in" education? In the main, this involves believing that certain kinds of entities are good, desirable, or deserving of protection; or believing that certain kinds of behavior are desirable, praiseworthy, or obligatory; or believing that certain human characteristics are worthy of esteem, praise, and cultivation. An inquiry into someone's values includes an inquiry into moral values, but it goes well beyond that. What is interesting, however, is that this first kind of inquiry into someone's values is essentially an inquiry into her beliefs. In this sense, to have certain values is simply to have certain beliefs.

I have distinguished value-beliefs (in this sense) from other beliefs because the propositions that are believed can typically be distinguished in virtue of their reliance on some evaluative/normative predicate, because of nagging philosophic concerns as to the logical and epistemological status of such propositions, and because in ordinary parlance we do use the term "values" to segregate off these kinds of beliefs. Nonetheless, from the point of view of the inquiry into the make-up of the self, they can be viewed as a very special sort of belief.

There is, however, a second sense, or perhaps I should say "facet," to an inquiry into someone's values. Here we might be largely unconcerned with what a person affirms or would affirm, and instead we are asking a question about the values that she embodies. But in what are a person's values embodied? Through what are they revealed? In particular, through what are a person's deepest values revealed?

When we seek to go beyond a person's assertions about what her values are, we turn to her conduct, her emotions and her desires. Consider emotions. When someone feels pride, or shame or guilt, or indignation, these emotions are not disconnected mental events *caused* by a person's values; rather they are *constitutively expressive* of the values that the person holds. Indeed, it is part of what is meant by saying that someone feels guilty about doing a certain act, that they feel that they did something wrong, or they feel that acts of a certain sort are wrong. Part of what it is to feel pride over some accomplishment is to value oneself highly (at that moment). The emotion is not some internal sensation that has can be identified in phenomenological terms that are totally distinct from the value judgments they express. Yet the fact that we have a tendency to use the term "feel" rather than "believe" in these instances reflects that one can have these value-embedded emotions in spite of the fact that in some explicit sense one does not believe the relevant value proposition. Thus, I can feel guilty about having done something even when I do not believe that what I did was wrong.

There are a variety of ways to characterize this situation. One can say that the person is of two beliefs, of unsettled belief, believes certain things in spite of herself, or perhaps has certain values in one sense but not in another. For present purposes it is not necessary to sort out these alternative ways of conceptualizing the situation. What is important is that it illustrates the variety of ways that an individual's values may or may not be integrated with other aspects of the self.

Distinguishing a person's explicit values (we might say value judgments) from his embodied values allows us to note the possibility of incoherence between these two. *One of the central integrations of the self is for one's value judgments to be embodied and for one's embodied values to be such that one does or would explicitly affirm them.*

Focusing on one's explicit values (judgments or beliefs), there are a variety of critically important ways in which these can or cannot be integrated. Since among the typical objects of such judgments are persons, their character and personality traits, their conduct, their aspirations, their values, their desires, their emotional life—(one might include all of these within a rich notion of an ego-ideal)—there is always the possibility of the conflict between the individual's value judgments and his own attributes. Here I am not talking about conformity between the individual's judgments and his beliefs about himself, but rather his judgments and his reality. One may be a narrow, selfish individual despite one's contempt for such people; one may have a desire to dominate others despite one's belief that such desires are base; one may feel envy of another despite one's belief that such emotions are contemptible. Since typically such realities about oneself are known to oneself, these situations represent a lack of integration between a person's moral beliefs and his beliefs about himself.

A conflict between one's values and one's beliefs about oneself becomes acute when that conflict is represented in a conflict between one's beliefs and one's self-identity. Having an ideal with respect to persons (e.g., having moral values as to which kinds of character traits are worthy of pride and which are shameful) is not the same as having a positive self-identity. If one has the latter, and many psychologists have postulated a need to see ourselves in these terms, then there can arise a conflict between that self-identity and specific beliefs that we have about those aspects of our reality that are not flattering. Here, in virtue of beliefs about that unflattering reality and beliefs about our conformity to the ideal, we have a conflict between beliefs about oneself—and because of the potential for this conflict, we may have a psychic need to not come to believe certain things about ourselves.

Interestingly, this need not take the form of denying the specifics of the unflattering reality; it might take the form of a wholesale denial of conformity to the ideal; indeed, it might take the form of a self-identity that is distinctly negative from the person's own point of view. Thus, there would be a lack of integration between the ego-ideal and the self-identity; between one's central values and one's central beliefs about who one is. Whether or not such beliefs are correct or well founded is itself, of course, a different matter.

The kinds of integration thus far considered, integration between beliefs (noncontradiction, probability, certainty); between beliefs and emotions; between beliefs and self-identity; between explicit values and embodied values; between explicit values and one's desires, emotions, projects, and traits of character; collectively capture much of what is meant by the integration of personality, or selfhood. If explicit values are included within the category of beliefs, then all of these modes of integration in one way or another involve beliefs—thus making clear the centrality of belief systems to the structure that is the self.

Yet, not all modes of integration involve beliefs. A set of desires may be internally consistent or inconsistent. By this I do not mean the absence of mixed feelings about things; one can with full integration both desire that something occur and also desire that it not occur, provided that the event in question has a variety of aspects, some of which one looks on positively and others negatively. Sometimes a complexity of desire is grounded in the complexity of the objects of desire.

Ultimately, however, there are relatively simple elements that one either desires or does not desire. A set of desires is internally inconsistent if it contains opposing desires towards the same thing in the same respect, that is, if there is a fundamental ambivalence. Thus, if we have as our most basic desires both a desire to be (a life instinct) and a desire to not be (a death instinct) and these are ultimate desires, not derived from something more basic, then we have within us a fundamental incoherence.

A set of desires may also be incoherent if it contains second-order desires that are inconsistent with first-order desires. Second-order desires are desires with respect to the kind of desires we want to have. I may not want to have certain wants. In this sense, a set of desires is incoherent if some of them are desires that one not have certain desires that are part of the set. This, of course, is very closely related to the conflict between values and desires, since one of the main reasons that one might not want to have certain desires is that one considers them base, wrong, not worthy of having.

Closely related to the coherence between desires is the possibility of coherence between a person's desires (and values) and his pleasurings—that is, between what he wants and what he finds pleasure in. Coherence takes several forms: (1) the individual wants what (he believes) leads to his own pleasure; (2) the individual does not take pleasure in that which he believes to be wrong or ugly or unfortunate; and (3) the individual takes pleasure in doing what he wants. The first two, properly speaking, involve integration with beliefs (beliefs about what will give one pleasure and beliefs about what ought to give one pleasure). The third of these, that the individual takes pleasure in doing what he wants, that is, in the exercise of his will, is a condition of a certain kind of vibrance and vitality. Taken collectively, these three integrations capture much of what it is to have a healthy will—that the will is towards that which gives it pleasure, that pleasure is found in objects that are approved of, and that there is pleasure taken in its exercise. When these different integrations are present, desire emerges in its wholeness and abundance.

These different aspects of human wholeness or selfhood are part of an idealized conception of self. Very few, if any, actual human beings meet all these conditions. Yet, despite the ideal nature of what has been presented, I suspect that these conditions are not sufficient. The problem is that these conditions are purely formal. Other than the constancy or continuity of beliefs over time, there is nothing about them that ensures the substantive consistency and constancy that is associated with the integrated personality. There are three areas where there is a need for substantive restrictions.

1. Thus far, I have placed no bounds on what the individual's experience may be, in particular, no bounds on *what* she finds pleasurable or on how this may change over time. It is easy to see that any erratic shifts in experience and tastes will cause violent shifts in the entire system. If there is no temporal consistency of basic attitudes, what was done on Monday may need to be undone every Tuesday. She may be forever rearranging her furniture, or her friends, or her activities, or her life as a whole. Certainly, selfhood involves some limit to these possible shifts in experience. With respect to her tastes or pleasurings, being an integrated person implies a fair degree of basic stability over time. Unfortunately there is no way of saying how much is enough.

2. A second difficulty is that I have placed no bounds on the

substance of the individual's basic concerns, desires, or values, nor upon the strength such elements may possess. For instance, suppose that a person has an overwhelming need or desire to be liked by others. Let us also suppose that he has an uncanny ability to know just what will enchant the person he is with. As a result he is always pretending to be something that he is not, and his pretense shifts radically from person to person. He is one sort of person when he is with *A*, another sort when with *B*, and still a third sort when with *C*. If these persona are sufficiently different, we may be dealing with a paradigm of a fractured or fragmented individual, yet the adoption of each persona may be highly integrated with his underlying fears and his calculations of how to deal with these dangerous situations.

There needs to be some way of indicating that the integrated person has a substantive consistency that goes beyond the formal agreement of the elements. Again, it is a tricky area; rigidity should not be confused with integration. Unfortunately, the problem is not even one of specifying an appropriate degree of permitted flexibility. Thus, a spy or a politician may engage in as complete and as numerous a set of pretenses as the person in my example. Yet, it would be an error to insist that the spy or politician lacks an integrated personality. It seems that the key difference has to do with the different reasons for the pretense. In the case of the spy, the goal may be to aid the country of his true loyalties, while in the other case the goal is to win everyone's affection. If the difference is merely in the substance of the goal or desire, then we are in an uncomfortable spot, for there is no obvious way of drawing the distinction.

We might say that the spy or politician, unless he loses himself totally, knows who he really is. He can separate fact from fiction, person from persona. But what if this is also true of the deeply fearful individual who knows that she is always pretending, but believes that she must.

In placing limits on the strength of certain fears, desires, or needs, I am essentially ruling out certain kinds of integration as being excessive. The wholeness that we associate with selfhood is *not that of maximum integration* where *everything* is tightly connected to everything else. Certain kinds of wholeness permit other kinds of loose relatedness. For instance, the fit between the individual's ideals, self-identity, and beliefs about herself may be such that it yields a security that serves to keep certain needs or fears in their place. Here their "place" is one of relative isolation—they should not be finding expression in all of the person's perceptions nor should they be generating a strong need to conform to the values or preferences of others. The absence of this openness to conflicting experiences is what was noted earlier in the discussion of the paranoid personality.

3. Finally, I have not thus far specified any limit on how conflicted someone's emotions, desires, or evaluations may be. While it is vital that there be consistency in terms of one's basic desires and values, I have been careful not to demand that the integrated personality be free of ambivalence. The reality that each person faces is complex, and most objects of desire and assessment have their pros and cons. It would be a serious mistake to confuse having an integrated personality with being integrated into one's social world. This would be analogous to confusing being alienated from oneself with being alienated from the social order. Nonetheless, there is something unsettling about a view of the integrated personality that allows the integrated individual to be someone who has mixed feelings about almost everything, who can't respond unambivalently to anything, who experiences every person with a variety of emotions, whose every choice carries a perception of serious drawbacks, and whose view of every important moral issue is that it has at least two sides to it. Carried to the extreme, this would allow an integrated individual to be someone who never really likes or dislikes anything.

Consider: every object of enjoyment has a complex set of properties. Our individual could be such that no natural clusters ever possess only the qualities she enjoys. She may like the taste of peaches, but not their texture. She may like the clarity of mountain air, but not the low pressure. She may like the prestige of being a doctor, but not the close contact with the diseased. Unfortunately for her, the world does not contain all possible combinations of basic qualities. In our everyday exchanges, such a person may seem to have no tastes. People might say of her, "She never knows what she wants, or what she likes, or what will make her happy." There is a sense in which this is true. If every real object or situation has various pros and cons for her, she may find it very hard to accurately predict how she will react to a given object. Thus, to take a trivial example, she may respond very positively to one strawberry, but not to the next, simply because they vary in the degree to which different qualities are present. Certainly, such a person may lose her grip on things. For any given class of objects, she may never be able to figure out to what it is that she responds, whether negatively or positively. In short, she may experience the confusing disarray of the existing social and physical world as her own confusion and inconsistency. On the other hand, she might not. If she does not, if she knows what she likes and values, and if she is aware that her ambivalence arises because the world she faces presents only heterogeneous choices, then perhaps it is best to set no limit to the amount of ambivalence she may feel.

FRAGMENTS OF THE SELF

The picture I have presented is one that allows for a great deal of diversity with respect to specific conceptions of the self. The previous discussion should be viewed as a sort of primer in "basic wiring." It speaks to relatively formal aspects of the ways in which components of the psyche are held together, but it does not really get to the broad strokes of orientation that characterize one or another broad conception of the self. Those were the differences I pointed to at the outset, the differences that separate the outlook of Aristotle from that of a Tibetian monk, and from both Nietzsche and Lawrence, and would further separate off Kant and Augustine.

As has been noted, few human beings have fully integrated personalities. Instead, the personality consists of various fragments or subsystems. These can be as small as an isolated element (e.g., a specific desire) or extensive enough to suggest that there are multiple personalities, or selves, inhabiting the same body. It is probably not too strong to say that almost every systematic view of human nature has not only made use of some notion of unity, harmony, or integrity of the personality, but also has had some distinctive way of perceiving and responding to the different fragments that make up the nonintegrated personality. While it is rather unusual to find an explicit formulation of these attitudes, they may be eked out of views on education, mental health, moral ideals, responsibility, self-transformation, authenticity, and so forth.

In these varied conceptions of the self, it is typical that certain kinds of elements (e.g., values, desires, emotions) are given special status as that from which acts of the self, or the true self, spring. In terms of the view of the self as the integrated personality, this specification of the locus of the true self can be interpreted not as meaning that the elements or fragments in question *are* the self, but rather that they *represent* the self. When the personality is integrated around these elements, then it will be a self.

Sometimes the self is defined negatively and certain elements are singled out as elements that must be eliminated or modified before selfhood is attained. A personality organized around these elements is *not* the self, or one's real or true self. For instance, certain desires might be viewed as inherently foreign to the self, and a personality that is woven around these desires is one that removes the person further and further from who he or she really is.

No analogy is every fully adequate for capturing the nature of the self, but some insight may be gained by considering musical instruments. In evaluating alternative ways of constructing a specific type of musical instrument, the most important question to consider is "How well does it play?" or "What does it sound like?" This offers an interesting analogy for thinking about the self. With musical instruments of a given type, we may have a conception of what it should sound like yet remain open to being *surprised* by the qualities that some new approach might bring forth—in short, we might retain some openness with respect to the specification of the standard of desirable functioning. And further, we would also accept that there are different types of instruments, each of which might be assessed in terms of how they sound with respect to other instruments of the same sort, and yet we would not demand that one type of instrument be determined to be better than another type. Although we might retain our preferences, we recognize that each type of instrument has its unique type of sound; each type has its own integrity, which yields a standard for assessing specific instruments of that type.

This question of adequacy of functioning is at the heart of debates about the self. But obviously there is no prior specification of what counts as functioning well. On some outlooks the key question is literally "does it play?" For instance, Nietzsche introduces playfulness as a central guide to the discovery or rediscovery of the self. But in more general terms, the analogy is to action and feeling—"What kinds of things does a personality organized in that particular way do?" "What sort of things does it feel or is it capable of feeling?"

As soon as human action and feeling becomes the touchstone for deciding what is self and what is not, it is clear that alternative views of moral behavior will penetrate into the theorizing. For instance, the issue of sexuality has always been central to discussions of the self—it runs from the Bible to Lawrence, from Plato through Freud. Insofar as the moral outlook is one that looks critically at much sexual activity, if self-realization is taken as desirable, the self will be defined in terms of that which inhibits and controls sexual activity. If the moral outlook is more Lawrencian, then it is clear that that which limits and controls sexual activity will be viewed as non-self.

But sexuality is only one of a variety of ways in which the question "How well does it play?" engages alternative moral outlooks in different ways. Another dimension has to do with social attitudes and conduct. In his discussion of when psychotherapy should end, Kohut refers to "functional reliability" as a test. He lays great emphasis on someone's being able to engage in his worklife in a particular kind of way. Speaking of a particular patient whose therapy was appropriately terminated, he writes about "his professional activities which now provided him with a reliable organized framework for the joys of self-expression."[32] Here joy and work are linked together to provide a touchstone in the process of personality shaping and reshaping. Without attributing this to Kohut himself, the formulation is compatible with the outlook of the modern corporation, which seeks to unify the individual within its structures so well that he or she experiences work "joyfully." Thus, it may be argued that to make "joyful functioning within one's professional life" a criterion for successful integration is to have built an uncritical social or political outlook into the therapeutic ideal.

In Chapter 9, I discuss the question of appropriate self-experience at the workplace, and I argue that being alienated from one's work is often required if one is not to be alienated from oneself. This only illustrates how much interpenetration there is between political philosophy and a metaphysical-sounding question such as "What is the self?"

This theme is brought out most sharply in Chapter 8, where I discuss Trotsky—his basic perspective being that we should not view as part of oneself any values that serve to constrain our ability and enthusiasm for revolutionary action. More generally, a Marxist perspective would argue that selfhood is not something that can be achieved individually—if it is achieved at all, it is as a result of social and historical processes that transform the individual but can themselves only be achieved through political change. On such a perspective, the issue of how to conceive of the self is made into an issue of praxis—it is a question of what conception of the self, when internalized by historical agents, will most fully contribute to the attainment of selfhood for humankind as a whole. Here too there is a conception of functioning, but an entire worldview is embedded in the answer. The question "What is the self?" is not something that can be neatly assigned to psychology or metaphysics or ethics. It is itself the most holistic question we can raise.

Once it is seen that a full specification of a conception of self includes a specification of the criteria of emotional and behavioral functioning that are to be used in assessing different patterns of integration, it should be clear that a theory of agency developed along the lines I have suggested will either have to be general enough to accommodate a wide variety of alternative moral, political, and aesthetic orientations, or it will have to fill in the blanks and be the formulation appropriate to a particular outlook and worldview. I have taken the former course, retaining the looseness of a general formulation. However, it is general in a very specific sense. It is not the case that it simply subsumes all other views regardless of where those views place the central locus of the self. On the framework I have put forward, the self per se does not have any particular locus. The fully integrated person is the self, regardless of whether the integration pattern is built around one or another alternative pole. Thus, potentially each of us might be integrated in very different ways, and thus have many potential selves. In this sense there is not a single "true" self that we are or become. But when a specific person becomes highly coherent in a specific way, then a self has been formed.

4

Agency

This chapter, building on the previous discussion of the self and activity, offers an account of the nature of human agency.

Let me recapitulate some of the central features of my account. Philosophers have viewed the question, "What is an action?" and the question "What is it to be an agent?" as two sides of the same question. Actions are those things that are done by agents; one is an agent whenever one has performed an action. Thus, the two traditional views, that which understands actions as events caused by a volition (or wants and beliefs) and that which understands actions as events brought about through the exercise of agent causality, are alike in that they do not separate the two questions.

The tendency to think that only one question is involved has been reinforced by an implicit aspect of much of the theoretical writings in analytic action theory—an atomistic perspective that takes as its starting point a simple event (e.g., the movement of a finger) and asks in relation to this event: "What is it for me to be the agent of this event?" For instance: "What is the difference between the mere movement of the finger, and my having moved the finger?"

So conceived, it is not surprising that the two questions tend to merge into one. When we focus on an event this simple, it is quite natural to suppose that whatever it is that makes me the agent of this event is exactly that which makes it an action.

The theory presented thus far has been characterized as molecular rather than atomistic. The notion of an activity molecule has been introduced as the central element of the theory. The activity molecule is conceived not as a simple event but as a process that is unified through what I call "indirect perceptual integration." This is a complex causal relationship whereby an ongoing perceptual assessment of an outcome causes an ongoing *series of events* to occur in a manner that shapes the outcome so that it conforms to a standard inherent in the perception. The typical events in the series are physical movements, and thus typically molecular activities are physical activities. In so understanding activities, a mental component (i.e., the perceptual assessment) is built into the notion of activity—molecular activities are thus psychophysical processes. They can be thought of as a very specific type of movement-feedback-adjustment process.

But having thus conceived of activities, and having understood them *apart* from any notion of volition, wants, desires, or agent causality, the question of agency emerges as a distinct question. Activities occur, but under what circumstances are we the agent of such activities?

The general answer I gave is that we are agents of activities when and only when the self is present in the activity. This in turn generated two questions: (*a*) What is the self? and (*b*) What is it for the self to be present in an activity? In the previous chapter I addressed the first of these questions. The self was analyzed as an integrated personality. Full selfhood implies a fully integrated personality, an ideal that can be understood in diverse ways that tend to embody moral, aesthetic, and therapeutic worldviews. The present chapter completes the theoretical account of agency by explaining what it is for the self to be present in its activities.

FREEDOM AND AGENCY

The term "freedom" is used in so many different contexts and senses that it would be bold to say there is no sense of "freedom" corresponding to what I have called "agency." But certainly agency is not the same as freedom in its central usage. A person can be the agent of his actions even when he clearly is not free, in the sense that he faces various threats and extreme penalties if he chooses certain courses of action that are in some more general sense "open" to him. But there is a particular notion of freedom that, even if it is not the same as what I have called "agency," appears to raise many of the same issues.

Traditionally actions have been viewed as caused by a desire (or a volition). Working off of this understanding of actions, some philosophers have distinguished free actions from unfree actions in terms of the nature of the desire. For instance, if the desire is the desire of a drug addict for heroin, and if it is so powerful that though she tries to resist it, she cannot, then it would make sense to say that she was unfree. Similarly, if through vast powers of manipulation, some evil power were capable of causing me to have desires quite contrary to my own values, we would also say that I was not free, even if I did what I wanted to do.

Viewed in this way, one analysis of freedom is that a person acts freely when he does what he wants to, provided that the want or desire from which he acts is truly his own. For this to be informative, what is required is an analysis of what it is for a desire to be truly one's own. This can be rephrased in the vocabulary I have been using as a need to provide an analysis of what it is for a desire to come from the self.

My interest is not in trying to explicate the concept of freedom, but rather in picking up on that discussion insofar as it is relevant to understanding what it is for an action to come from the self. Even though I have rejected the analysis of actions as events caused by desires, it still is possible to maintain that being caused by a desire, or a desire that is truly mine, is exactly what makes an action (or activity) mine. Thus, agency could be understood as being caused by a desire that comes from the self.

I reject this as a necessary feature of agency because I want to maintain that actions can come from the self even if there is no desire that is their direct cause. Even so, it remains possible that a sufficient condition for agency is that the action in question comes from a desire that emerges from the self. Without, at the moment, going into whether or not this is sufficient, it is at least highly relevant to agency. Thus, it will be useful to consider how certain philosophers have dealt with this question: What is it for a desire to be truly mine?

Harry Frankfurt, writing of free will, says that it involves "satisfactions . . . which accrue to a person of whom it may be said that *his will is his own.*"[1] Frankfurt centers his discussion on what it is to have a will that is one's own, and on what it is to be a person. He writes that "one essential difference between persons and other creatures is to be found in the structure of a person's will." He goes on to say that "It seems to be peculiarly characteristic of humans, however, that they are able to form . . . second-order desires." By "second-order desires" he means desires about other desires, for instance, the desire to not have a desire to eat ice cream.

But, according to Frankfurt, the essential feature of persons is not that they have second-order desires, but rather that they have desires that certain desires be the motives out of which we act. He calls these "second-order volitions," and says,

> it is having second-order volitions, and not having second-order desires generally, that I regard as essential to being a person. It is logically possible, however unlikely, that there should be an agent with second order desires but with no volitions of the second order. Such a creature, in my view, would not be a person.[2]

He introduces the term "wanton" to refer to such creatures who are not persons (they have desires, but not second-order volitions). Frankfurt makes clear that the stance adopted towards first-order desires by the second-order volitions need not be a moral stance. It suffices merely that the person has preferences with respect to what desires he or she will act from. He then goes on to identify *freedom of the will* with being free to have the will one wants (the "will" for Frankfurt is that desire which is actually acted upon). Thus, to have a free will is to have the ability to determine whether or not one will act on one or another of one's desires. For instance, if the drug addict has two competing desires, the first to take the drug and the second to not take the drug, and if she also has a second-order desire that she not act out of the first desire (the desire to take the drug), then her will is free if and only if this second-order desire is controlling. If despite this desire to not act on the desire for the drug, she is unable to resist the desire for the drug, then her will is not free. Put differently, the person has an unfree will because her will is not subject to determination by her preferences with respect to it.

Frankfurt further distinguishes between having a free will and acting freely. He maintains that even if one doesn't have a free will, one can be said to act freely if one acts in accord with second-order volitions. Thus, he cites the case of the happy addict, a person whose will is not free in that her addiction is too strong, but who is quite happy to be acting out of her desire for the drug. This "happy addict" acts freely, while the unhappy addict does not act freely.

Certainly, there is a useful distinction to be made between people who have a capacity to determine which desire they will act on when desires conflict and people who do not. But is this capacity to be equated with freedom? The key issue is why should an action in accord with a second-order desire be viewed as emerging from the self? Why give this particular locus to the self, or this particular authority of being genuinely mine to actions that are in accord with these particular desires?

Frankfurt has adopted a particular stance within a general category of positions that can be called "locus theories of the self." Locus theories pick out a particular mental state or a particular part of the personality and view these components as having a special authority in determining what is truly mine and what is not. The theory of the self developed in the previous chapter is a nonlocus theory. The self was understood as the integrated personality without identifying any particular component as necessarily the central point in that integration.

Frankfurt doesn't argue in a straightforward way for the proposition that a desire is one's own if it is the subject of a second-order desire that we act from it, but his view on this seems linked to his claim that having second-order desires (desires about what desires we act from) is "essential to being a person"—it is the basis for his distinction between persons and the class of beings he calls "wantons."

The term "essential" and its variants have a long and perilous philosophical history. In one sense they are used to identify a distinguishing characteristic, a necessary feature. I would hesitate to accept Frankfurt's view that having second-order desires is a necessary condition for being a person. But even if this were to be true, it would not follow that such desires were "essential" in a different sense, in the sense in which we might speak about the "inner essence," or that which is most truly one's own.

These two senses of "essential" are quite distinct. For instance, it is perfectly possible to accept that having the ability to act from second-order desires is an essential (i.e., necessary) characteristic of persons *and* to maintain that this very ability to act from second-order desires is in fact the ability to act from desires that are not truly one's own. Thus, it may be that a necessary feature of persons is an ability to act from what is not one's self. And thus, Frankfurt's outlook could be turned completely around. Wantons (e.g., animals) might be viewed as creatures whose desires are always their own (and thus free), as distinct from persons who end up often acting from second-order desires rather than from their truer more natural selves.

Consider the Puritan who views his lust as sinful and desires to not act on it. Are his actions through which he avoids being alone with members of the opposite sex free actions? Would he not be acting on a desire that was truly his own if he acted on a sexual impulse? Why are

his moral strictures, which find their way into his second-order reflections on his own desires, more genuinely his own than are the prompt-
ings of his body?

Sometimes it seems that in addition to saying that to act out of a
second-order volition is to act freely, Frankfurt also believes that one
acts freely only if one acts in accord with a second-order volition. That
is, that acting in accord with a second-order desire is not only sufficient
for acting freely but necessary. But what reason is there to maintain
this? Is the open and spontaneous and unreflective sexuality of the
Somoan youth not fully his own? Is he acting unfreely when he acts
naturally?

Consider the act of telling someone that you love them. On Frankfurt's account this would be wantonly done if the person had no
reflective views with respect to the motives he or she was acting on.
But for a healthy person, the natural expression of love to a loved one
may be completely without reflection upon one's motives. Acting
directly out of love, simply giving it verbal expression without any
second-order desire to do so, would appear to be acting freely and
performing an action that was truly one's own.

My point is not to argue for the direct expression of emotion as the
only mode through which the self emerges in action, and thus to argue
against the significance of alternatives. Rather, it is to argue against
the centrality and exclusivity that a locus theory such as Frankfurt's
involves.

Frankfurt does not intend to give a special priority to second-order
volitions as opposed to volitions at any possible higher level. He
recognizes that one may have a critical view of one's second-order
volitions. Suppose I am someone struggling against my Puritan background. I have a lust that I find myself viewing as sinful. Thus, I find
that I have a second-order volition to not act out of that lust. But I
might also have a third-level perspective on this Puritanical view of
lust. And on this third level I may have a desire that I not act out of
my second-level volition, but rather out of my first-level lust.

Frankfurt does not clearly address the question of whether it is
always the highest level volition that reflects the self and thus is the
guide to the free act. Rather, he says, "When a person identifies
himself decisively with one of his first-order desires, this commitment
'resounds' throughout the potentially endless array of higher orders."[3]
Some commentators have urged that this expresses a more refined
view, according to which Frankfurt is saying that a sufficient condition

for acting freely is that a person identifies decisively with the desire from which he or she has acted.[4]

An identificationist view can be stated as follows:

> An action is truly one's own (and therefore free) if and only if the person identifies with the desire from which he or she acted.

This is not a refinement of the emphasis on second-order volitions. It is a different analysis. To have a desire to not act from sexual desire is one thing; to identify with a desire to not act from sexual desire is something different. Suppose I have a second-order volition that I not act from lust; it is still possible that I identify with the sexual impulse. I can identify with a desire yet still not desire to act from that desire. To identify with a desire is to experience it as truly mine; it need not be the case that I approve of all that I so experience.

Whether or not Frankfurt's view is to be understood in terms of a second-order volition or an identification with a first-order desire, both formulations are essentially answers to what it is for a desire to be truly one's own. The action is truly one's own because the desire is truly one's own. And if the action is truly one's own then it is freely done.

Both formulations treat having a certain attitude (an approving desire or an identification) towards a desire as sufficient for constituting that desire as one's own. There are basic problems with this position. If the key factor is the attitude towards the desire, it may be asked, *when* does the attitude in question have this certifying perspective on the desire? Attitudes, be they desires about desires or identifications with desires, change. I can at some later time come to be quite estranged from the desire that I today identify with. Thus, in retrospect, having understood that I was acting largely out of the views of my parents and their (I now think) distorted moralizing, I now see as foreign many of my desires that I once identified with or approved of.

When we identify with a desire, this identification has within it, it would appear, a judgmental component, a judgment that the desire is my own. When I at some later point no longer identify with the desire out of which I acted, my lack of identification reflects a change in judgment. I am no longer judging that desire to have been truly mine. If having an attitude towards a desire (whether an identification with it or an affirmative second-order attitude towards it) is sufficient to make it one's own, then given the fact that these attitudes change, either "ownership" is relative to a particular point in time or is itself noncognative. On this latter perspective, assertions that a desire is mine or not mine would be understood in a fashion analogous to the way emotivists portrayed assertions in ethics. The "judgment" that the desire is truly mine would be treated as a pseudo-judgment that fails to affirm any matter of fact, merely expressing some attitude.

The alternative that I am maintaining rejects both the claim that having an attitude towards a particular element (e.g., a desire) is sufficient to make it truly my own, and further rejects the noncognative interpretation of such statements. To say that a desire is one's own is to posit the existence of a structural relationship between the desire and one's self. Similarly, to say that an action is one's own is to posit the existence of a structural relationship between the action and the self. Because our identifications embody judgments about the presence of such structural relations, they may be erroneous. The exact nature of the structural relationship that makes a desire or an action one's own is extremely complex and theoretically open.

A particularly jarring example that suggests that identification is not sufficient for somethings being really one's own is found in the television commercial for a popular brand of face cream. It shows an attractive, late thirties or early forties woman. She muses to herself about the wrinkles that have appeared. She says, "There is a part of me that says 'Age gracefully,' but then the real me says, 'why?' " As she says "then the real me says," she smiles a somewhat devilish, somewhat sexy smile. The viewer is presented with a woman who is experiencing inner conflict. On one level she affirms an ethic that challenges youth-based ideals of beauty and advocates aging with acceptance, grace, and dignity. On the other hand she has a powerful desire to continue to appear young. But the viewer witnesses her having resolved the conflict through an identification with the will to struggle against aging. The smile "tells" us that this indeed is the real person coming through, and it relegates the "age gracefully" perspective to something foreign, perhaps the superficial imperative of a feminist subculture.

The intent of the commercial is to get the viewer to take over the perspective of the woman in the ad. It seeks to cause the women viewing the ad to have the same kind of identification that she does, to not fight against their attachment to youth-based conceptions of beauty or the will to appear younger than they are, but rather to embrace such impulses as genuinely their own and instead to reject those values in terms of which such impulses might be overridden (and face cream neglected).

Suppose that such advertising campaigns are effective in getting women to have the identifications they seek to establish. If identification is sufficient to establish a part of oneself as really one's own, then the advertisers have brought it about that the woman's real self lies not in her "age gracefully" values, not in her reflection upon what is wrong with the face cream culture, but rather in her will to resist the appearance of aging. I would deny this. At some later time the very same woman who now identifies with the will to resist looking one's age may come to see that her identifications themselves were manipulated, that her identifications were not really her own. Something more than identification is required to establish an element of the self as genuinely one's own. Identification is neither necessary nor sufficient.

Watson, in his essay "Free Agency," puts forward a view that comes closer to the structural perspective I am urging. Watson seeks to "develop a distinction between wanting and valuing which will enable the familiar view of freedom as able to make sense of the notion of an unfree action." He contends that in the case of an unfree action, the person is "unable to get what he most wants or values, and this inability is due to his own motivational system."[5] In developing the distinction between wanting and valuing, Watson emphasizes that when we want something because we value it, the source of the want lies in our *judgment* with respect to the good. Watson is careful to explain that some moral attitudes are merely the result of acculturation and do not emerge from the person's judgment. In the sense in which he is using "to value" these situations would not be instances of valuing.

He defines the valuation system of an agent as "that set of considerations which, when combined with his factual beliefs (and probability estimates) yields judgments of the form: the thing for me to do in these circumstances, all things considered, is a."[6] He defines the motivational system of an agent as "that set of considerations which move him to action."[7] He then concludes that the possibility of unfree action consists in the fact that an agent's valuational system and motivational system may not completely coincide. He says, "The free agent has the capacity to translate his values into action; his actions flow from his evaluational system."[8]

Watson then considers the approach Frankfurt has taken. He disagrees with the emphasis on second-order volitions. He writes:

the "structural" feature to which Frankfurt appeals is not the fundamental feature for either free agency or personhood. . . .

One job that Frankfurt wishes to do with the distinction between lower and higher orders of desire is to give an account of the sense in which some want may be said to be more truly the agent's own than others (though in an obvious sense all are wants of the agent) the sense in which the agent "identifies" with one desire rather than another, and the sense in which an agent may be unfree with respect to his own "will."[9]

Watson goes on to ask, "What gives these volitions any special relationship to 'oneself'?" Watson argues that the status of the second-order volitions comes from first-order practical judgments concerned with whether or not a given action is worth doing. If we judge that it is, then we want to act out of the desire to do it. Watson then draws the explicit parallel with Plato:

Therefore, Frankfurt's position resembles the platonic conception in its focus upon the structure of the "soul." But the two views draw their divisions differently; whereas Frankfurt divides the soul into higher and lower orders of desire, the distinction for Plato—and for my thesis—is among independent sources of motivation.[10]

Essentially, Watson shares Frankfurt's view that an agent is free when he or she acts from desires that are in the fullest sense his or her own. But Watson claims that these are not as Frankfurt would have it, desires that are the object of second-order desires, nor are they the second-order desires themselves, nor are they desires that one identifies with. Rather they are desires that emerge from first-order evaluative judgments.

Watson quite correctly points out that Frankfurt has not demonstrated the special status he attaches to second-order volitions, and Watson then goes on to suggest that the special status actually should be given to our first-order evaluative judgments.

Watson's view may be recast as:

A desire is one's own if is integrated with the individuals valuation system; and, a desire is one's own only if it does not conflict with one's valuation system.

Harmony between values and desires ensures true ownership, and conflict between values and desires disqualifies ownership of the desire.

It is important to see that Watson's outlook is also a form of locus theory. He is not requiring harmony per se as a condition of ownership of any element of the self, but rather as a condition of ownership of desires. They must fit with the values. The values have the elevated position. Conflict between the two systems does not call them equally into doubt.

What I want to emphasize about Watson's perspective is the importance he gives to a structural relationship. He is not saying that any moral or evaluative attitude per se is one's own. There must be some *set* of views that results in an evaluative judgment.

In his reference to valuation systems and motivational *systems*, and the need for "harmony" between those systems, Watson is describing aspects of what I have referred to as the integrated personality or self. One difference between Watson's view and my own is simply that in my analysis for an action to come from the self it is neither necessary nor sufficient that it come from a desire that is part of a larger evaluative system.

It is not sufficient because the *evaluative* system need not be truly one's own. It may run powerfully in conflict with other emotions and desires of the person. Suppose that I have not only a belief that sex is wrong and ugly, but a *system* of beliefs in which I believe that man is evil and that sex is the source of that evil, and further I believe that there are religious authorities of great stature that have laid down these findings. Thus, I have a value system, a structure of judgments. Does it follow from this that my sexual impulses are not my own? Does it follow from this that I am unfree if I yield to a desire in conflict with these judgments? Watson and Frankfurt would say yes.

Against both Watson and Frankfurt, there is the Lawrencian position. In D. H. Lawrence we have the total rejection of desire that emerges from some notion of the ideal, whether it be second-order volitions as to which first-order desires we want to act from, or first-order judgments of the worth of contemplated actions. Lawrence's rejection of action that emerges from notions of the ideal would encompass actions done in pursuit of one's ego-ideal or in fulfillment of notions of virtue.

Both Watson and Frankfurt represent certain specifications of linkages between self and action. Watson's view is more structural and powerful than Frankfurt's but it remains just one possible way of giving signification to these connections. A Lawrencian outlook maintains an alternative view of the self that takes these exact connections and treats them as criteria for concluding that the action is *not* really one's own. Not only are different factors given different weight, but the same factor, on a different conception, may count against, not for, presence of self.

Consider:

> Experience is true to the person when he is himself alone. . . . There are no goals to pursue, directions to follow, or techniques to use. . . . Self expression is not persuasive and is without special purpose or function.[11]

And

> Not voluntarism, but spontaneity, or grace, not the ego but the id.[12]

In these passages, which reflect the influence of D. H. Lawrence, the authors give emphasis to that which is done for its own sake, rejecting that which is instrumental, calculative, or goal oriented—central elements in the evaluative system Watson emphasizes.

And within a Nietzschean perspective, an individual whose moral beliefs are in conflict with his or her impulses and who engages in an activity *out of a sense of duty*, does not manifest the presence of his or her self in that activity. It is exactly the opposite.

Both Lawrence and Nietzsche represent alternatives to Watson's view that the locus of the self is to be found in the evaluative system per se. In pointing out the limitations of Watson's view, I am not maintaining that the kind of linkages he points to *must* be insufficient. Rather, a great deal depends on the individual self in question. For instance, unlike Lawrence, I am not saying that the sexual is the locus of the true self and of authentic desire. If the person has a sufficiently integrated personality in which his judgments and beliefs about the sinfulness of sexual impulse are deeply and richly integrated, then that is who he is. And in *that* case his acting in ways that conflict with sexual impulse are genuinely actions of his self. But because I am not attributing to the value system some general role as the locus of the self, the degree of integration required would be considerably more than that demanded on a view of the sort Watson holds.

As an alternative to all locus theories, I would argue that there is no single psychic element or subsystem that is the carrier of the self, and thus no special entity that must be related to desires in order that they be my own. Rather the question of ownership is specific to the individual in question. If his personality is integrated around an evaluative system, and if his actions emerge from that system, then they emerge from himself. But if his personality is integrated in ways quite different, if, for instance, desires and emotions play a more central role and judgments are less central, then when there is conflict between his values and his desires or emotions, he is more fully expressed when he acts out of his emotions.

THE STRUCTURAL WEB OF AGENCY

Agency can be viewed as a complex structural union between actions and the self. In virtue of this structural connectedness, the self may be said to be present in actions. But it is more than that. Agency is not a single simple relationship. It is not a matter of the exercise of some irreducible power of agent causality, nor is it a matter of the general existence of a single causal thread that connects volition or desire with physical movement. Agency is a union of self and action that is different in each and every token of every type of action. Moreover, it is not merely a structural connection between the self and the action, but typically a structural relationship through which the self is directly present in the activity molecule and thus accounts for our sense that we are literally alive and active through our actions.

There are two radically different dimensions to this structural connectedness. On one end of the spectrum the connectedness in question may have nothing to do with the experiential qualities of the activity performance. Indeed, as I will maintain, this non-immediate structural connectedness can even be constructed by the person years after the performance of the action itself.

On the other hand, there is a second dimension that involves the direct and immediate presence of the self within the activity itself. This dimension has both phenomenological and behavioral aspects. It is not a mere matter of causal connectedness between activity and self, but of actual presence of self in the activity.

In this section I consider the first dimension—the web of structural relations that constitute agency, whether or not they result in direct presence of self. In the next section I will consider direct and immediate presence of the self within the activity.

A person performs an action. Is it really hers? As both Watson and Frankfurt realized, the central structural linkage involves consideration of why the individual performed the action. On traditional accounts, since something is an action only in virtue of being caused by wants and beliefs (or volitions), there are always wants and beliefs that are linked to the action. Thus, the issue of whether or not the action is truly an act of that person tends to focus on whether or not the wants and beliefs are truly her own.

On the account provided in the earlier chapters, an activity is a free-standing process that is an activity in virtue of its inner structure. This inner structure involves a causal interaction with a mental element (the ongoing perceptual awareness) but does not necessarily involve wants and beliefs.

As previously noted, it is possible to imagine a situation in which, through electrical or chemical stimulation of the brain, scientists would be able to cause a person to engage in some activity. They could do this without causing her to have the wants and beliefs that would typically explain the action. Suppose someone picks up a violin and plays it. And suppose that not only do her hands behave in ways necessary to bring forth music from the instrument, but the performance is brought about through the ongoing perceptual assessment of the music as it is generated. We have a clear case of an activity. In some minimal sense it would be her activity, in that it was her body that was active and the movements of her body were being guided by mental states that were hers. But she would not be the agent of that activity. There would be no connection to the self at all.

Suppose we ask this person why she played the violin. And suppose that she can give no reason, and that we can find no reason. And suppose further that the "default" explanation—"because I wanted to," or "because I felt like it," turns out to be completely empty. The individual had no experiential desire to play the violin, and when checked we find that the typical brain states people are in when they have such a desire were not present. Essentially we have activity with no motivation. Under these circumstances, we might maintain that the person was completely passive with respect to the activity. She was not an agent of it at all. Just as we can imagine the story where the explanation for the behavior lies in the manipulation by the scientists, it is completely possible for something, perhaps not quite this stark, but similar, to happen in ordinary life without any external forces doing the manipulation.

The question of motivation is the central issue, but not the only issue, in considering the way in which a person is linked to his actions. The various factors raised in the accounts given by Watson and Frankfurt all have their place in the story, but none occupies the throne.

Typically actions do not occur just by themselves. They arise out of a constellation of wants, beliefs, attitudes, evaluative judgments, and emotions. In establishing agency, the first task is to identify these connections. The question "Why did he do it?" typically elicits this kind of connectedness: "because he was angry"; "because he hates her"; "because he wanted to"; "because he thought it was right"; "because by doing that he was able to do X."

Any of these connections can serve, and there is no need to try to squeeze them into one particular model. Further, as both Frankfurt and Watson recognized, these kind of linkages are insufficient to establish that the action is really his own. It must be more deeply connected to some larger structure of self, typically by showing that the desire, emotion, belief, value, or judgment from which the action emerged is itself authentically the person's.

Where Frankfurt's and Watson's approaches go astray is in their efforts to specify a particular kind of linkage, whether to second-order desires or to evaluative judgments, which is either necessary or sufficient. Similarly, a person's identifications, which are clearly also of relevance to agency, are neither necessary nor sufficient. As I argued earlier, identification reflects a judgment about the existence of a deeper structural relationship.

A much stronger formulation, which brings together Watson's emphasis on values and Bergmann and Frankfurt's focus on identification and that ensures a powerful structural tie between self and action, would be to require that the action emerges from some element that is part of someone's self-identity. For instance, that it emerges from *certain* values, the holding of which is part of how the person understands himself to be the person he is. This is a nonphenomenological linkage, which may be expressed in an identification experience, but need not be.

But this condition is far *too* strong and would be met only relatively infrequently, and further, as strong as it is, might still prove insufficient as even a person's identity structure could prove to be not authentically his own. (This possibility is considered further in the discussion of Trotsky in Chapter 8.)

What I conclude from this is that agency has to be conceived as a kind of webbing, as a connectedness between self and activity that has no particular specification. It might be thought of as analogous to the webbing that supports suspension bridges. There is no engineering specification that covers all cases, being necessary to all circumstances and sufficient to all eventualities.

Moreover, some elements of webbing that connect the self to its activities can be very indirect, and nonetheless quite central to establishing that the action is genuinely one's own. Thus it may be a matter of a connectedness that is nothing like the following:

> At the time of the performance, the desire that actually causes the act-token must be accompanied by another occurrent desire that the first desire be acted upon and this second desire must itself be a cause of the fact that the first desire causes the action.

Rather it may be that:

- The person's self-identity tends to be confirmed by the fact that he does A (a deeply religious person engages in a ritual prayer, almost on automatic pilot)
- The skills that are utilized in A have been acquired as part of a central project of X (a figure skater does a dance routine at the Olympics after having rehearsed it for years)
- The opportunity to do A was the result of X's efforts to obtain an opportunity to do A (an immigrant finally gets the opportunity to pull the lever in a voting booth)
- Doing A is expressive of X's deepest emotions and concerns (without reflection or even conscious awareness a mother comforts her child)

Put in general terms, the structural connectedness between the person and his or her action needs to be such that the action is linked to the self rather than to some element that itself floats freely. Insofar as a particular theorist maintains a conception of the self that places specific elements at the center of the self complex, it would be expected that that theorist would view agency as requiring a linkage with elements of that sort.

In presenting a view of the agency relationship as a web of diverse connectedness, I want to stress just how complex and how *theoretically* open this relationship between an action and the self is. This can be seen by reflecting on the way in which at later points in our life we can give meaning to earlier points, and appropriate as one's own actions from one's distant past. For instance, some event is made into a decisive turning point by the things I do later; I give it its deeper significance by making something out of it.

Consider a man who for years worked tremendously hard, accumulating a good deal of money and power and the ability to cut his way through obstacles that would thwart most others. One day he begins to look back on much of how he has lived his life, on all that activity and expended energy, and it seems strange and pointless. He wonders about it. What was his life about? Were those wasted years? Why was he so motivated to earn money? He now looks back upon much of his life with a kind of confusion. He doesn't understand what point there really was in his having devoted so much time to accumulation. From one perspective, it may seem as if his life was never his own. Yet it may be within his ability to appropriate those years, to give them a meaning that becomes their central meaning even though they were not seen that way when they occurred. For instance, in turning his attention towards the future, towards some grand project in which he deeply believes but has never until now undertaken, he may find that it is only made possible because of how he lived all those previous years. His wealth and power and personality now are seen differently. He weaves them into a larger structure, into the project of his life, and through this his meaning and fulfillment emerge. Their meaning is revealed. They were the years of preparation, the years through which he became who he had to be in order to do what he must do in life.

A perspective such as this is common in fairy tales and in some fictional writing. Usually it is a story of someone who does not know his real identity, a prince raised as a pauper. But the conception of identity in fairy tales is as something externally given, through birth or through an oracle or through some supernatural agent with the power to confer identity. In reality, identity is to a considerable extent self-conferred, and with the conferring of identity we have the reformulation of the self, and thus the realignment of past actions in relationship to that self.

The basic point is that the connectedness that constitutes agency is not limited to a connectedness that exists prior to or at the time of the action. It can come into being at a later stage, and thus agency, which in the main is a matter of causal relations through which the self gives rise to the action, cannot be limited to just linkages of that sort.

IMMEDIATE AND DIRECT PRESENCE OF THE SELF IN ACTIVITY

It was noted above that the union of self and action has two dimensions. The first is a diverse web of connectedness that links the self to the action. The second is something rather different—it is the direct and active presence of the self within the activity performance.

If we think of actions or of agency as the "making happen" of some simple event, some bit of behavior—say the movement of a finger—we may not even notice this aspect of agency. And indeed, it has been largely ignored in the vast literature of action theory. Yet it is something that we are all familiar with in everyday life.

The expression "present in the activity" corresponds to our experience when we are engaged in an activity. We do not experience our hand as moving and merely believe that there is some connection between the movement of the hand and our self; rather, we experience the movements as the movements of the self. Not only is the movement self-generated, but it is the movement of an embodied self; in some sense I am both in and active-in the activity of the moving hand. This goes way beyond merely causing it. Of course, *experiencing* oneself as present in an activity is neither a necessary nor a sufficient condition for *being* present in that activity. It is always possible, for instance, that someone, through confusion or self-deception or freak circumstances, fails to experience himself as present in some activity where he is present (fails to experience himself as an agent when he is an agent), or experiences himself as present when he is not. The question to be answered is this: In virtue of what characteristic is someone's experience of himself as present or not present in his activity correct or incorrect?

When we are engaged in an activity, when we are most active, there is a sense that we are somehow alive within the very activity itself; it is in and through the activity that we are rendered visible, concrete, and external. This is not the only sense in which someone might be said to be present in his activity, but it is phenomenologically the sharpest.

But to what does this phenomenological experience of ourselves as alive *within* the activity correspond? Are we dealing here only with imperfect metaphors for something very difficult to describe? Or is it literally true that the self is present in the activity? On the account of activity offered earlier, literal presence is possible.

The expressions "presence of mind" and "absent-mindedly" suggest that activities can be performed with different degrees of presence of self. And the admonition to do something with presence of mind suggests that it is in some sense possible to put oneself into the activity—where this means more than just to watch it from afar, even if watched carefully. But if the self can be present in the activity, how does it gain access?

It will be remembered that activities are organic wholes unified

through "indirect perceptual integration." There is an ongoing perceptual assessment of the outcomes such that the other elements (e.g.,
movements) are caused to occur in such a way as to bring the outcomes
into conformity with the inherent assessment. In a direct primary
sense, the self gains access to the activity molecule through the
perceptual assessment. Perceptual assessments are not uniform across
the entire domain of activities. The perception may be intense; it may
be wavering; it may be sensitive to aspects of concern to the self; it
may be impulsively blind; it may be the highly developed result of
years of practice or it may be amateurish; it may constitute all of X's
awareness or it may compete with other mental states; it may be
absorbed or it may be detached.

The perceptual assessment was characterized as a form of "seeing-
as," that is, as a phenomenologically rich perception whose particular
richness involves the seeing of the outcomes *as* too-this or too-that or
as just-right. To speak of a perceptual assessment is to say that the
unfolding outcome is perceived against the backdrop of a standard or
bench mark or image of adequacy. The perceptual assessment is,
however, an occurrent mental event.

In the discussion of perceptual assessments, I argued that they are
not wants or beliefs and maintained that they cannot in all cases be
understood as expressive of the individual's wants and beliefs. Thus, I
offered examples in which an individual may not want her craft to be
aesthetically right (e.g., she does not want to give her best to this
employer given the low wages she receives) but she finds that she
cannot avoid seeing the work as not-right (her seeing it as not-right
should not be viewed as an expression of a desire of hers that it be
right or that it be not-right—it is just the way she sees it). Nor is it
always the case that the perceptual assessment is expressive of the
individual's beliefs. For instance, in driving my car behind another car
I regulate the distance between the two cars by way of a perceptual
assessment of the distance between the two cars as "okay" or in terms
of a perceptual assessment that a certain distance is "too close." Not
only do I not have to have the thoughts "I'm getting too close to that
car and I had better slow down," it is not necessary that I even have
such beliefs. All the fact of activity requires is that I have the perceptual assessment and that it causes me to move in ways that result in
my getting the distance between my car and the other to conform to
my perceptual sense of what is "okay." It is perfectly possible that I
know, and thus believe, that I am vastly over-cautious and believe that
in fact it is perfectly safe to be much closer than I am. I can have these

beliefs and nonetheless have a perceptual assessment of the car ahead as "too close." Thus, I argued that the notion of activity can be articulated without reliance on wants, volitions, or beliefs of the individual.

However, to point to these possibilities of activities that are divorced from the individual's wants and beliefs does not mean that they *must* be divorced. On the contrary, typically it is the case that the perceptual assessment *is* expressive of the individual's wants and beliefs. If I see the car ahead of me as "too close" it is because I don't *want* to be in an accident and because I have some general *belief* that at this distance there is danger of an accident. It typically is in virtue of my having wants and beliefs of this sort that I come to have perceptual assessments of this sort, and while it is the case that the perceptual standard, once formed, can have a life of its own, it is generally responsive to the wants and beliefs that one has in the specific context.

Suppose that I am giving someone an account of a particular incident; it may be that the way I tell the story, the detail, the speed, the tone I take, and so on, are regulated via my perception of their reaction as I speak. I might not have any preexisting standard that corresponds to what I view as too-close when I approach another car—rather my telling of the incident is regulated by my desire to get a certain kind of response from this particular person, and by my belief as to whether or not I am getting that response. While these desires and beliefs may be fully operative during the activity, they need, of course, not be desires or beliefs that I am conscious of as I speak. Indeed, the awareness of the fact that I am regulating my activity in the light of such wants and beliefs tends to break the flow of the activity. It fragments it into separate components. Its wholeness is better preserved when the regulation merely occurs—thus, at the heart of activity there is an element of passivity. Or to put it differently, activity may be at its core nonvolitional.

The normal coherence between the individual's wants and beliefs and the perceptual assessment inherent in the activity is the most basic way in which the self is directly present in activity. The wants and beliefs are typically part of the integrated unit we are calling self, and their reflection within the activity *is* the presence of self in the activity. The perceptual assessment is their expression. This linkage is our base case of normal, minimal agency. It implies nothing about the centrality of the wants and beliefs to the self, and it corresponds only to the minimal sense in which we are typically the agent of our activities.

It can, of course, be the case that the aspects of the self that are directly present in the activity are quite central. Thus, consider the standard that is implicit in the perceptual assessment. For instance, is this standard tied to the individual's self-identity—as it might be if the activity in question was an artistic activity (e.g., ballet), and being a person who has such and such a standard of how it should be done, or being a person who is able to perceive the differences between its being done well or poorly, were central aspects of a person's sense of worth.

Wants and beliefs, however, are not the only aspects of the self that can be directly reflected in the activity molecule. Recall Searles's remarks quoted earlier about the individual whose vocal feeling tone did not fit with the content of what she was saying. This relationship between the content of the speech act and the tone of the same act is intelligible because both content and tone are expressive of emotions, moods, and attitudes. There is conflict when tone and content seem to express contradictory attitudes. But our nonverbal behavior also has an emotional tone to it; the way in which we do certain things is not merely a matter of conformity to some perceptual assessment, it may also be the result of the fact that we are in a particular emotional state. The emotion is directly expressed through the activity; it colors the activity. Thus, the emotional tone of an activity, while not a matter of bringing the shape of the activity into conformity with an implicit standard, does, in a parallel way, reflect the direct presence within the activity of mental states that may constitute or be connected to central elements of the self.

Consider, for instance, a single act—a woman kisses a man. The kiss is never just a kiss. It is always a certain kind of kiss, and its being this kind or that kind is itself reflected in the very structure of the kiss. Compare then:

1. *Purely instrumental*—a kiss delivered to a stranger for one dollar at a country fair kissing booth. In this case, without pleasure or emotion of any sort, performed solely in order to raise money for charity

2. *Perfunctorily*—the marriage has gone stale. It is the regular bedtime kiss

3. *Affectionately*—she greets her good woman friend of many years

4. *Sensuously*—she is in bed with her lover; they have the whole afternoon ahead of them

5. *Tenderly*—her husband is asleep and she does not really want to wake him, but she is filled with love for him

6. *With repugnance*—out of a sense of obligation as a wife married to a man she finds physically repellant

7. *Passionately*—overflowing with sexual desire, she tries to devour him

In these different situations, the woman feels different things, and the kiss has different causal histories. But it would be a serious mistake to assume that the kiss itself is always the same, and that the situations differ solely with respect to antecedents or concomitant mental states. Quite the contrary. The sensuous kiss is not the same as the perfunctory kiss, and neither is the same as the tender kiss. There are observable differences, different not only to the one doing the kiss but to the person being kissed and to a third-party viewer. If it were in a play, the director might tell the actress what kind of kiss, and in teaching acting one might need to show someone the differences.

The sensuous kiss is slower. The lips themselves are more exploratory, and are pushed forward and perhaps slightly parted. This much can be seen by the observer. But it is more than observation. For the person doing the kissing, it is not just a matter of behavior. To kiss someone sensuously is to locate one's consciousness in a certain way. One cannot kiss sensuously while thinking about something else.

This feature of the kiss—the character of consciousness during the kiss—is not something extra that occurs at the same time as the kiss, rather it is itself inside the kiss. The activity molecule that is the kiss is held together by it. The awareness of the lips of the other is not the same in the sensuous kiss as in the perfunctory kiss. Not only is it longer in duration, but it is a more acute awareness. It involves a full attentiveness of the person to the lips of the other as they are found by one's own. But it is more than that; it involves a finding of the other's lips as delicious (at least typically so). Thus, the person is in it in a special way that is not the case with the perfunctory kiss. That kiss is almost pure behavior. It is stiff and unexploring, and brief.

In the loving kiss there is yet another difference. It is not merely that the person loves the person she is kissing. One can kiss a loved one other than lovingly. The loving kiss itself is saying something through the activity. An emotion is being expressed. The emotion of love is not only expressed in the kiss, it conditions the kiss. Because the kiss emerges from love it is different in certain ways. There is a language of expression. It is not critical whether it is purely conventional or whether there is some universal and natural way in which feelings of certain sorts are expressed through behavior. What is germane is that because the kiss expresses love, and possibly because it is intended to express love, it is done in a certain way.

And it must be remembered that the activity molecule that is the kiss is made up of more than that which is logically necessary for a kiss—a kiss is in reality more than something we do with our lips. It involves the entire body. It involves holding the other or touching the other in certain ways. Two hands hold the head in a way that is coordinated with the lips. The eyes are closed just in order that consciousness of all else be obliterated; just in order that sensuous engagement is possible.

These correlative elements of the kiss are quite different in different kisses. In the country fair kiss, there may be elements exactly the opposite of the loving kiss. The body is held back so that there is no physical contact except that between the lips themselves. This may be how the woman says, "This is just a country fair kiss."

The broader point is this: the activity molecule itself, whether it is the perceptual assessment, the standard implicit in the perceptual assessment, or the movements themselves (what do the lips do, and how long, how forcefully do they do it), or what the arms and hands and head and eyes do in the kiss—all of these elements possesses the capability of modification that may reflect aspects of the self. They are all vehicles through which other elements of the self are present in the kiss.

An important distinction needs to be made. Part of what I am saying is that the kiss itself has within its very structure elements that are modified to express a broad array of attitudes, motives, emotions, and desires. And the perfunctory kiss is in its way just as expressive as the sensuous kiss. That is, it too reflects and embodies something quite large. An entire universe of understanding might be read out of one perfunctory kiss. So in one sense the self is to be found, perhaps revealed and expressed, in the perfunctory kiss. Yet there is another sense in which the difference between the perfunctory kiss and the sensuous kiss is precisely that the self is *not present* in the former and is present in the latter.

The fact that we make this distinction tells us that by presence of self we mean something more than that components of the self are revealed or expressed or manifest in the activity. Just what we mean is not easy to say. A first thought is that the difference is that the perfunctory kiss expresses or reveals the absence of certain feelings, while the sensuous kiss actually is the manifestation of their presence. But this is hard to sustain. The perfunctory kiss certainly is not the manifestation of love, but it might be the manifestation of something else—perhaps in some instance a sense of duty. And the kissing of that which is experienced as repugnant may manifest emotions as powerful as love—it may manifest hatred.

The difference at hand is a difference that has to do with being wholly engaged (or not) in a performance. The term "wholehearted" might be used as well, but that term is ambiguous. In one sense it is synonymous with "wholly engaged," referring to the phenomenology of the performance as it occurs, but in another sense it has to do with the absence of any conflict about what it is that we are doing. This typically is reflected in the phenomenology, but it need not be. So we may not be wholehearted in kissing an illicit lover, in that we may believe that it is wrong, yet it may be the case that some of these illicit kisses are kisses that we are wholly engaged in when we deliver them.

One aspect of what we mean by being present in an action is that we are fully present in it when we do it. It suggests the absence of conflicting tendencies, in that conflict tends to affect our consciousness during the very performance. Consider these diverse examples of a kiss that does not fully engage the person as she performs it.

- *Purely instrumental*—the kiss at the country fair previously described
- *Against her will*—a woman kisses a man who threatens her with a knife. It is a rape. She is almost frozen with fear
- *Conflictedly*—she kisses an illicit lover, feeling that it is wrong to be doing so
- *Ambivalently*—it is the first date. She kisses him but is unsure of whether or not she really wants to
- *Perfunctorily*—the marriage has gone stale. It is the regular bedtime kiss

In none of these kisses is the person wholly engaged in *the performance*. Being distracted, remote, frozen, or troubled are all ways of being not-present when we do something. Yet the absence of the whole engagement of the person connotes rather different things in each case. In the instances of fear, guilt, and ambivalence there is conflict; either conflicting tendencies, conflicting motives, or conflicting desires. But in the instances of pure instrumentality and the perfunctory kiss, it is not conflict but rather the absence of an occurrent (noninstrumental) desire to kiss.

In that which is spontaneous, joyful, delightful, in that which is play, there is an immediacy to the performance. And sometimes we speak of the immediacy of a person, meaning their capacity to be right-there in that which they are doing. Thus, the presence of the self is not merely a matter of the expression of elements of the self in the activity, but also the immediate presence of the self.

When we do something naturally, spontaneously, rather than purely instrumentally, there is a creativity that emerges. One discovers who one is by relaxing and letting one's self come out. And this relationship between self and action when the self is emerging is perhaps what gives us the sharpest sense of the activity of the self. It is not merely that there is a preexisting self that is expressed or reflected in the activity, but rather the self emerges for itself in the very activity. In this regard there is a basic difference between a performance that is rehearsed and one that is spontaneous. It is not that in delivering a rehearsed performance one is not an agent, or that the self is not present in the performance. It may be fully so. But in the spontaneous performance, be it an exciting conversation or a jazz performance, there is the element of novelty. We do not know exactly what we are going to do or say prior to our doing or saying it. Yet rather than this lack of forethought and lack of explicit intention reflecting an absence of agency, it is exactly this feature that permits the self to be most active, to rise to and break through the surface. In creativity the self is both revealed to itself and constituted. Ironically, this greatest activity of the self occurs when we abandon volition, when we just let ourselves happen.

As was noted in an earlier chapter, some activities, in virtue of the kind of activities that they are, have a particularly great *potential* for the self to be present. These expressive activities are those in which the self can most fully be directly present in the activity itself. Thus, playing the violin offers far greater possibilities for the direct presence of self than does stapling papers together. The perceptual assessment of the ongoing outcome is rich and subtle and sensitive to the variety of possibilities. The perceptual assessment serves as the eye of the needle through which the self emerges.

The fact that certain kinds of activities have an unusually rich and distinct potential for being vehicles for the direct presence (expression) of the self results in their being separated off as "expressive," "artistic," or "aesthetic" activities. The potential that they have, which we might term "aesthetic potential," is not unique to them. All human activity has *some* aesthetic potential; what makes aesthetic activities unique is the range and scope of this dimension.

The fact that an individual engages in such activities, however, does not mean that he or she avails of that potential. Rather, it is typically the case that one has to learn how to do so. This is a great part of what training in these activities consists of. Thus, consider sculpture—it is the plasticity of *the clay itself* that provides the potential, but the individual must learn how to express himself through it. And this direct expression is a matter of learning how to make the clay conform to the standards inherent in one's perception of it as it is modeled (which is itself in part dependent on the education of our eyes as well as our hands)—and also of learning how to transmit to or through the clay an emotionality.

Yet artists or practitioners of any aesthetic activity may be thoroughly alienated from what they are doing. Often there is a failure to perceive or understand how this can be so, because it is not recognized that self-expression is not guaranteed merely in virtue of the type of activity that is performed; it is a question of the relationships of the self to the actual token, and these relationships may be quite diverse. They may also be quite weak, even where great aesthetic potential exists. There is no type of activity that cannot be done without immediacy, without involvement, without presence of self. We always may be elsewhere.

The actualization of the aesthetic and emotional potential of an activity, what we are calling the immediate and direct presence of the self within the activity, is of great importance. For some people participation in such modes of self-expression is the central pleasure/confirmation that life has to offer. But we should not make the mistake of assuming that direct presence is the only way the self may be present in an action; nor should we assume that it is necessarily the most significant.

It is often the case that even when aesthetic potential is very limited, and thus there is limited *direct* presence of self, the *indirect* presence may be quite powerful. Digging a hole may be a mechanical operation, performed with crude tools and little or no critical perception or adjustment of outcome; yet it may embody a great deal of the self—as when one is planting trees in a reclaimed desert. The simple act of handing someone an object is not rich in aesthetic potential. Yet if the object is one's teenage diary and a mother is passing it to her daughter, the *act* of giving it to one's daughter may express much that is central to the self of the parent—though the activity in physical terms expresses little. Thus, both aspects of agency—the web of connectedness and the immediate presence of self— stand on their own feet. Indeed, for all the power of the experiences of immediate presence, at bottom they are features of the phenomenology of the performance. They are properly thought of as the marks of presence, rather than being fully constitutive of presence itself. And thus I might at some later point look back on actions in which I experienced myself as immediately present and conclude that that wasn't really me after all.

Kohut's discussion of what he terms "pseudovitality" is suggestive of how a better understanding of the psychological dynamics that lie behind the marks of engagement can contribute to our understanding of agency.

He writes of

> the overt excitement. Behind it lie low self-esteem and depression, a deep sense of uncared-for-worthlessness and rejection, an incessant hunger for response, a yearning for reassurance. All in all, the excited hyperactivity of the patient must be understood as an attempt to counteract through self-stimulation a feeling of inner deadness and depression.[13]

This is an important caveat. If we are to go along with Lawrence and Nietzsche in their emphasis on spontaneity, we must remember that the truly spontaneous may be quite hard to discern.

With this I conclude the discussion of presence. At bottom it is presence of the self that is at the heart of the notion of agency. The concept of presence is multidimensional and remains a rich field for future work. In the pages above, I have called attention to many of its central dimensions; they are listed below.

I. *Ways in which the self gains direct presence within an activity*
   1. The perceptual assessment is expressive of the wants and beliefs of the individual
   2. The standard inherent in the perceptual assessment is itself an expression of X's basic values, standards, projects, sensibilities, etc.
   3. The emotional tone of the activity is expressive of central emotions or concerns of X

II. *Immediacy: marks of presence in the performance*

    4. While doing A, X does not experience moral qualms about doing A

    5. X enjoys doing A

    6. While doing A, A seems a reasonable thing to be doing

    7. While doing A, X does not feel that he would rather be doing something else

    8. While doing A, X does not dwell on the alternatives he might be doing instead of A

    9. X's sole attention is on A

    10. X "forgets" or "loses himself" in doing A

    11. When he does A, he experiences himself as free, or as acting out of his real self

    12. X performs A with enthusiasm; it rushes out of him

INTERLUDE

Interlude

This concludes Part One of the book. Before moving on to Part Two (Alienation) let me try to bring together various threads of the analysis of action and agency that I have presented.

1. With respect to actions, I have put forward a molecular rather than an atomistic theory. Actions are not seen as the making happen of individual movements. The basic concept is that of a molecular activity. These are complexes marked by indirect perceptual integration. This relation holds between the parts of the activity; an activity *is* an activity because of its internal structure and not because of its external relations.

2. Thus something is not an activity because of the way it is caused. I have separated the question "When is something an activity?" from the question "When is someone an agent?"

3. Agency is a web of relations that constitute the presence of the self in the activity. It is this presence of the self that makes the action truly one's own. The self can be either directly present in an activity or indirectly present. Direct presence is possible because the elements of the activity molecule are themselves variable and subject to modification depending upon other aspects of the self. Direct and immediate presence of the self is a feature of the performance. It reflects a structure of relations between the self and the action, but it is not equivalent to this structural relationship. The structural relationships are also evidenced in a variety of indirect ways in which the self is present in the activity or action.

Locus theories can be seen as attempts to identify specific connections between self and action that are adequate for agency. I have rejected all locus theories, viewing them as the expression of larger aesthetic, ethical, and therapeutic outlooks, reflecting broad cultural alternatives between which it is not possible to find convincing resolution. Instead, I have maintained that "presence of the self" should be seen as something of a formula whose content will vary depending on the kind of personality we are dealing with. Alternative types of personalities may have very different kinds of structures. In some the evaluative or rational elements may be central; in others these connections may be less well defined, and unification of the elements may be on a different basis (e.g., emotions may play a far more central role).

With respect to one specific relationship—causation by wants and beliefs (or volitions)—which plays a central role in the dominant accounts of action/agency, I do not view this causal role per se as critical to agency. With respect to agency, *only* those wants and beliefs that are *part of the self* are relevant. Thus, the person may perform activities that are caused by and integrated with wants and beliefs, but if these wants and beliefs are "aspects of hers that are not hers," she is not an agent. And I do not regard causation by wants and beliefs as necessary so long as other forms of coherence are present between the self and the activity.

Moreover, because the role of wants and beliefs is to link the person to his or her activities (in the relation I term agency), what is critical is not the presence of wants and beliefs in the occurrent sense, but rather long-standing wants and beliefs that are central to the personality, buttressed by wants and beliefs relevant to the context of the action itself. The occurrent mental event that is present in activity is a perceptual assessment, not a want, volition, thought, or belief.

4. By understanding agency as the presence of self in the activity, I have avoided any need for occult senses of agency but have not been forced to exclude as cases of ageny much that is interesting in human activity. Thus, novel occurrences in a conversation, or jabs in a boxing match, or thoughts while writing, or steps while dancing, while they do not fit well into traditional models of human action, may on my analysis be central instances of human agency despite the fact that they do not conform to some rationalistic notion of what an act is, one modeled around a highly deliberate isolated act. Rather than finding agency only in such rare cases we find it *potentially* all around us, in everything we do, but to greater and lesser degree depending on the

degree of existence of the self, and the degree of integration between the self and the activity.

In making agency a matter of self, agency is as variable as the self is, and the sense of agency as variable as the sense of self. Deliberate, intentional action is not the paradigm case of agency. On my account, not only may we be the agents of activities that it would be strange to speak of as intentional, but it is possible that there is an absence of agency in cases of intentional actions. It is possible to have entire cultures in which the conception of the self is such that actions done after deliberation and choice are just those that are the most inadequate expressions of the self. People in that society might say, "Oh, don't judge him badly for that, he was letting himself be dominated by his thoughts and calculations. If you want to see him as he really is, you must see him when he acts naturally and smoothly, and not out of an intention."

PART TWO: ALIENATION

5

Alienness: The Experience of One's Own Incoherence

From Plato to the present day, the human psyche has been thought of as consisting of parts, and mental health has been thought to require certain degrees and kinds of relatedness between the parts. Plato used the metaphor of political justice to characterize the ideal relationship between the parts; contemporary theorists may emphasize the elimination of "dissonance" between cognitive elements. However it is formulated, be it in terms of "integration of the personality," "internal coherence," or "cognitive dissonance" there is an enduring tendency to think of human healthfulness as requiring a certain unity or wholeness.

Closely linked to the tradition that emphasizes wholeness is another strain of thought that emphasizes honesty and authenticity as central to the health ideal. From the Socratic injunction to "know thyself" through contemporary efforts to uncover one's real feelings, the attainment of healthfulness has been associated with overcoming internal dishonesty and self-deception. It is an ancient wisdom that human beings not only have, at times, false beliefs about themselves, but that the "falseness" is not innocent.

The "wholeness" tradition and the "honesty" tradition are intimately connected. Not only is a lack of internal honesty one example of a lack of wholeness, but internal dishonesty is typically thought of as a response to a yet more fundamental incoherence. This disunity, which may be characterized as "conflict" or "threat" or less dramatically as "dissonance," gives rise to the falsity. Thus mental health is thought to involve not only self-knowledge, but also the elimination of internal discord, which generates falsity. The honest recognition that one is terribly conflicted, that one's emotions are not consistent with one's judgments, or that one has inconsistent views of oneself, is but a way station on the road to a fuller health.

But what if it does not work this way? What if it turns out that the *more* we follow the injunction to "know thyself" the *more* we encounter incoherence? And what if it turns out that that incoherence is not rooted in malleable features of our individuality, but instead is rooted in rather permanent features of the human condition? And what if it turns out that the discovery of this incoherence is so unsettling that it makes it impossible for us to engage in the normal activities and relationships that we take to be the hallmark of the healthy life?

Just such a conflict is articulated by the Underground Man in Dostoyevsky's *Notes From Underground*.

"I am a sick man."

"People do pride themselves on their diseases, and I do, maybe more than any one. We will not dispute it; my contention was absurd. But yet I am firmly persuaded that a great deal of consciousness, every sort of consciousness, in fact, is a disease."

"I do not respect myself. Can a man of perception respect himself at all?"

"I invented adventures for myself and made up a life, so as at least to live in some way. How many times has it happened to me—well for instance, to take offense simply on purpose, for nothing; and one knows oneself, of course, that one is offended at nothing, that one is putting it on, but yet one brings oneself, at last to the point of being really offended."

"Anger in me is subject to chemical disintegration. You look into it, the object flies off into the air, your reasons evaporate."

"Oh, if I had done nothing simply from laziness! Heavens, how I should have respected myself, then. I should have respected myself because I should at least have been capable of being lazy; there would at least have been one quality, as it were, positive in me, in which I could have believed myself. Question: What is he? Answer: A sluggard."

How are we to characterize the Underground Man?

1. He sees himself as sick

2. He finds himself unable to remain involved in any activity

3. He feels that he lacks an identity; his perception of himself is as a being without any characteristics

4. His emotional life is unstable. Emotions are not sustained; instead, they seem to dissolve. They never flow smoothly into conduct

5. He claims to take pleasure in his pains, and pride in his problems

6. He constantly feels that he is acting some part that he gives himself

From our everyday standpoint, from the way in which we actually experience people with whom we are in contact, we would recognize the Underground Man as a person with serious mental health problems. And surely, if he were to follow standard advice and seek professional assistance, no psychiatrist would suggest that there is nothing wrong with him. Clearly this man has "psychological problems."

We might, if he is forceful, pause at his knowing that this is precisely what we will think of him. Indeed, he characterizes himself as sick. He seems to be aware of how we will see him, yet he seems to be beyond us. He is mocking our categories and contends that actually there is some logic to his situation. We may *pause*, but surely his having an intelligible perspective on his own being would not lead us to doubt that he has serious problems. It is now a commonplace that the patient has a rational structure within which his conduct makes sense.

Yet there is something different here. The Underground Man does not explain the peculiarities of his conduct and being by putting forward any facts that are unknown to us. He seems to perceive things quite accurately, with no trace of fantasy. Rather, he claims that it is our conduct and way of being that are in question; that he is the way he is, not out of response to special features of his situation that are unknown to us, but out of appropriate response to the most general features of a situation that we all share. All he is, he claims, is a man honestly responding to the truths of the human condition.

His claim that his experience is authentic or valid is tied to the claim that *it is grounded in consciousness*, that is, accurate awareness or true belief. Even if true, this does not, however, settle the question of his mental health. Accordingly, for the time being, let me put the question of mental health on "hold." What I am concerned with is the *appropriateness* of his experience of incoherence, and the validity of what he says. Though this has bearing on the question of mental health, it is not the same issue. We may discover that there is a conflict within our concept of health; for instance, we may discover that one's general well-being, one's ability to be happy, take pleasure, feel whole, and be productive are not compatible with an authentic response to one's condition.

The existence of some incoherence is the general condition of the human psyche; it is possible that there have never been any human beings that have achieved complete unification. In what follows I shall explore the different kinds of fissures and seek to distinguish those that are ultimate givens of the human condition from those that are personal and in principle remediable, and both of these from those that, while neither purely personal nor universal, seem to compellingly arise in the central contexts of human life (e.g., in situations of deep political commitment).

To say that incoherence is a general condition of the human psyche is not to say that people are generally aware of their own lack of unity. Indeed, it may be as the Underground Man suggests—only a rare few, those with heightened consciousness, are aware of the emptiness at the center. It may be as Sartre says—that we are regularly drawn towards an inauthentic posture of wholeness.

In what follows I will argue that incoherence abounds and that its discovery awaits us at every turn. It is revealed by reflection on the most intimate details of our personal life. It is to be found in our basic projects: our personal relationships and our work. And it is inherent in our social projects: our efforts to shape and control the terms of our relations with others—our existence as political agents.

Thus, broadly speaking I am in agreement with the Underground Man. For the most part, people are not aware of the extent and nature of the incoherence they contain. When they are aware of it, it is usually manifest in feelings of uncertainty, doubt, confusion, hesitation, and ambivalence. These are the everyday forms of experienced incoherence; but under greater reflection these experiences may be transformed into something much sharper, into a dramatic perception of one's own lack of internal connectedness. I use the term "alienness experiences" to designate these intense experiences of inner fragmentation.

"Alienness" refers to a felt experience, something that occurs at a given time and place and occupies one's consciousness. It is a part of our mental phenomenology. While the term has been invented, the experience has not. That is not to say that it is a regular experience or even that all people have it at some time. Nor is it to say that it is an experience that has existed from time immemorial. I doubt that cave dwellers felt alienness. Human experience has a history, and it makes sense to suppose that the first experiences of alienness came relatively late in that history. This does not make them any less real, and it may make them particularly interesting.

Let me hasten to explain that I am *not* talking about alienation or alienness experiences primarily in the social sense of being alienated from society, or of feeling alien at a party or in a foreign country. These uses have some relationship to what I am concerned with, but my primary interest is in the experience of one's self as alien, or more specifically, the experience of some *aspect* of oneself as alien. Consider:

Experiencing one's past actions as alien. I am alone. I am eating. I have been indulging myself, eating all my favorite foods, especially chocolate ice cream. For a moment I pause with the ice cream in my mouth. I am playing with its creaminess; I attend to it sharply. I notice the taste, but it is strange, for the taste is not particularly good. Perhaps it is just something in my mouth, or this ice cream, but no, I come to realize that I have no special fondness for this taste; more than that, I realize now that I never had, that during those years when I was adamant as to which flavors I would eat and which ones I liked I had never really paid any attention to the taste of the ice cream. It all seems strange; all of that behavior looks now like some sort of act that I was going through, a series of movements that weren't really mine. I want to say that I didn't really do this, that there was something else that must have been acting through me.

Experiencing one's ongoing actions as alien. A similar case: lovemaking. So much activity is organized around this, so much perception and engagement. The world seems divided into two kinds of objects, sexual and nonsexual. So much is involved: the pursuit, the seduction, the anxieties that follow. The centrality is immense. Yet in the very act to pause and wonder, "What the hell am I doing!" Amid the strain and exertion to recognize that, if anything, I am feeling tense and fearful rather than ecstatic! What is it all about? What am I inhabited by? I continue through the act. Very little changes, everything goes on as before, organized around this pursuit, but now it is all weird, as though it is not me at all. I want to deny that I am doing this.

Experiencing one's emotions as alien. I oppose the war. There is no question about this. Indeed, if I have any sympathy, it is with the "enemy" and not with my country. But actually I oppose it all, the actions of trapped men, entrapping their children in struggle, each killing the other, the tremendous waste and injustice. Yet, sitting in front of the television, hearing news reports of fighting, hearing the passion of the newscaster, I experience all the emotions of a booster. What is this? What are they? These emotions are foreign. They are not mine, that's not the way I feel! I want to shout, "these emotions are not mine!"

Experiencing one's beliefs as alien. We are sitting at a table, my friend and I and a woman I am with. Somehow it sneaks up on me—a suspicion: Is he touching her foot? He seems to be just talking and she is eating, but are they really doing nothing? It is not an ordinary question. I know that there is nothing going on. There is not a shred of evidence. I have no reason to believe. . . . Yet even now I am unable to control myself; like a fool I glance under the table, careful that no one sees me looking, for how could I possibly explain what I was looking at? Yet my suspicions are eased only while I can see under the table; the very second I look up I am again assailed. What is wrong with me? What are these thoughts, these invasions? These beliefs are foreign matter, I don't believe that there is anything to be seen, yet again *it* comes. I want to deny that these beliefs are mine.

Experiencing one's life as alien. What am I to do? There is not really any alternative to doing something. I am caught within the necessity of deciding, of taking stands, of taking sides. Even adopting skepticism constitutes a position. I am engaged in major projects of all sorts: I marry, choose a career, live in a certain country, adopt a certain life style, accept a position, buy a home, have children. These are all terribly significant actions; they are irrevocable. To turn away from them once they are done entails a total alteration. And yet I know that I enter into them without having sufficiently appraised the question. I am unsure of my wants and beliefs, and, to the extent that I am confident, I know that I ought not be. Yet I go on, as I always have. I make decisions. Yet they don't seem to emerge from me as much as absorb me. My entire life seems strange. I tend to say, "my life is not my own" or "it's as if I'm not alive."

Experiencing one's entire self as alien. I think of myself in a certain way: I am a certain kind of person; there are things about me that are central. Perhaps I am an artist or a writer; I have a special concern with truth, or with understanding; or I live according to certain standards, and evaluate myself and others by them. But I see these aspects of myself as arising from rather simple conflicts and insecurities at an early age; I chose these standards and self-images in order to judge, in order to feel superior. I pursued them in order to feel secure within my own world. This is especially true of those identifications that are not even superficially grounded in assessments, but are simply mine: the way *I* see things, the way *I* do things, the kind of person *I* am. Once understood, it looks so different. My entire personality seems to be that of a buffoon, a pathetic creature. I would replace it wholesale, and even this concern with identity, this concern with who I am; this too is the hallmark of that very same fear-ridden, needful, or merely habitual person. I turn away in disgust. But where am I to go? I feel as though I were inhabited, as though I were not myself, as though I don't really exist.

Let me say a few words about these experiences. First note that in each example there is *something* that the person experiences as alien, be it an emotion, a belief, an action, or his entire personality. As such the experience of alienness is unlike certain other conscious states such as feeling chilled or dizzy.

To have an alienness experience is to experience something as-alien. In this it is similar to many phenomenologically rich modes of experiencing. A child can experience one of her stuffed animals as terrifying, or as malevolent, alive, hungry, lecherous, and so on. We arrive at a party where we know no one—we may experience it as forbidding, cold, unfriendly, or perhaps as sparkling, exciting, inviting. Sartre speaks of arriving at the cafe and experiencing Jacques as "not-there." Alienness is a particular way of experiencing oneself.

Alienness is *not* the same as merely experiencing something as not belonging to oneself. After all, I do not experience *your* actions as belonging to myself; I do not experience *your* personality as being mine; I do not experience *your* past as being mine; nonetheless, I cannot be said to have alienness with respect to any of these objects (your actions, your beliefs, your personality). It is only *my* personality, *my* actions, *my* beliefs that are possible candidates for alienness. Thus, alienness is the experience of something *as* one's-own and also, at the same time, as *not*-one's-own. It is the experience of an aspect of one's self as my-own-yet-not-my-own.

It is useful to consider how such experiences have been hitherto understood. However, the psychological and psychiatric literature contains no term that corresponds exactly to the phenomena I am considering. The closest resemblance is found under the heading, "depersonalization." Karl Jaspers gives the following definition:

Every psychic manifestation, whether perception, bodily sensation, memory, idea, thought or feeling carries this particular aspect of "being mine" of having an "I" quality, of "personally belonging," of it being one's own doing. We have termed this "personalization." If these psychic manifestations occur with the awareness of their not being mine, of being alien, automatic, independent, arriving from elsewhere, we term them phenomena of depersonalization.[1]

For Jaspers, the objects of depersonalization are psychic manifestations. What is experienced as alien is something "mental" or "internal," a content of consciousness that can be placed in time precisely. One can say, at a specific time *t*, I had a manifestation of sort *S* and it did (or did not) have the quality of being-mine. In the phenomenon of alienness, what is experienced as alien includes not only psychic manifestations, but also beliefs, emotions, desires (in the both occurrent and dispositional senses) as well as the person's body or self or actions. Second, in depersonalization (as Jaspers describes it) the manifestations (thoughts, emotions, etc.) are experienced as merely alien, often as belonging to others, but in alienness they are recognized as one's own, yet not one's own. They are experienced as mine-but-not-mine.

Various authors use the term "depersonalization" in somewhat different ways.

The experience is distressing and seems to be essentially one of unreality; the world feels unreal; the subject feels that he is unreal, totally or partially; the symptom never seems to have a delusional quality. . . . The patients have insight. They do not say "I am unreal" but "I feel that I am not real, although I know I am." When they speak of a change in their personality, they seem always to refer to a sense of loss.[2]

Another describes depersonalization as:

an experience pertaining to either the bodily or the mental self. In the first case the person will complain that his body or rather certain parts of the body do not feel like his own, as belonging to him. He may describe them as estranged from himself or as being dead. . . . Not rarely we detect states of depersonalization pertaining to the genitals and to the sexual act. . . . They perceive themselves as going through the act without being "present"; the penis performs as if it were not their own. Whenever depersonalization extends to the mental self there is a feeling of unreality of the self and of being "outside the self." The depersonalized patient will think, react, act; but his experience is that of a detached spectator who is observing another person's performance. Not only his actions but his own thought processes appear to him unfamiliar and strange.[3]

And still another says:

> The outer world appears substantially unaltered, but yet different; not so essentially, so actually, near or far, clear, warm, friendly and familiar; not really and truly existing and alive; more as if in a dream and yet different from a dream. At heart the patient feels as if he were dead; and he feels like this because he does not feel. His feeling, wishing, thinking and memory processes have become different, uncertain, intolerably changed, and yet the patient knows everything correctly; his faculties of perception, of intellect and of logic have not suffered at all. . . . In still more severe cases even the unity of the ego is only perceived, not felt.[4]

The fact that there is no generally accepted definition of "depersonalization" seems to reflect the absence of any satisfactory theory to explain the phenomena. Without theoretical insight it is difficult to see how to classify diverse phenomena, and different classifications may reflect different intuitions as to where an explanation is to be found. Such differences will even affect the description of the phenomena to be explained. Is depersonalization the same as alienness? At this time there is little point in maintaining that we are dealing with one, two, or three different phenomena. It is only from the position of having a theory of alienness that we will know how to relate it to depersonalization.

Returning to the examples of alienness, I note that each example involved a rather rich context, and setting the experience within the context was critical to understanding just how one could come to feel the way one does in the alienness experience. In each case the person has some *beliefs* about the object he experiences as alien. In the examples, the relevant beliefs included: (1) my actions have not been motivated by what I have always understood as my reasons for acting as I do; (2) my beliefs make no sense, yet they remain my beliefs; (3) my emotions do not emerge from my beliefs but in spite of them.

We also find certain verbal formulations or tendencies to verbalize alienness. These statements about the object—that it is not one's own, that one did not do it, that one is not oneself—emerge as complaints within the clinical situation. One complains that one feels *as if* one were not the agent of one's actions, or as if one's emotions were not one's own, or as if one did not exist. Understanding alienness calls for grasping the relationship between (1) these verbal formulations, (2) the experience of alienness, and (3) the beliefs and realizations about the object of alienness.

I reject the general assumption that these experiences are in themselves pathological, and reject the general assumption of the psychoanalytic approach that they are had *in order to* protect or defend the individual from some unpleasant realization about himself or herself. Along with this last, I reject the view that these experiences are part of some general self-deception on the part of the individual. I wish to show that these experiences *may be* accurate perceptions of reality, and that they play a central role in authentic human life.

Consider the following passage from R. D. Laing. Laing is describing a patient he refers to as "David."

> His self was never directly revealed in and through his actions. It seemed to be the case that he had emerged from infancy with his "own self" on the one hand, and "what his mother wanted him to be," his "personality," on the other. . .
>
> The central split is between what David called his "own" self and what he called his "personality." This dichotomy is encountered again and again. What the individual variously terms his "own," "inner," "true," "real," self is experienced as divorced from all activity that is observable by another, what David called his "personality." One may conveniently call this "personality" the individual's "false self" or a "false self system." . . .
>
> The "self" in such a schizoid organization is usually more or less unembodied. It is experienced as a mental entity. . . . The self is not felt to participate in the doings of the false self or selves, and all its or their actions are felt to be increasingly false and futile. The self, on the other hand, shut up with itself regards itself as the "true" self and the persona as false.[5]

It is important to realize that the falseness of the false self is a part of the schizoid's perspective. *He* has split himself in two. *He* sees one part as real and the other as not real. Laing's way of making the schizoid comprehensible consists of two components. First, he explains *why* the schizoid does this, why he erects the false self. It is done as a defense. He seeks to protect himself from his underlying "ontological insecurity." Second, he endeavors to move inside the schizoid's world. The key to understanding what the schizoid is saying and experiencing is to remember his sense of identity. We can understand *if* we remember *his sense of identity.*

If the individual delegates all transactions between himself and the other to a system within his being which is not "him," then the world is experienced as unreal, and all that belongs to this system is felt to be false.[6]

Laing has remained within the accepted psychoanalytic outlook. He remains on the level of compassionate understanding. He says that what the patient says is "existentially true." But, for Laing, this means that it follows from the patient's own sense of identity. Such "existential truths" remain self-deceptive!

Laing reminds us, "And yet, of course, this isolation and inner non-commitment are not without self-deception." He tells us that, "There is something final and definitive about an act" and then he goes on to quote Hegel:

The act is something simple, determinate, universal, to be grasped as an abstract, distinctive whole; it is murder, theft, a benefit, a deed of bravery and so on, and what it is can be said of it. It is such and such, and its being is not merely a symbol, it is the fact itself. It is this, and the individual human being is what the act is. In the simple fact that the act is, the individual is for others what he really is and with a certain general nature, and ceases to be merely something that is "meant" or "presumed" to be this or that.[7]

Thus, for Laing, to not see one's actions as one's own is inherently self-deceptive and pathological.

My approach differs from Laing's in several ways. Most importantly, I wish to get beyond having to speak of "existential truths" that are self-deceptive. In the previous discussion of the self, I used a distinction between a person and a self, as does Laing. But I was seeking to articulate a real, structural distinction between a loosely related and sometimes deeply conflicted set of elements that we can call "the person" and the more unified compound called "the self." The person/self distinction is not essentially something in the schizoid's sense of identity (though he or she may make that distinction) but rather it is a distinction within the personality itself. The experience of the schizoid and alienness experiences more generally are possible because they embody conceptual structures we all share. The analysis of agency and activity presented in Part One provides the basic tools for understanding the alienness experience.

In discussing the examples considered at the beginning of this chapter, I noted that the experience of alienness was brought on by one's coming to have certain beliefs. I do not wish to construe this as a merely causal relation, or even as a motivated response (e.g., a defense against something seen as threatening). There is a more intimate connection, one in terms of which the experience of alienness might be appropriate and accurate, and as not necessarily involving self-deception.

In Part One, agency is understood as involving the integration of the self with an activity. The self was conceptualized as the integrated personality, and activities were seen to be a complex of elements held together through "indirect perceptual integration." Thus the account of agency calls for integration in three areas: among the components of the activity, among the components of the self, and between these two complexes.

Alienness with respect to one's actions is the experience of an absence of integration (wholeness, unity) in one or more of these three loci. Moreover, it is possible to provide parallel analyses for alienness with respect to other aspects of the self (e.g., experiencing one's emotions as alien, experiencing one's personality as one's own but not one's own).

Thus far I have grouped together a variety of verbal articulations of the experience of alienness:

- "I feel as if *I am not the agent of my actions.*"
- "I feel as if *my actions are not really mine.*"
- "I feel as if *I never really do anything.*"
- "I feel as if *everything just happens to me.*"
- "I feel as if *everything I do is done by something else.*"

I have spoken as if there were only one experience of alienness. But having understood wholeness as involving integration in three distinct loci, it is possible to distinguish three distinct experiences of alienness, each corresponding to the experience of a different lack of coherence.

First consider the normal experience of oneself as the agent of one's activity, or as the genuine holder of one's beliefs or values, or as someone whose desires and emotions are really his or her own (see Figure 5.1). Integration in the three areas may be characterized as follows: (1) there is a complex integrated in the manner that is constitutive of its being a particular kind of element (e.g., an emotion, a belief, a value, an activity); (2) there is a unified complex that is oneself; (3) there is an appropriate relationship between the self and

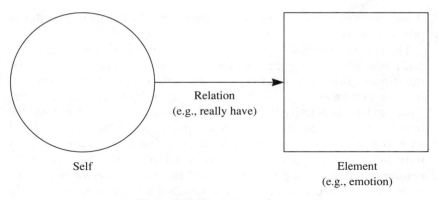

Relation
(e.g., really have)

Self   Element
                                        (e.g., emotion)

Figure 5.1   Normal experience

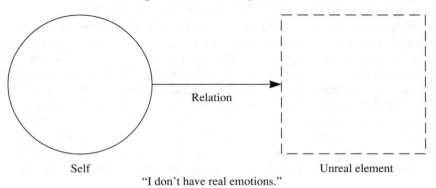

Relation

Self   Unreal element
              "I don't have real emotions."

Figure 5.2   Reduction of aspect

the element such that the element can be said to "belong to," or "come from," or "really express" the self.

The first contrast with normal experience may be termed *reduction of aspect* (see Figure 5.2). Here the necessary integration is missing within the aspect or element itself. There exists an aspect of mine that appears to be an activity (or an emotion, or a belief, or a value) but is really something else ("I don't have real activities, emotions, beliefs, values, etc."). Here there is no challenge to either the existence of the self or to the connection of self to the aspect. It is rather that the aspect is seen as failing to really be the kind of aspect it is originally taken to be; in reality it falls short of the required fullness; it is correctly seen as reduced to something else. For instance, they are not actions but merely movements; they are not beliefs but merely thoughts; they are not personality characteristics but merely patterns of past behavior.

The second contrast with normal experience may be termed *person/ self ambiguity* (see Figure 5.3). Here the reality of the element is not questioned. It is a real activity, emotion, desire, and so on. Moreover, it is the expression of some entity, but that entity is not truly oneself. There exists an activity that was done by the person I am but not by my self. *I* am not the agent of it; something or someone else is. This is an expression of the absence of the fully formed self. Rather than a fully integrated personality, the individual confronts two fragments neither of which is fully whole. Person/self ambiguity is introduced to refer to these two complexes. That which the individual calls self is the complex with which he or she identifies; the theorist may from his or her third-person point of view identify one or the other fragment as representing the self, or he or she might be neutral between the two fragments. There is no challenge, however, to either the aspect itself (it is a real activity, emotion, belief, etc.) or to the linkage between the aspect and the fragment from which it emerges. What is at issue is the status of the fragment: "It comes from the person, but not from me."

The third contrast with normal experience may be termed *alternate relation* (see Figure 5.4). Here there is no challenge to the full-fledged existence of the element. It is a genuine emotion, value, action, and so on. Nor is there any question of the existence of the self. But the necessary integration between the self and the element is missing.

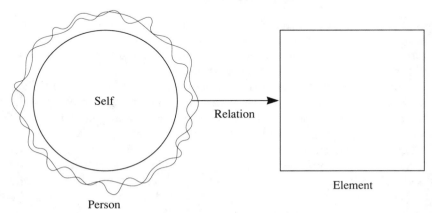

Self

Relation

Element

Person

"My emotions don't come from the real me."

Figure 5.3 Person/self ambiguity

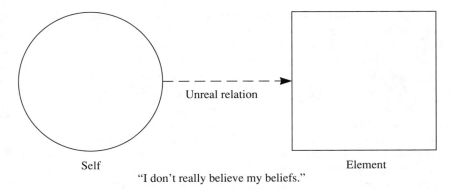

Self   Element

"I don't really believe my beliefs."

Figure 5.4 Alternate relation

There exists an activity of mine but I am not the *agent* of it; I have it, but I have not done it. (It is my desire, but I don't *really have* that desire, it's not really mine. I have the belief that *p*, but I don't *really believe* that *p*.) Here the incoherence is experienced as located *between* the aspect and the self. The self exists and so do the particular actions, emotions, desires. But they are not the actions, desires, emotions of the self. The self is not really present in them; it has some other relationship to them.

Thus, corresponding to each of the three loci of possible incoherence there is a distinct kind of alienness experience and distinct ways in which the experience will be characterized or expressed verbally. If we look at these verbal expressions, at what is in clinical situations, sometimes referred to as "the verbal complaint," we find that typically they take the form: "I feel as if _____." The underlined segment, which we can refer to as the embedded belief, asserts the existence of some state of affairs (e.g., I am not the agent of my actions, my emotions are not mine, I have no personality traits). I have identified above several of these verbal complaints from the agency/action family of alienness experiences.

The fact that the verbal formulation typically begins with the disclaimer "I feel as if" reflects the fact that the individual having the alienness experience is no more able than anyone else to say what it is to not be the agent of one's actions, or to have emotions that are not one's own. He or she is groping for a verbal formulation that will capture an experience of himself or herself that is deeply perplexing. I have spoken of the experiencing of some aspect of the self as being one's own and not one's own, but it would be a mistake to imagine that the experience itself exists in full clarity and that the problem is merely how to translate it into words. Our experience of ourselves is mediated through the conceptual structures that we use to think about the self. In my analysis of agency I have sought to articulate the conceptual structures that are implicitly present in these experiences. But by making the implicit explicit, there is the risk of presenting the experience as though it has greater clarity than it does.

These experiences remain paradoxical for the person who has them, and she realizes their paradoxical character. She does not have the delusions of the person who claims to be inhabited by beings from another world. Because she is in touch with the paradoxical nature of her experience of self, she uses the "as if" formulation. In view of this, one might say that Figures 5.2, 5.3, and 5.4 better convey the phenomenological quality of alienness if we erase the words that explain the symbols.

The general explanation of alienness is this: the beliefs that cause or give rise to the alienness experience do so, typically, because they serve as *grounds* for the assertion contained in the embedded belief. They constitute reasons for believing the embedded belief to be correct. Thus, in the analysis of agency, I have provided an account in terms of which it is meaningful to ask if someone is an agent with respect to his or her activity. The identification of something as an activity does not carry with it the implication that the person who "has" that activity is an agent with respect to it. The beliefs that give rise to the experience of oneself as not the agent of one's own activities are just those beliefs that suggest there is insufficient integration to conclude that the agency relationship holds between self and activity.

The explanation that I am offering, however, could not be correct if the individuals who have the alienness experience do not share the conceptual framework in terms of which the embedded beliefs of alienness complaints are made intelligible. While the analysis could render "I am not the agent of my actions" intelligible, it could not explain how or why such experiences occur for people who do not embody this conceptual framework. And it should be remembered that there is a diversity of ways in which the self as integrated personality can be understood. Thus, an understanding of any particular person's experience would require knowing what particular conception of the self they hold. Put differently, it can be said that we all carry with us philosophic theories that condition our experience of ourselves.

Insofar as the analyses I have provided go beyond our pre-analytic conceptual framework, the analysis should to some extent modify the alienness experience. In particular, it should render that experience somewhat less paradoxical. The internalization of the philosophical analyses presented should result in the elimination of the "as if" quality of those experiences. At the same time, the ability of the analyses of activity, agency, and self to render intelligible our experiences and our verbal characterization of those experiences is additional confirmation of the theory. All philosophical theory, even that which seeks to radically revise ordinary language, must bear some connectedness to our linguistic intuitions. Action theory is rather tightly connected to the fact that we do distinguish between "my hand went up" and "I raised my hand." Theorists have looked for an account of action that would articulate the criteria that lie behind these linguistic discriminations. In the search for a conceptual analysis that would explain the experiences of alienness and thus make them rationally intelligible as opposed to inherently pathological, there is a broader intuitive base, which serves as a touchstone for the adequacy of philosophical analysis.

ALIENATION AND AGENCY

Throughout the previous discussion I have been rather careful to speak of the experience of *alienness*. In general, I have avoided using the term "alienation," and at no point have I said that a person who experiences some aspect of self as his-and-not-his is alienated from that aspect. Nonetheless, it is clear that there is an important relationship between alienness and alienation, and this should be made clear.

The relationship can be stated succinctly: Alienation is the *state* in virtue of which a given *experience* of alienness is valid. In the alienness experience an individual experiences some aspect of self to be his and not his. This is a veridical experience if and only if he is truly alienated from that aspect of self. Thus "alienated" can be defined as follows:

X is alienated from aspect *A* if and only if it is his and not his.

As defined, alienation refers to an underlying structural relationship, essentially the lack of integration between *X* and the aspect in question. To say that a person is alienated from such and such an aspect does not imply that he feels alienated or has an alienness experience in relationship to that aspect.

It should be recognized that as defined the notion of alienation is schematic. No specific characterization of what it is to be alienated from some aspect of self is given because the account is intended to be sufficiently general to encompass alternative understandings of the self and the necessary modes of integration.

It was pointed out above that judgments of the validity of an *experience* of alienness are based on a conception of the self and on a view as to what integrations must hold for a given aspect to be fully of the self. Thus, from a third-person perspective the theorist (therapist, friend, other) may assess some other individual's experience of alienness, embodying in the assessment a conception of the self that is quite different than that embodied by the individual who has the alienness experience. This can be restated in terms of alienation; in making judgments about whether or not an individual is alienated from some aspect of himself, the theorist may employ a notion of self different from that of the individual himself.

Implicit in this view of alienation as a state that underlies the valid experience of alienness is the circumstance that one may be alienated from an aspect and not experience it as being-and-not-being-one's-own. Indeed, one may even have no experience of the aspect at all. One may not even know that it exists. Thus, one may be so deeply alienated from one's emotions that one is not even aware of their existence. By contrast, the person who is alienated from A and does have the experience of A as being-and-not-being-her-own is the person who is in touch with certain features of her reality. She experiences her relation to the aspect in question as it is. Thus, it is an error to take the absence of alienness as signifying unity. In many cases there is not only a lack of integration but a lack of awareness of the lack of integration.

Having linked alienness and alienation, and having understood agency as the presence of the self in its activities, we can now define "agency" in terms of "alienation."

> X is the agent of some activity A if and only if A is an activity of X and X is not alienated from A.

Thus agency is the opposite of alienation. This, in a nutshell, expresses my theory of agency. Both agency and alienation are understood in terms of a structural relationship between the self and the element in question (e.g., an activity). To ascribe agency is to affirm the existence of that relationship. To ascribe alienation is to affirm the absence of that relationship. Paralleling the structural side, there is the individual's own experience of the presence or absence of the relevant structural connectedness. When she experiences it as present, she experiences herself as an agent; she identifies with herself as the source of the activity. When she experiences an absence of a required relationship, she experiences alienness. This experience, as noted, differs depending on where the incoherence is experienced as residing.

The basic point is that alienness emerges from coming to believe things that serve as grounds or reasons for concluding that the embedded alienness beliefs are correct (i.e., that the required structural connectedness is indeed absent). If I am correct that alienness is rooted in belief that serve as its grounds, then the alienness experience can be explored by situating it in the kinds of reflection or practical contexts that give rise to such beliefs.

Three central contexts within which alienness emerges are: (1) psychological inquiry into one's own nature as a specific individual; (2) philosophical inquiry into the most general features of the human condition; and (3) political activity that aims at basic changes in our social world. In the remaining chapters of this book I examine the dynamics of alienness within each of these contexts. Collectively they demonstrate the centrality of alienness to what it is to be human.

Table 5.1 shows the linkages between the alienness-generating beliefs, the contexts in which they arise, the verbal expressions and experiences they give rise to, and the conclusions they support.

Table 5.1   Alienness-Grounding Beliefs

Belief	Context	Verbal Expression	Useful Model	"Warranted Conclusion"
A. My actions are motivated by values I reject	psychological/ political	"My actions do not come from the real me"	p/s	The actions are integrated with something belonging to the person but not to the self
B. My actions are not motivated as I had thought. I don't know my motives	psychological	"My actions do not come from the real me"	p/s	Integration with person but not self
C. My values were implanted in me by others, by society, etc.	psychological/ political	"My actions don't really come from me"	p/s	The actions are integrated with values that are not really his own
		"I feel as if another acts through me"	a-r	Action is merely done by him but it expresses another
D. There are no answers to value questions (nihilism)	philosophical	"I never really do anything"	p/s	There is an absence of "reasoned" integration between all values and other aspects; thus they do not belong to the self
E. Everything one does is fully determined by events that occurred long before one's birth (determinism)	philosophical	"I never really do anything"	r.a.	There are no actions, just movements
		"I never do anything. I am not the agent of my actions"	b/p/s	Actions come from something that is not the self (e.g., the body). One is never a real agent

Table 5.1 (cont.)

Belief	Context	Verbal Expression	Useful Model	"Warranted Conclusion"
F. Mental events never are causes of movements (Epiphenomenalism)	philosophical	"I don't do anything"	r.a.	There are no mental causes, no indirect perceptual integrations, no actions, just movements
		"My actions don't come from me"	b/p/s	Actions are caused by bodily states
G. One can never know what effects actions have (Scepticism)	philosophical/ political	"My actions do not *really* come from me"	a-r	Since one never has good grounds for doing the things one does, they are not really one's own
H. If one had by chance been born in a different culture, one would see things in a radically different way and pursue a radically different life.	philosophical	"I don't really do anything"	p/s	Actions are integrated with values and beliefs, but these are not grounded in the way they must be to be really one's own
I. What I am doing violates own values	psychological/ political	"I am not the agent of my actions"	p/s	His actions don't come from his self as they violate his essence
J. The existence of the self does not involve some "deep fact"— there are no Cartesian egos (Parfit)	philosophical	"I do not really exist. There is no real me"	p/s	He is not really the agent of his past and future actions

Key: p/s = person/self
    a-r = alternate relation
    r.a. = reduced aspect
    b/p/s = body/person/self

6

Alienness and the Human Condition: The Philosophic Context

In the previous chapter I pointed out the marginality of alienness experiences. There is no sustained literature that discusses such experiences, and insofar as anything very similar to them has been a subject of discussion it has occurred under the heading "depersonalization."

Occasionally within the philosophic literature we find an author who says something of the sort, "If that were to be the case then my experiences would not be mine." But there are few sustained examinations of the experience of one's own experiences as not one's own.

At the moment, I want only to say that the status of what I have called "alienness experiences" is unsettled. There is probably little question that something of this sort exists. But certainly my claim that such experiences are sensible because in them reality is experienced as it is, or as it quite reasonably appears to be, cannot be readily granted. For this view implies that paradoxical utterances such as "my act is not my act" or "my emotions are not really mine" are not just the expression of some attitude that I have about the act or the emotion, but meaningful statements that quite possibly are true. Moreover, they are meaningful not because they are ways of saying what we say with some familiar idiom, such as "I was not myself." On the contrary, they assert some rather shocking truth, something that is hard to accept and, indeed, hard to understand—that I am not myself.

And as such, they might just as well be made in the third person, as "his acts are not his" or "his emotions are not really his."

In some situations people do occasionally talk this way, and when we hear such things we usually try to find some sense that we can make of them. In broad terms the theory I have put forward with respect to agency, a theory that allows us to ask without paradox, "Is he the agent of that action of his?" can be viewed as an expanded and formal approach within this same practice of looking for a way of making sense of what is being said. Within the theory of agency developed earlier, these utterances loose their paradoxical character. Because these distinctions and analyses do not fully predate the theory, they cannot have been, in a full sense, what the individual was saying. They are what he was trying to say but lacked the conceptual framework to clearly say.

Because these paradoxical locutions and experiences of alienness are responses to a confrontation with a reality that surprises us, the beliefs that express how that reality is understood may be termed "alienness-grounding" beliefs. Alienness-grounding beliefs are beliefs that trigger the alienness experience because they provide grounds for the conclusion that is at the heart of the alienness experience (e.g., the conclusion that my actions are not my own). And because different kinds of reflection—reflection on one's own psychological make-up or history, reflection upon one's own conduct and one's own understanding of what one is doing—can result in the formation of such alienness-generating beliefs, alienness is an experience that typically emerges in contexts of reflection.

It is, however, not necessarily psychological reflection or self-examination that leads to the use of alienness locutions. To get a sense of this we can consider an imaginary case. Not a great deal hangs on this case, but it may serve to broaden the context.

Every person has the capacity to engage in "silent soliloquies" with himself or herself. Sometimes this is what we mean by thinking or having thoughts. These silent soliloquies are much like speaking and hearing. They occur in a particular language, they are uttered to oneself in a particular tone, and speed, and loudness. In some instances they have the character of actions, in that I can deliberately say certain things to myself. In other instances they appear to be happenings whose occurrence is out of my control.

Suppose that a person has agreed to follow instruction cards. When we show her a card that tells her to think a certain sequence, say to count from one to ten to herself, she does so. Working with two such persons, we then discover that by intercepting an electrical impulse in one person's brain and switching it with that of another, we can tell the first person to count from one to ten and the second person to recite the alphabet, and what each will experience is what the other initiated.

In a situation of this sort, it would be natural to say, "my thoughts are not really my thoughts," or "each person is having the other's thoughts." This kind of thing can be made more and more complicated. Suppose that by a similar process, we could take two people, one who responds to horror movies with fright and one who responds with laughter, and have them experience the emotional states the other would have had. We might say that they are having each other's emotions, or that their emotions are not really their own.

The point of this example is that under certain circumstances, circumstances that *are terribly out of the ordinary*, the most natural way to describe the situation is with the use of one of the alienness locutions. Since the use of an alienness locution in characterizing this example is not about oneself or anyone real at all, it should be clear that the use of such locutions need not be seen as motivated by any project of defense or denial. It simply seems the most natural way to describe the unnatural situation.

The locutions that emerge from alienness-generating reflection are varied. I earlier called attention to three kinds of alienness experiences. The three can be seen to be related to three different aspects of what we are saying when under normal circumstances we say something such as "John ran home," or "John was angry," or "John is a nasty person." These normal assertions can be viewed as composed of three assertions: (1) a specific person (John) exists; (2) certain specific elements (e.g., an emotion, an action) exist; (3) that person stands in a relationship (e.g., ownership, agency, really having) to those elements.

Alienness-grounding beliefs can then be more formally characterized as beliefs that in a paradoxical manner call into question any of these three claims. By "paradoxical manner" what I mean to call attention to is that the alienness-grounding beliefs on the one hand undermine the claim and yet on the other hand seem to leave it intact. Or to put it differently, the alienness-grounding belief leads us towards the conclusion that there is an odd factual complexity as to the existence of that person, that entity, or the relationship between them. If the entity does not exist, it is not a simple case of its not existing. Under normal circumstances when we challenge the claim that someone performed a specific action we are maintaining something rather simple: that it is not true that the person did it. But the alienness-generating beliefs pull us towards saying something like, "Well in one sense he did, but in another sense he didn't, except that I can't quite say what the two senses are." In other words, alienness emerges at points in which we sense a factual complexity or ambiguity that seems to stretch our language. It is an ambiguity of a sort that we never anticipated could exist and that we don't quite have words to characterize.

Earlier I suggested that each of the three statements considered above involve a claim that a certain kind of integration exists. The first affirms the existence of sufficient integration to constitute a person. The second affirms sufficient integration to constitute the elements in question (e.g., an emotion). The third affirms sufficient integration to constitute the relationship of "ownership," or "agency," or "really having." The term "integration" is used as a place holder for a multiplicity of linkages; it has no single meaning.

Philosophers have traditionally been concerned with these kinds of linkages. Sometimes the concern is quite general, for instance concern over whether there are causal relationships between mental events and physical movements. Sometimes the concern is quite specific, for instance, over how thoughts, values, and sensations seem to be bound together in emotions. And sometimes the concern is indirect, for instance, over what kind of considerations support a moral claim, and thus only secondarily over what kind of beliefs a person would have to have for his or her moral attitudes to be well founded.

Within these investigations, at one point or another, there typically emerges a school of thought that challenges the common viewpoint by denying that such linkages can exist at all. These are radical theses, and they recur throughout the history of philosophy under the headings such as skepticism, epiphenominalism, and emotivism. At certain points in the history of philosophy, such radical conclusions have been viewed as the insight and wisdom that philosophy imparts. At other times, they have themselves been viewed as expressions of a philosophical immaturity; it being maintained that the starting point of philosophic analysis is that we exist, that we have knowledge, that we can support ethical claims, and so forth. Most often, there is no general denial and no general affirmation, but rather separate positions on rather separate matters.

The basic point, however, is that philosophic inquiry can call into question the very possibility of the most fundamental forms of integration, whose presence we assume in our normal experience of ourselves. When this occurs, because of the generality of the claim that the required integration is not to be found, philosophical speculation can lead to the conclusion that *alienness is the authentic experience of the human condition*. Thus alienness, which on the one hand lurks in the shadows of known experience and is even a bit too confusing to talk about, can emerge as somehow being that experience to which we are all called, insofar as we are to experience ourselves as we really are.

In this chapter I will consider some of the relationships between philosophizing and alienness. In the first section I will consider ethical nihilism. My concern will be with the implications of ethical nihilism with respect to possible integration of the self, and with the implication for the person who believes the thesis. Nietzsche's views on this will be considered. In the second section, I will consider the writings of Derek Parfit. They link to the present discussion in a variety of ways, as will become clear. And finally, I will focus on a central thesis in Sartre's writings. I will argue that much of Sartre's discussion of the problem of authentic self-experience (in *Being and Nothingness*) can be seen as involving the problem of how to experience oneself when one has discovered that reality is inherently and paradoxically fragmented. In other words, that Sartre's philosophy is itself one vast alienness-grounding set of beliefs, and that if Sartre is correct about reality then it follows that alienness is the authentic experience of oneself.

My reasons for focusing on nihilism, Nietzsche, Parfit, and Sartre are the following. The nihilist thesis stands out as the single radical philosophic speculation that is often espoused by ordinary people of good sense. Probably more than any other philosophic speculation, it does affect the way people experience themselves and their world. I consider Nietzsche because he stands out as the philosopher who most deeply concerned himself with the mental health implications of the nihilist outlook for the individual who accepts the thesis. I consider Sartre because he stands out as the philosopher who espoused the most radical and unbridgeable fissures in our being, concerning himself most basically with the question of what it is to be authentically in touch with those fissures. And I consider Parfit because he is a contemporary, because he comes out of a very different philosophic tradition than do Nietzsche and Sartre, and because his work too, in its quiet way, is concerned with the issue of authenticity as it presents itself in response to philosophic speculation about the nature of the self. My general thesis is that philosophic speculation can provide the grounds for alienness. I find it illustrated and partially explored in the work of these three diverse thinkers.

ETHICAL NIHILISM AND ALIENNESS

Ethical nihilism has been a recurrent thesis in the history of philosophy and has, unlike many other philosophical theses, struck a strong resonant cord with much wider publics. We can distinguish between nihilist theses in terms of whether they apply only to matters of ethics or to a more general notion of value. For our purposes we will lump them together under the heading "meta-value nihilism." Here we are talking about a philosophical thesis about values and/or knowledge and *not* a psychological condition of being without norms or preferences. Meta-value nihilism may be expressed by claims such as "there are no answers to value questions," "nothing really has any value; people just imagine that there is such a thing," "it is meaningless to assert that something is right or wrong," "ethical claims are really just emotional expressions," "there are no value propositions," "there are no value facts."

When one says that there are no value facts, one is not denying that there are people who have values. What one is saying is that those values are mere attitudes, prejudices, tastes, preferences—but in no way can be said to be true, correct, valid, rational, or warranted. But the individual with strongly held values does believe that certain states of affairs are more valuable, desirable, moral, preferable than others. Under normal conditions having such normative commitments involves believing that some things are more valuable than others, and thus that one can be correct or incorrect in holding something to be valuable.

I am not concerned with whether or not nihilism offers an adequate or true account of reality. My concern is with two questions: (1) What are the implications of nihilism for the existence of the integrations requisite for the unity of the psyche? and (2) What are the appropriate experiential implications for the nihilist's own experience of the fact that he or she holds a nihilist thesis? The first question concerns itself with the implications if the nihilist thesis is true; the second with the implications of believing the nihilist thesis.

If meta-value nihilism is correct, then there is no relationship of grounding between an individual's values and his or her beliefs. This particular form of integration, which we had thought capable of existing, and which we thought to exist at least some of the time, is in principle impossible. No one is integrated in this way because that type of integration is impossible. It is impossible for my beliefs to be integrated with my values in this way, because the propositions that I believe do not and cannot constitute a justification for the value statement. For instance, if it is impossible to derive any proposition of the sort "My duty is to do X" from propositions that are empirical in a straightforward manner, then this absence of logical derivation is mirrored in its absence between the individual's belief that his duty is to do X and his empirical beliefs.

It might be thought that this means that within the individual's belief structure the value elements (we can refer to them as beliefs about what his duties are) are totally isolated. But this does not follow. They may be part of a large complex that includes other value elements as well as beliefs about empirical matters. Thus, a great deal of factual knowledge may be connected to the person's belief that capital punishment is wrong. For instance, if the person operates from a consequentialist principle that asserts that social practices are wrong if they lead to a net increase in human suffering, this principle (or a belief that it is correct) and the specific belief or attitude about capital punishment and numerous other beliefs about the causal consequences of capital punishment may all hang together.

Nihilists have not had to deny this. Charles Stevenson, the central figure in twentieth-century emotivism, noted that there is great space for argumentation in ethics because there may be agreement on the definitions or on the principles. But if there is disagreement on this fundamental level, he maintained, there is no rational way of resolving it. Translated back into the psyche this gives us a different picture of what the inner make-up of a person looks like, even if nihilism is true. There is a great deal of variation that is possible.

The psyche, if nihilism is true, need not be one in which each ethical judgment stands isolated and revealed as arbitrary. Value judgments may each be thoroughly embedded within a larger outlook. People differ in this respect. What the nihilist tells us is that there are limits. This larger cluster of integrated beliefs itself floats loose.

Moreover, it is doubtful that any value attitude floats entirely loose. Thus, consider someone who believes that some specific type of act is wrong, for instance the belief that masturbation is wrong. The nihilist tells us that there is no possible relation of justification between any beliefs that the individual has about matters of fact and her belief that masturbation is wrong. But suppose that we are dealing with someone who has no more of a basis for her view that masturbation is wrong than that her parents said so. Even in as "weakly rational" a case as this, we might find some complex connections between this belief and other beliefs of hers. Her logical structure may be: they said X, they are authorities, and thus there is reason to believe X. And while if nihilism is true it cannot be the case that anyone is an authority on moral truth, since the conception of such truths is itself incoherent, it does not follow that the belief that someone is an authority on moral truth is itself unsupportable. For any given individual it may be woven into a very rich fabric that includes her own beliefs about the limits of her own knowledge and her confidence in the wisdom, capacities, wider experience, and knowledge that others possess and of their ability to know and understand what she does not.

What all this tells us is that nihilism, even if correct, can only rule out certain kinds of integrations; that in the main, even if nihilism is true, an enormous amount of inner connectedness is possible. And that even if nihilism is true there can be enormous differences with respect to how thoroughly someone's values are integrated with the rest of his or her make-up. In short, nihilism doesn't reduce ownership to much of a muchness, even if it rules out the possibility of a psyche structure that is the analogue of adequately justified belief.

But if nihilism doesn't carry devastating conclusions about the nature of the self, it may still have devastating implications for the self of the nihilist. Thus, there is a second question. Up to this point I have asked, "What implications does nihilism have for the possible structure of a self?" The second question is, "What does the inner connectedness of the nihilist himself look like?"

Given his nihilist views, the nihilist knows that he has various views but he believes them to be without foundation. There are values that he has, but he may see them as rather *accidental* aspects of himself. They lack, and of necessity must lack, the kind of rational connectedness that belief elements have when we know certain things to be true. Since to a considerable extent it is my apprehension that there are reasons in virtue of which a belief is valid that serves to make it truly *my* belief, value nihilism, for those that believe it, by denying the ultimate possibility of rational connections tends to dissociate values from the self. If one sees one's values as no more valid or correct than any others, if one sees that one's having those particular attitudes is merely the result of chance or circumstance and that one could have not only had other values but that one would not have been in any sense wrong, ignorant, or in error had one had radically different values, then one's values are to some extent detached.

The nihilist may say, "Yes, I have these values, but they are accidental facts about myself, just as accidental as the fact that I have ten freckles on my arm. To explain why I have these values is not very different than to explain why the freckles. Neither provides a basis for action, for life." So viewed, being a person with those values tends to no longer be part of his self-identity. He has these values but there is no reason to hold onto them, since they have no particular validity. If they change then they change, but no longer does he define himself in terms of the values he holds. The explanation of how he came to have these values may vary. They may have resulted from education or upbringing; they may have served certain psychological functions, making him feel good about himself and superior to others. Whatever their genesis, they had no basis in fact. Given this view of himself, he may say things like, "my values are not really mine," or "I don't really hold to be valuable the things I hold to be valuable," or "I don't really have these values, they are just there" (all forms of alternate-relation). Given the constitutive role of value judgments within certain emotions, the meta-value nihilist confronting his own emotions, but aware of the fact (in his eyes) that the core value judgment has no validity (or invalidity), may come to feel that his emotions aren't really emotions, that he lacks the inner conviction needed to have real emotions. And as a result his emotional experience itself is transformed and perhaps stifled.

When the mine-ness of one's values and emotions is shaken in this way, it may spread to other elements that are integrated with one's values. When we turn to the things he does in pursuit of his values, we may find that the nihilist doesn't experience his actions as emanating from himself. "Yes, I live out a life in accord with these values, but there is no real point to it. Indeed, that is the deep truth, there is no point to anything."

The nihilist, even if his values are themselves embedded in a vast network of other valuative and factual beliefs, leaps right to the final conclusion, which is that however carefully one might bind each arbitrary assertion in a bundle of other assertions, the entire package is itself ungrounded. Given that he is a nihilist, whatever inner webbing exists is irrelevant to him. His nihilism represents a meta-perspective on each of his values, desires, emotions, and actions and says of each one that there is no warranted ground for them. This being so, he says that they are not really his own, they merely happen to be the ones that are his.

What I have described is certainly one way of responding to having come to believe a nihilist thesis. But is this detachment from one's self merely one possible response to coming to believe the theses of nihilism, or is it a rationally required response? If it is only one possible response, then what determines which response will occur and what is expressed by having one response rather than another?

It is Nietzsche who more than any other philosopher wrestled with these issues and placed them within a complex therapeutic program, a program within which the philosopher is part therapist. Nietzsche's thought is rich, subtle, and not straightforward. Let me offer the answer to my question that I find suggested in Nietzsche.

Nietzsche himself was a meta-ethical nihilist. He calls on the philosopher to

> take his stand beyond good and evil and leave the illusion of moral judgments beneath himself. This demand follows from an insight which I was the first to formulate: that there are altogether no moral facts. . . . Moral judgments are therefore never to be taken literally: so understood they always contain mere absurdity. [1]

Nietzsche's affirmation that God is dead can also be seen as a philosophic thesis about the absence of any external grounding for values or for self-identity.

While Nietzsche does not explicitly work his way through the question of how someone who believes a meta-value nihilist thesis will come to experience his or her own life, his answer is that there are two paths—the way of sickness (the world weary), and the way of health.

The way of sickness involves a turning away from life and can be understood as a general change in one's experience so that one no longer experiences anything as of value. Within the framework I have been developing, it can be identified with a general alienness within which all experience of anything as having value is viewed as not really one's own. This is basically the reaction I have just described.

This general psychological nihilism is for Nietzsche the greatest of dangers; it represents the loss of the greatest of treasures. He writes:

> Verily, men gave themselves all their good and evil. Verily, they did not take it, then did not find it, nor did it come to them as a voice from heaven. Only man placed values in things to preserve himself—he alone created a meaning for things, a human meaning. Therefore he calls himself "man" which means: the esteemer. To esteem is to create: hear this, you creators! Esteeming itself is of all esteemed things the most estimable treasure. Through esteeming alone is there value. . . . [2]

But the alternative to psychological nihilism is not to be found in a simple affirmation of all one's attitudes as one's own even though they are without external grounding. Once the external props are removed, the inherently healthy individual will see some of his or her values as not really having been his or her own, as being alien. This is because our culture is in fact alienating. It imposes on us moralities that are not authentically our own. We internalize those moralities, and turn them against the self. Philosophical nihilism is a path to freedom, as is the recognition that God is dead.

Over time the healthy individual will come to discard what is artificial. She may be left with nothing. But this need not last. She can come into contact with what is genuinely her own. The test of what is one's own is that it is willed for its own sake, that it comes spontaneously, that one meets it with delight, that it provides for a release of energy and creativity. And with respect to her own valuings, to those that emerge spontaneously, she will come to feel that they are uniquely her own. Rather than the absence of an external justification for her desires being the cause of her viewing them as less her own, they will be viewed as even more intensely her own.

Thus, in answer to the question I raised about how one might respond to a realization of meta-value nihilism, Nietzsche can be said to go in two reinforcing directions at the same time. Accepting nihilism serves to reveal an underlying alienation that lay hidden—the fact that many of one's values, objectives, motives, emotions, and projects *were* never really one's own. Now they are seen to be what they were all along—alien elements that had taken over one's life. But now, having been stripped down by this baptism of nihilism, there is that which survives, or is newly discovered, that which is genuinely one's own. By stripping oneself of the need for external justification, one intensifies one's capacity for self-generated esteeming. And one comes into a more direct contact with oneself. Thus nihilism becomes a tool of completing a process of alienating that which is alien.

That which remains is affirmed all the more forcefully, but it is not affirmed as it once was. It is not affirmed as a general rule for the self or the other. Nietzsche writes:

> My brother, if you have a virtue and she is your virtue, then you have her in common with nobody. . . .
>   Then speak and stammer "This is my good; this I love; it pleases me wholly; thus alone do I want the good. I do not want it as divine law; I do not want it as human statute and need: it shall not be a signpost for me to overearths and paradises."[3]

As an alternative, the meta-ethical nihilist often calls upon his or her listeners to recognize that the ethical claims they make are assertions of their will or volition, and he or she sometimes further maintains that this should cause no problem. Thus, Hans Reichenbach exhorts his readers to:

> Open your ears to your own will. . . . There is no more purpose or meaning in the world than you put into it.[4]

And,

> let us forget about the appeal to obligation. Let us throw away the crutches we needed for walking, let us stand on our own feet and trust our volitions, not because they are secondary ones, but because they are our own volitions.[5]

What is it that determines whether or not someone will be able to vigorously affirm as his own that which he sees as lacking in external grounding? Nietzsche's answer is essentially the same as that which I have offered: it depends on how the individual understands the self. For Nietzsche there is no self that is a decider, a chooser; no self that stands back and surveys the alternatives.

> It is only the snare of language (of the arch-fallacies of reason petrified in language), presenting all activity as conditioned by an agent—the "subject"—that blinds us to this fact. For, just as popular superstition divorces the lightening from its brilliance, so does popular morality divorce strength from its manifestations, as though there were behind the strong a neutral agent, free to manifest its strength or contain it. But no such agent exists; there is no "being" behind the doing, acting, becoming; the "doer" has simply been added to the deed by imagination—the doing is everything.[6]

Instead the model of full selfhood is the self-propelled wheel, the child. Here there is no felt need for justification or reasons to motivate one to activity. The self is active without having to be moved to action, for the self is the body:

> "Body am I, and soul"—thus speaks the child. . . . But the awakened and knowing say: body am I entirely and nothing else: and soul is only a word for something about the body.
> The body is a great reason. . . .

"I" you say and are proud of the word. But greater is that in which you do not wish to have faith—your body and its great reason: that does not say "I" but does "I."[7]

Thus for Nietzsche, one will be acting out of one's self when one is acting out of one's body (e.g., one's spontaneous emotionality). Given a conception of the self of this sort, the belief in nihilism does not lead to a conclusion or experience of one's actions as not one's own.

It is important to remember that the nihilist's attitude towards his own value beliefs is not the same as that of one who comes to doubt the adequacy of his own belief system as opposed to that of another. For instance, someone may, as he becomes an adult, become aware of the diversity of ethical outlooks, and upon reflecting on his own beliefs may realize that he has simply internalized the perspective of his parents, and he may conclude that he really has no solid basis for many of the attitudes he has. This person still believes in the applicability of the concept of truth and of warranted ethical belief; he comes to have a meta-perspective on his own beliefs in which he now believes that his beliefs may not be true. Here the situation is the same as it would be with respect to any belief. To believe that one does not have a solid basis for beliefs that one holds is to believe that one does not really know to be true what one believes. It is to reduce one's beliefs to mere beliefs, which is to not fully believe what one had believed, or to have beliefs that are not real beliefs or beliefs that are not really one's own.

The nihilist is in a different situation. The nihilist (in the philosophical sense of someone who holds a specific meta-value position about the noncognitive status of value sentences) does not suspect that his beliefs are in error. Rather he comes to see that they are not really beliefs, but merely positive or negative attitudes towards certain states of affairs, attitudes such as "I like it" or "I want it to be the case." The issue then is whether or not he can maintain a full connectedness to these attitudes if he no longer experiences them as capable of having a grounding.

Ironically, it would seem that the nihilist is in a better position to retain his attitudes than the non-nihilist who has doubts about the truth of his specific orientation. The nihilist would not see his holding these "beliefs" as irrational since there is nothing inconsistent with reason in his doing so. Rather, he could (on some analyses) simply assimilate these views to the category of his preferences. They may not have any grounding, but they remain his preferences. This at least seems a possibility. Indeed, the nihilist could perhaps turn the issue around and say that the individual who reacts to the acceptance of the nihilist theses by experiencing a detachment from his values and beliefs is himself treating them as if they were candidates for a rational attachment when they are not. And he may further say that that individual who cannot find a vibrant life without "external" props suffers from an inability to identify himself in any other way than as a rational decider. This inability is itself a disease that seeks to subject the will to some rule of reason; the conception of the self reflects the disease. To note that alienness is appropriate in relation to this conception of the self is only to indict the conception.

When Nietzsche introduces categories of health and sickness to characterize these different orientations he is making a certain kind of claim about other features of life and personality that go with these outlooks. For instance, insofar as it can be shown that greater human creativity is associated with one rather than another conception of the self, this would seem an important showing. Nietzsche would claim that these two orientations lead to radically different responses to the death of God (the realization that there is no external grounding for values or identity), and this being so, only one of them is capable of being healthy (exuberant, creative) in the face of reality.

The power of this is quite significant if one accepts the claim about the nonexistence of God. For then it is a meta-thesis about how to adjudicate between alternative conceptions of the self by reference to the criterion that the conceptions provide for the reconciliation of authenticity and health. But it must be remembered that "the death of God" is more than an atheistic claim. It stands for a more general proposition about the absence of external (i.e., rationally grounded) frameworks for life. And here, be it with respect to ethics, aesthetics, or one's own identity, there are credible perspectives from which it can be maintained that there is something there to be discovered. And if there is something to be discovered, rather than just affirmed, then a counter-factual such as how one would respond if one discovered that there was nothing to be discovered, known, or appreciated, is not a decisive consideration. It says if the human condition is such and such, then authenticity (facing that condition rather than running from it) and health require X.

Moreover, I am not fully comfortable with the idea that the alienating dimensions of nihilism can be fully avoided for the nihilist through an assimilation of values to acts of will and an identification with what we continue to affirm once we have been liberated by nihilism. Can't those for whom philosophical nihilism emerges as psychological nihilism say:

> Look, it is all very well to maintain that values are essentially projections of the will, but it is one thing to simply want a piece of chocolate—for that I have and need no justification. But it is something different to want it to be a world in which people cooperate rather than compete, a world in which no one tortures one another, and a world in which everyone has a full stomach. What is genuinely mine is not just my will that it be this way, but my belief that it should be and that there is a basis for making claims on the other.

Of course, the nihilist is likely to respond:

> There is never any basis for making claims on the other, but that is not to say that the other has a right to not have claims imposed upon him, for there is not a basis for rights either. If one makes claims then one does that as a projection of one's will—not out of a belief that one is supported by some underlying truth.

The effects of philosophical nihilism are in a sense easier to bear if the stripping-away process Nietzsche describes reveals an artificiality to the individual's commitment to a morality of interpersonal rights and obligations. But what if one finds both that this is what one really does affirm and that one believes there is no warrant for it? Of course, it is possible that one's philosophic commitments may themselves be bracketed and kept in place. The philosophizing may be reduced to a quiet intellectual exercise never allowed to be integrated with the rest of one's life. In short, it can itself be an alienated activity. But if instead philosophic reflection is allowed to penetrate the emotional sphere, then the implications of a philosophical nihilism are not fully met by Nietzsche's response. The nihilist may be left with claims that he makes on others and that others make on himself, which he does feel are valid, and yet he maintains that no claims can have the kind of validity he affirms.

In the end we may be left only with Hume's experience of the disorienting power of philosophizing:

> The intense view of these manifold contradictions and imperfections in human reason has so wrought upon me, and heated my brain, . . . I am confounded with all these questions, and begin to fancy myself in the

most deplorable condition imaginable, environed with the deepest darkness, and utterly deprived of the use of every member and faculty.

But fortunately it happens that since reason is incapable of dispelling these clouds, nature herself suffices to that purpose and cures me of this philosophic melancholy. . . .[8]

At least for a while.

PARFIT'S ANALYSIS AS AN
ALIENNESS-GROUNDING BELIEF

The denial of the possibility that required integrations can exist (e.g., between one's values and other beliefs) is not the only way in which philosophical speculation can generate alienness. One striking contemporary example of philosophic speculation that may give rise to alienness from a different basis is Parfit's *Reasons and Persons*. Here Parfit is centrally concerned to argue that the existence of a person consists in *nothing but* the existence of certain kinds of psychological integrations. What he denies is that persons exist in any other sense.

Parfit bears on the larger discussion of alienness in a variety of ways. The most direct, however, is that Parfit undertakes to show that at the most basic level we are not what we take ourselves to be.

> The truth is very different from what we are inclined to believe. Even if we are not aware of this, most of us are Non-Reductionists. . . . We would be strongly inclined to believe that our continued existence is a deep further fact, distinct from physical and psychological continuity, and a fact that must be all-or-nothing. This belief is not true.[9]

Parfit considers the kinds of experiences or attitudes that are appropriate for someone who comes to share his philosophic conclusions. His basic idea is that seeing things his way should cause us to change the way in which we feel about our own lives and death.

> When I believed the Non-Reductionist view, I also cared more about my inevitable death. After my death, there will be no one living who will be me. I can now redescribe this fact. . . . My death will break the more direct relations between my present experiences and future experiences, but it will not break other relations. This is all there is to the fact that there will be no one living who will be me. Now that I have seen this, my death seems to me less bad.[10]

Thus, Parfit falls within that philosophic tradition that believes in the overwhelming power of philosophic speculation to radically and appropriately transform our experience of ourselves. Philosophy involves speculation that can reveal to us a hidden or misunderstood human condition and can thus lead us to a more authentic self-experience, more authentic in the sense that it is an experience in touch with the realities of our condition.

I will argue that at least one appropriate experience for someone coming to believe what Parfit believes is that of alienness. In particular, an alienness with respect to oneself through time. This might be expressed in "my past is not really my past" or "my memories are not really mine" or "my projects are not really mine" or "I am not really myself."

In all of these expressions use is made of the term "really." This use needs to be clarified. Parfit makes frequent use of the term, and one aspect of what Parfit is seeking to do is to reveal what we really are. He frequently says things like "we really are not what we think we are." That is, in truth we turn out to be different from what we had taken ourselves to be. This is not meant with respect to any particular property that we might have, as when someone discovers that in truth he is not as attractive a person as he took himself to be. Rather, what Parfit is saying is that we are not the kind of entities that we take ourselves to be.

When Parfit says that we are not what we believe ourselves to be, he is saying that there is something that we believe persons to be, something so basic that it is almost impossible for us to think of persons in any other way, and yet it turns out in fact to be the case that this is not what we are. This kind of realization is not merely a matter of some unexpected fact, of some surprising new truth about persons; it goes so deep and so thoroughly challenges our understanding of what person's are, that from the prior perspective we are tempted to say that if that is what people really are then there really aren't any persons.

What we believe ourselves to be, according to Parfit, is an entity that somehow exists distinct from and apart from our body and our experiences. With respect to our continued existence, Parfit tells us, we are nonreductionists. We believe that our existence is more than a matter of continuities. We believe "it involves a further fact. It is natural to believe in this further fact, and to believe that, compared with the continuities, it is a deep fact, and is the fact that really matters."[11] That is, we believe our existence consists in a fact that is a fact in addition to facts about the existence of a body and certain experiences and relations between them. Parfit sees this belief as so fundamental that he feels compelled to argue that it is psychologically possible to not believe it.

The analogy Parfit uses for his vision of the nature of persons is that of a nation. The nation is not something that exists as an additional fact beyond and in addition to all the facts about people and territory. This view of persons Parfit characterizes as reductionist. It contrasts with the view that I exist as a separate entity that has mental experiences and inhabits a body, but could just as well not. Cartesian egos are one example of a nonreductionist vision of persons.

Parfit maintains that because our existence is not some separate fact, the question of our existence is not a *determinate* question. By this he means that it is not always the case that there is an answer as to whether or not I exist. Sometimes this is an empty question, in the way that it may be an empty question to ask whether or not a certain club exists when it shrinks to two members or just one member. Other than simply knowing the facts about the number of members, there is no additional fact to know. There is nothing to be right or wrong about when we say the club exists or does not exist. Consider a central passage in Parfit's discussion.

> My Division. My body is fatally injured, as are the brains of my two brothers. My brain is divided, and each half is successfully transplanted into the body of one of my brothers. Each of the resulting people believes that he is me, seems to remember living my life, has my character, and is in every other way psychologically continuous with me. And he has a body that is very like mine.[12]

What emerges then are two human beings, each of which is psychologically continuous with the first. Parfit notes four alternative ways of characterizing the situation:

1. The first person has died

2. The first person has survived in brother *A*'s body

3. The first person has survived in brother *B*'s body

4. The first person has survived in both bodies

The argument against (1) is that since people have in fact survived with half their brain destroyed, the person would survive if half of his brain were successfully transplanted into A's body. And if he is surviving in A's body, he could not be said to have died just because a second operation succeeds in transplanting the other half of his brain into B's body.

But if the first person survived, then where is he? He can't be both of the persons that emerge because they are not the same as each other. And since he stands in the same relation to each of them, there is no basis for saying that he is one and not the other. Thus, all four alternatives are implausible.

Parfit suggests that rather than believing that there is an answer to the question, "Has the first person survived and if so where is he?" it may be that there simply is nothing more to know. The four alternatives listed above need not represent four different situations, but merely four choices we have for talking about this situation. But this, Parfit points out, could not be the case if we are separately existing entities such as Cartesian egos.

Parfit regards it as empirically possible that we are Cartesian egos. He believes that there could be evidence that such things exist. For instance, it could be discovered that the brain is not the carrier of memory, and that even when there is no brain there can be a continuation of memory. But, Parfit maintains, the evidence is not to be found.

For someone who believes that persons are Cartesian egos or something similar, Parfit's discussion of the evidence is unlikely to be satisfactory. And it cannot be said that he shows conclusively that there are no such things. Rather, he develops and explores the implications of an alternative way of viewing what we are. Repeatedly he comes back to the analogy of a nation, saying that at bottom his claim is that the being of a person is something like that of a nation, and that our existence through time is a matter of the holding of certain psychological connections and continuities. He doesn't go into great detail in specifying what these are.

Calling relationship R the relationship of psychological continuity and connection, he offers the formula: $PI = R + U$; personal identity over time is the unique (U) holding of relationship R. On this formula, when the person divides, R is satisfied, but not uniquely. Thus, personal identity is not maintained. But Parfit sees this formula as secondary. It is something he is introducing as a way of *deciding* what to call certain difficult cases.

Having argued that our being is not some additional fact beyond psychological connections, and that therefore the continuation of the numerically identical person that we are is indeterminate, Parfit goes on to say that "identity is not what matters." He argues rather that what matters is the relationship R, which is the relationship such that when it holds uniquely it confers identity.

> Can the presence or absence of U (uniqueness) make a great difference to the value of R? . . . This is not plausible. If I will be R-related to some future person, the presence or absence of U makes no difference to the intrinsic nature of my relation to this person. And what matters most must be the intrinsic nature of this relation. . . . If adding U (uniqueness) does not greatly increase the value of R, R must be what fundamentally matters, and PI (personal identity) mostly matters just because of the presence of R.[13]

Thus, his argument in the case in which my brain is divided and two persons emerge, neither of which is me (since personal identity requires uniqueness according to the formula), is that it would be irrational to view this ending of personal identity, this death, as like ordinary death, since what we have is internally the same as what we have when there is only one person (i.e., survival). So division, although it involves the going out of being of the numerically identical entity (i.e., death), must be quite close to survival in its inherent value even if not the same. And since with division there is not identity, identity per se is not what matters. The continuation of ourselves in the sense of numerical identity is not, at bottom, what our concern with death is about. Although death involves the ending of the numerically identical being, what matters about death is that it also (typically) involves the ending of the chain of R-related entities and experiences. Parfit believes that if we come to change our beliefs about what we are, if we come to change them to the correct belief, namely that we are like nations and that our continued existence is a matter of R holding uniquely, then our attitudes towards ourselves and what happens to us should rationally change.

My central concern at this point is not whether Parfit is correct in his primary theses, but in his meta-thesis. Parfit holds a meta-thesis of the sort that I have been arguing. It is that coming to believe certain philosophic theses should significantly and appropriately alter the way in which we feel. Or to put it differently, that there are some feelings that are appropriate to certain philosophical conclusions. Or more powerfully, that if these philosophic conclusions are in fact true facts about the human condition, then there are certain feelings or experiences that are authentic modes of experiencing the human condition.

Parfit does not use this kind of language, but this is his meta-thesis about his own work. And it is a thesis that I agree with. What I have been arguing is that alienness is such an experience. That to experience the alienness of the self or of some component of the self may be the appropriate experience of those objects, given that the person holds a specific philosophic thesis.

And I believe that Parfit's own thesis about the nature of a person is an alienness-grounding belief. Parfit is correct in saying that almost all of us are nonreductionists. We almost all believe that our existence is some discrete fact in addition to facts about continuities and connections. And Parfit is correct in maintaining that it is almost impossible to rid ourselves of this way of thinking about ourselves. But if this is how we tend to image ourselves, then how are we to relate to our own being if we come to accept the reductionist view?

The transition from nonreductionism to reductionism is not something easily made, nor is it even clearly understood. Parfit himself says that "It is hard to explain accurately what a Reductionist claims."[14] He is almost unsure that it is psychologically possible to believe about oneself what the reductionist believes.

Parfit cites a number of philosophers who are one in maintaining that if the reductionist position is true, then there is no reason for us to be concerned about our own futures. He describes one as maintaining that "if there is nothing more to personal identity than these continuities, we should be indifferent whether we live or die."[15] What these claims express is not primarily a view about death but a view about being. Coming from the nonreductionist position, they are saying that if reductionism is true then in some sense we don't exist, or at least our existence is a very different sort of thing than we took it to be and therefore so is our death.

Thus, someone coming to believe what Parfit believes might express herself by saying "I don't really exist." And when this is applied to personal identity through time, she might say doubly, "Not only don't I really exist at a given moment in time, but I don't persist through time."

Parfit's vision of what it is for a person to exist and to continue to exist through time does not tell us that a certain integration fails to exist or cannot exist. Rather, it tells us that a certain kind of entity (e.g., a determinate extra entity) fails to exist. And because all we are is an integrated sequence, what happens to me in the future or what happened to me in the past did not really happen to *me* in the same sense as we had previously meant it, because the "me" isn't the same in the same way. This it would seem is the implication of coming to accept Parfit's account of what we really are—of coming to accept that we are not what we think we are.

Parfit goes beyond this. Building on his account of persons as coherent bundles persisting through time, Parfit addresses the possibility of successive selves within what we would ordinarily take to be the lifetime of a single person. Parfit thus distinguishes between the person and the self, seeing the person as a more encompassing but more loosely coherent entity. This is similar to the way I use the self/person distinction, though I have spoken primarily of their coexistence at a single point in time. Parfit writes:

> On my proposed way of talking, we use "I," and the other pronouns, to refer only to the parts of our lives to which, when speaking, we have the strongest psychological connections. When the connections have been markedly reduced—when there has been a significant change of character, or style of life, or of beliefs and ideal—we might say, "It was not I who did that, but an earlier self."[16]

What Parfit suggests is that a person who looks backwards or forwards in "his life" and does not think of that earlier (or later) person as being really himself may actually be correct. Thus, Parfit's writings on personal identity constitute a set of propositions that fall into the category of alienness-generating beliefs. That is, someone who believes what Parfit has to say about personal identity through time, and who then internalizes Parfit's conception of persons, and who then further discovers that there isn't sufficient integrations between different parts of his life, might simply come to regard his (past) self as not himself, or that past life as not having been his.

In short, Parfit's writings serve as an example of how philosophic reflection can generate alienness in two ways. First, by revealing that given what we thought persons were, persons do not exist. And second, by developing a conceptual structure for thinking about persons, in terms of which it would make good sense to say of someone who lacked adequate integration through time that he is not that former person. In this latter project, Parfit's theory works in a way quite similar to my own.

On the account I have offered there is also a distinction between the self and the person. However, since I have envisioned the self as a highly coherent personality, it is unlikely that we will find many instances of successive selves within the lifespan of any given person. Rather, what we may find is a succession of different partially integrated personality compounds, each falling significantly short of the integration required for selfhood. Thus, I would speak of a succession of persons existing within a larger person-shell. Insofar as the components achieve the integration required for selfhood, they would tend to be elongated through time. Selfhood is not a matter of a momentary integration at some time-specific cross section, but a unity that also extends through time. Thus, selfhood (the existence of the self) would tend to be inconsistent with a sharp clumping of the personality into numerous distinct units over time.

The question emerges with respect to the factors whose presence or absence tend to provide for this clumping of the personality into successive compounds. Of central importance is the extent to which a person does identify with the person he or she has been and the person he or she will become in the future. We can look forward or backwards, and be largely indifferent to what has happened to "oneself" in the past or what may happen in the future. Alternatively, we may live intensely in the past or the future, feeling with great immediacy what has happened or will happen to that person we see as ourselves.

The extent to which people do identify with themselves either in the past or the future varies considerably. Not only are there differences between individuals, but there are broad cultural differences as well. Some people actively engage in replaying and reliving their earliest childhood experiences through their entire lives. Some children at the earliest ages see themselves in terms of who they will be at the most distant parts of their lives. And alternatively, some people live only in the present in a very literal sense of identifying only or largely with their present self.

Identification with past and future selves or with oneself in the past or future (depending on one's metaphysics) is what makes it possible to have an extended project. It is what allows a person to have "a life" in the sense of a single extended coherent set of experiences.

In one sense, of course, everyone has a life. But for some people their own life is an object of their experience. They are involved in crafting their life and, in so doing, crafting their being over time. This is a distinct phenomenon. No doubt it is limited to the human species to so perceive oneself, and it differs significantly person to person, culture to culture.[17]

It is a familiar point that a person's self-identity plays an enormously powerful role in the dynamics of the self. A person's self-identity typically involves strong identifications with oneself over time. One sees oneself as being the person with this particular past or that particular future. This is a contingent but tremendously basic fact about human beings that results in powerful shaping tendencies. What are these tendencies? In brief they are tendencies to integrate the self through time. They function in a self-fulfilling manner, bringing into being the connectedness that is affirmed in the identification experience. Identification with self over time is in fact one aspect of psychological continuity. Indeed, it is possibly the single most important aspect. Furthermore, it is self-fulfilling because it tends to give rise to other continuities, such as having at a given point long-term objectives and having them over time continue to be one's objectives. Thus, it gives rise to and sustains long-term projects.

Being engaged in a long-term project is in fact a particular mode of identification with oneself over time. To view some extended series of activities that the self will engage in over a lengthy time period as essentially one project is to identify with oneself throughout the expanse of that project. Thus, what I have spoken of as agency, that is the presence of the self in its activities, may involve a very long-term interaction between self and activity. Not only is the self present in the project over its long existence, but the long existence of the project contributes to the creation of the continuities that constitute the self.

It was noted earlier that sometimes people come late in life to see the true meaning of what up to that point seemed to lack coherence. For instance, a person may come to see all of his life as having been a preparation for something that he is about to do. This "seeing" is not a matter of a single belief, but of giving or finding a coherent interpretation that unifies what is otherwise discrete. In so unifying all of one's life, not only is the true meaning of one's life revealed but the true identity of oneself. This true identity is something not just in the present, but the true identity of the single extended self that one has always been, which has been obscured and hidden.[18]

Literature has this power because of the power of the author to write the story. The author imposes these definitions on events and the character comes to accept them. People, and entire civilizations, have at times seen themselves in just this way. Certainly to view human life as a God-written narrative is to see it as having exactly these kinds of meanings, and the drama of an individual life is often to discover and respond to these discovered meanings.

Part of what is involved in the "death of God" in the Nietzschean sense is the stripping away of this way of seeing the self and life. This can have a variety of implications. But most essentially it is to say that it is the individual person who creates these meanings, gives them to his life and himself. They are not there to be discovered.

If these meanings that link different phases of a life are not present or are not found, then the individual is contracted in time, possibly lightly integrated from moment to moment, or possibly becoming the kind of lumpy creature Parfit imagined, tightly integrated for discrete phases that are not tightly connected to each other. Because our future actions offer us the ability to go back into the past and find or create meanings that smooth out the lumps, we may be said to retain the ability to make a coherent self out of a succession of persons. In this sense we might be said to retain a freedom to bring ourselves into being.

SARTRE

The tension between human freedom and being is at the core of Sartre's great work, *Being and Nothingness*.[19] Sartre is centrally concerned with the appropriateness of our ways of experiencing ourselves. His basic thesis is that the being of persons is radically different from the being of physical entities. Because we are inherently free there is a fundamental lack of integration; this lack of integration is experienced as a lack of being, as a nothingness that is at the heart of our being. Yet this is not something that we can readily accept about ourselves; it is something that we are in flight from, and this flight takes the form of denying the most fundamental aspects of our being. Thus a second lack of integration exists, that between what we are and what we think we are. Moreover, this second lack of integration is maintained through an active project of denial of our reality.

So described, it is clear that there are certain parallel's between Parfit and Sartre. Like Sartre, Parfit denies that we are Cartesian egos, or that our being as person's is some deep additional fact. And like Sartre, Parfit maintained that in general we do not know what we really are, that is, we have a fundamentally false vision of our own being. Also like Sartre, Parfit is maintaining that it is almost impossible for us to believe what is true about ourselves. And finally, like Sartre, he is maintaining that to believe the truth about ourselves would be to undergo a major change in our attitudes.

There are also important differences. I doubt that it would make sense to categorize Sartre as a reductionist in Parfit's sense. Parfit's basic image is that the existence of persons is like that of nations in that there is no extra Cartesian-like ego-fact. But for Sartre, the being of a person cannot be reduced to merely facts about coherences and connections. After all, this is exactly what is true about physical objects, that the bicycle is nothing more than the parts. For Sartre our being always escapes being summed up by such statements because we are free, because we sustain the various parts and connections in existence through free acts.

And while both Parfit and Sartre see their work as pointing towards transformed emotional responses towards one's own being, for Parfit this takes the form of being less concerned about one's death, while for Sartre the awareness of our perpetual absence of being is itself an awareness of a kind of death. And our project of misconstruing our own being is a project of flight from this awareness of non-being so that it is not a simple error about which Parfit can correct us. Indeed, this flight is so central to what we are that it could be said that we are that which flees from non-being.

Like Nietzsche, Sartre is maintaining that there is no external grounding of our identity. And like Nietzsche he sees philosophy as carrying within it deeply disturbing realizations. Yet Nietzsche is clear in his own mind about the possibility of an exuberant being who revels in the very absences that we are in flight from on a Sartrean perspective. For Nietzsche that flight is not a given; to the contrary it is the reflection of a lack of health.

In this section I will attempt to assimilate Sartre into the general framework I have developed. I will attempt to show that what he says about "angoise" is more properly said of alienness, and that much of Sartre's work can be interpreted as an instance of philosophic inquiry that both generates alienness and that, if he is correct, leads to the conclusion that alienness (not anxiety) is the authentic experience of the human condition.

Sartre's discussion of bad faith captures the core of his outlook. He begins with a complex example. A woman is involved in a flirtation; and the man says something that is rich in meaning; but she "disarms this phrase of its sexual background."[20] "She restricts this behavior to what is in the present, she does not wish to read in the phrases which he addresses to her anything other than their explicit meaning."[21] The man takes her hand but she manages to not notice it. "The hand rests inert between the warm hands of her companion—neither consenting nor resisting—a thing."[22]

Sartre then explains, redescribing within his ontological theory, what is going on. "She has disarmed the actions of her companion by reducing them to being only what they are; that is, to existing in the mode of the in-itself."[23] He says that the existence of bad faith rests on the utilization of "the double property of the human being, who is at once a facticity and a transcendence."[24] He then explains:

Although this meta-stable concept of "transcendence-facticity" is one of the most basic instruments of bad faith, it is not the only one of its kind. We can equally well use another kind of duplicity derived from human reality which we will express roughly by saying that its being-for-itself implies complimentarily a being-for-others. Upon any one of my conducts it is always possible to coverage two looks, mine and that of the Other. The conduct will not present exactly the same structure in each case. But, as we shall see later, as each look perceives it, there is between these two aspects of my being no difference between appearance and being—as if I were to myself the truth of myself and as if the Other possessed only a deformed image of me. The equal dignity of being, possessed by my being-for-others and by being-for-myself permits a perpetually disintegrating synthesis and a perpetual game of escape from the for-itself to the for-others, and from the for-others to the for-itself.[25]

Sartre then points out that one may also play on the quality of being-in-the-world and being-in-the-midst-of-the-world, that is, the difference between being an active agent who causes there to be a world of human meanings and projects, and being a passive object with an inert presence among other objects. He also notes the possibility of playing on temporal aspects.

Affirming at once that I am what I have been (the man who deliberately arrests himself at one period in his life and refuses to take into consideration the later changes) and that I am not what I have been (the man who in the face of reproach or rancor dissociates himself from his past by insisting on his freedom and on his perpetual re-creation)."[26]

He sums up these qualities, "In all these concepts which have only a transitive role in the reasoning and are eliminated from the conclusion . . . we find again the same structure. We have to deal with human reality as a being which is what it is not and which is not what it is."[27] This characterization of the nature of persons can be expressed as the most fundamental lack of integration, not now between two disparate elements, but with respect to any given property itself.

It is crucial to remember that Sartre says there is *equal dignity* to these two perspectives, that one does not correspond to appearance and the other to reality. Rather, they represent two limited but valid perspectives on human reality. It is as though we had two languages in which to talk, and as it suited us, we talked first in one and then the other, only we are not so much dealing with languages as with theoretical or metaphysical structures for apprehending reality, each with its own epistemology. This then is the "inner disintegration at the heart of being" that Sartre is talking about.

The far-reaching import of Sartre's position emerges when we turn to his remarks about the opposite of bad faith, sincerity. The ideal of sincerity is "that a man be for himself only what he is."[28] But this is "not merely an ideal of knowing, it is an ideal of being."[29] Thus, from a normal perspective, one of the most basic forms of integration is self-knowledge, for there to be a fit between what we really are and what we believe ourselves to be. But this fit, which we so readily accept as a possibility, is actually an impossibility.

He offers as an example the cafe-waiter. Here we have not any matter of belief about which the waiter might be deceiving himself. The only proposition that could be formulated about which there is any question is, "I am a cafe-waiter." But of course there is no doubt that this is true. The issue of bad faith is one of how one relates to oneself as a cafe-waiter, or how one understands what it means to be a cafe-waiter. A man is never, for Sartre, a cafe-waiter in the way that an inkwell is an inkwell. He tells us, "From the very fact that I sustain this role in existence" I "transcend it on every side," I "constitute myself as one beyond my condition. Yet there is no doubt that I am in a sense a diplomat or a reporter? But if I am one, this cannot be in the mode of being-in-itself. I am a waiter in the mode of being what I am not."[30]

It should now be clear that Sartre is not limiting himself to what we normally think of as self-deception, which emerges as an unfortunate translation of "mauvaise foi." He considers the case of sadness—not now as an instance of someone pretending to be sad when he is not, but rather a paradigm instance of the person who is truly sad.

I am sad. One might think that surely I am sadness in the mode of being what I am. What is sadness, however, but the intentional unity which comes to reassemble and animate the totality of my conduct. It is the meaning of this dull look with which I view the world, of my bowed shoulders. . . . The being-sad is not a ready-made being which I give to myself as I can give this book to a friend. I do not possess the property of affecting myself with being. If I make myself sad, I must continue to make myself sad from beginning to end. I can not treat my sadness as an impulse finally achieved and put it on a file without recreating it, nor can I carry it in the manner of an inert body which continued its movement after the initial shock. There is not inertia in consciousness. If I make myself sad, it is because I am not sad—the being of sadness escapes me by and in the very act by which I affect myself with it. The being-in-itself of sadness perpetually haunts my consciousness (of) being sad, but it is as a value which I can not realize; it stands as a regulative meaning of my sadness, not as its constitutive modality.[31]

Sartre is putting forward his general theory of what he calls "psychic objects." The conclusion that he reaches is that our normal ways of thinking about objects of the psyche and of the self are themselves self-deceptive, or in bad faith, and that our language is part of the project of trying to pretend that we have being.

We tend to think of objects of the psyche, such as sadness, as a state that we are either in or not in. We think of it as having its own independent existence. Part of what it is to be in this state is to be passive. It has a grip on one. One slips into it as one might sink into mud. This is what Sartre denies. The falseness of our normal view does not emerge because we are making a simple mistake. It is a fundamentally false view of ourselves. At every moment we hold together psychic objects that are our creations, and so from the perspective of our in-itself language, which demands passivity, it is always false to say: I am sad; I have an emotion; I have a certain character trait.

For Sartre, consciousness itself does not exist apart from being made. It is, only insofar as it is experienced. It has no being to be experienced beyond itself, before or after it is experienced.

It [consciousness] is because it makes itself, since its being is conscious-ness of being. But this means that making sustains being; consciousness has to be its own being, it is never sustained by being; it sustains being in the heart of subjectivity, which means once again that it is inhabited by being, but that it is not being: consciousness is not what it is.[32]

Thus our conscious states are ours only in virtue of our creation of them. This, in turn, gives us a *power* of alienating; we can cast off aspects of self by no longer sustaining them in being. He writes,

Shall I uncover in myself "drives" even though it be to affirm them in shame? But is this not deliberately to forget that these drives are realized with my consent, that they are not forces of nature but that I lend them their efficacy by a perpetually renewed decision concerning their value.[33]

But if this is so, then drives are not really drives. And just as drives are not really drives, so character traits are not really character traits. He writes, "Shall I pass judgment on my character, on my nature? Is this not to veil from myself at that moment what I know only too well, that I thus judge a past to which by definition my present is not subject?"[34]

One final example. Sartre talks of the homosexual who refuses to draw the conclusion that he is a homosexual from the evidence before him. The man rejects his homosexuality in the mode of not-being-in-itself.

He would be right . . . if he declared to himself, "To the extent that a pattern of conduct is defined as the conduct of a paederast and to the extent that I have adopted this conduct, I am a paederast. But to the extent that human reality can not be finally defined by patterns of conduct, I am not one."[35]

To this we are tempted to say that it all depends upon what is meant by "paederast." But the point is that we mean something more than patterns of conduct; we mean tendencies that the person has. But for Sartre, the person doesn't have these tendencies. It is not that a specific person lacks these tendencies and thus he is not a homosexual while another person might be. On the contrary, no one ever has these tendencies because we are free beings and free beings cannot have tendencies in the same way that an object has tendencies. What Sartre is saying can be reformulated as: (1) the thesis that our language for talking about persons (e.g., for ascribing character traits) involves the assertion of counter-factuals, assertions about what they would have done or felt if circumstances had been otherwise; and (2) that the reality of free beings will not support the required counter-factuals. It is always open whether or not the person will feel or behave in the required way.

Sartre's critique focuses on two points. First, attention is directed at what I have called the aspects of the self. His point is that the *paradigm* instances of these elements fail to meet the necessary criteria for being the elements they are. This paradox whereby we learn language by applying terms to instances that are not really instances of the property in question occurs because language itself is one of our devices for masking our freedom.

The second point of focus is on the relation between the individual and the element that is his. For Sartre, we never really have these aspects even when we are paradigms of someone who does have the aspect, because we never stand in the relation of "having." Sartre is claiming that one is in bad faith whenever one experiences oneself as not having some aspect of self when one has satisfied all the public criteria for the attribution of this aspect to the self: this is ordinary self-deception. And one is equally in bad faith when under these circumstances one does experience oneself as having the aspect: ordinary sincerity.

By introducing two kinds of being, the in-itself and the for-itself, Sartre provides an ontological framework that allows us to reinterpret experiences of self that have been thought of as pathological. Now the tables are turned; normal self-experience is seen as inauthentic, and a wide range of denials that were seen as instances of commonplace self-deception may represent a confused but authentic recognition that one never has any attribute in the mode of possession of the in-itself.

Sartre's outlook can be readily assimilated within the preceding discussion of alienness. Sartre himself is in the position of the person who asserts a wide variety of seeming paradoxes:

- Sadness is not sadness
- The sad person is not sad
- I am not what I am and am what I am not
- The homosexual is not a homosexual
- The drive is not a drive

These paradoxical conclusions can be viewed as verbal utterances within the general class of expressions for which I offered noncontradictory interpretations in the preceding chapter. Instead of seeing a person who says things of this sort as someone attempting to flee from himself, but unable to fully deceive himself, it is possible to uncover the rational structure of what he is saying just as it was with the person who says, "I am not the agent of my actions."

Of the three modes for interpreting verbal utterances of this sort, the model I have termed "person/self ambiguity" is not very helpful. It might be suggested that we analyze "I am not what I am" as: there is a person who is a certain way and a self that is not. However, this approach is rather misleading because for Sartre the self is itself something that can be analyzed along the first model (i.e., there is something that seems to be a self but is not a self). For Sartre, there can never be a self because there are never the necessary aspects of a self (e.g., character traits), and the modes of integration necessary for selfhood are always absent. The integrated personality cannot exist. There is a disintegration at the heart of being. Wholeness is impossible in principle.

On the first model, reduction of aspect, these utterances are ways of denying that an element, say sadness, is really sadness. Instead it is something like sadness, except that one gives it to oneself from moment to moment. Thus one ends up saying "My passions are not passions," "My drives are not drives," and so forth.

The third model, alternate relation, is also helpful. Sartre writes, "The waiter in the cafe can not be immediately a cafe waiter in the sense that this inkwell is an inkwell, or the glass is a glass."[36] We can understand him as claiming that there are two different ways in which something may "have" a property (i.e., two alternate relationships). Within this metaphysical distinction, there are a wide range of properties or attributes that it is false to ascribe to us in the mode appropriate to objects. Thus, when we are sad, it is the case that we are-1 sad, but not the case that we are-2 sad. Thus, Sartrean metaphysics can be seen as an attempt to spell out a set of distinctions that are implicit in someone's feeling or saying "I am sad and I am not sad," and in terms of which such a claim may be noncontradictory. In this way, his distinction between modes of being occupies the same explanatory role vis-à-vis the utterances and experiences he considers as does the distinction between having an activity associated with oneself and being the agent of that activity, except that on the account I have offered it is sometimes the case that a person is the agent of his actions; for Sartre a person is always suspended between the two modes of being.

The chain of reasoning that leads Sartre to make these utterances and that would justify the introduction of two kinds of sadness and two ways of having an attribute, has as a major premise the claim that we are free in a categorical sense. This includes the claim that consciousness cannot be determined. From this premise Sartre argues that we can never be sad, nasty, cheerful, and so forth. Implicitly, his argument involves an analysis of the ordinary meanings of emotion terms and character trait terms. The unstated view is that such concepts can only be applied to beings that are not free. To fully explore his outlook would require subjecting such concepts to an analysis that would parallel the analysis provided earlier of actions and activity. If Sartre is correct, then we should find that our ordinary concepts carry with them an implication that we are not free beings. And since we are free, there is some sense in which it is never true that these terms apply to us.

Our freedom and our role in maintaining ourselves in being is never something that is fully unknown to us. Thus, it is not necessary for someone to come to accept Sartre's outlook in order for her experience to be transformed. Rather, the individual has to accept what she is already aware of, the nothingness at the heart of her own being. Sartre identifies this authentic experience of our own being as anxiety.

Anxiety is not the same as alienness. How are they related? Anxiety is itself an emotion and it carries with it the notion of flight; the flight from that which produces anxiety. Alienness is an experience of lack of integration. It is a perceptual mode in which the self or one of its elements is experienced as being mine and not mine. But alienness is not in itself a specific emotion. It is conceivable that one could calmly experience the alienness of oneself, and it is even more likely that one would have this experience with terror. Sartrean anxiety is built upon alienness. But just as less cosmic forms of alienness need not result in ordinary anxiety, so too the ontological anxiety identified by Sartre is one of several possible responses to the perception of alienness. Thus, given Sartre's analysis of being, I would maintain that it is alienness, not anxiety, that can claim to be the authentic experience of the human condition.

This might be denied. One could agree that alienness lies at the inner core of anxiety but maintain that to calmly experience one's own alienness is to be denying that very reality. Thus it might be maintained that anxiety is the only appropriate response to a realization of the inner lack of being.

How would a claim of this sort be established? If in more ordinary contexts we asserted that fear was the appropriate emotional response to something, we would be saying that to calmly experience something as dangerous rather than to fearfully experience it is on some level to deny that it is dangerous. To calmly experience that which threatens what is valuable is to treat what is valuable as if it were not, which is to say that nothing valuable is endangered. Thus, to not have fear is to deny that something destructive of something valued may occur.

To say that alienness, per se, is the authentic experience of the human condition, is then to say that experiencing one's very being as not-there need not be terrifying. It is, for instance, to say that one possible alternative mode of relating to one's not-being is through quiet acceptance.

Is this possible? I think it is. Indeed, this is one way of characterizing Buddhism. Interestingly, Parfit makes this connection. In discussing his own reductionist view of the person, he asks if it is psychologically possible to believe that our existence is not some extra fact beyond anything constituted by physical or psychological connections. He writes:

> Nagel once claimed that it is psychologically impossible to believe the Reductionist View. Buddha claimed that, though this is very hard, it is possible. I find Buddha's claim to be true. After reviewing my arguments, I find that, at the reflective level or intellectual level, though it is very hard to believe the Reductionist View, this is possible. My remaining doubts or fears seem to me irrational.[37]

There is a difference here. Parfit is asking whether it is possible to believe that in some sense there is no self. The question I have asked goes beyond his question. I am not even asking if it possible to believe without fear that there is no self, but whether it can be appropriate to respond calmly to an awareness of the absence of self. Yet it is this that Buddhism affirms.

Sartre might have responded to this by saying that to react calmly is to deny the loss of being that is revealed. But in response, Buddha might have said that to react anxiously is to think that one has lost a being that one now sees one never had or could have had. To experience oneself as having lost something is to deny the nothingness that is revealed. In short, Buddha might maintain that Sartrean anxiety is only a first step to Buddhist calm. The claim I am making is that alienness is the common experience that exists within either Sartrean anxiety or Buddhist calm.

This concludes my discussion of alienness as it arises within the context of philosophic reflection. The philosophers and philosophic issues I have discussed were selected as powerful illustrations of a general point about alienness. Alienness is an experiential mode that is grounded in a person's coming to have certain paradoxical beliefs about himself or herself. Philosophy is a central context of speculation that often enough gives rise to such beliefs, and if the philosophic speculation that results in alienness-grounding beliefs is itself valid, then alienness is the authentic mode of experiencing the human condition.

7

Alienness and Self-Understanding

This chapter is concerned with the dynamics of alienness and identification as they arise in a person's inquiry into himself or herself.

IDENTIFICATION, SELF-IDENTITY, AND A CONCEPTION OF THE SELF

The relationship between the individual's *identification* with some aspect of his self (his experiencing some aspect of his self as his own), his having a *conception of the self* in which the locus of the self is situated in a certain component of the mental geography, and his having a particular *self-identity* needs to be clarified.

I have distinguished between the concept of the self and specific conceptions of the self; if, as I have suggested, the self is best thought of as an integrated personality, then the various conceptions differ with respect to the patterns of integration, including differences about the central locus of the self. Each of us has some implicit conception of the self. Within this conception we not only formulate judgments about ourselves, but also about each other. Thus, from a third-person perspective, an observer with a conception of the self in terms of which an individual's value system is the core of the self might hold the view that someone who found himself having desires that sharply conflicted with his values would be having desires that were not fully his own, especially if those desires were induced through some process of social conditioning. Thus, our perspective on how to properly identify a particular person reflects our general understanding of the self.

Similarly, a person's conception of the self is reflected in analogous judgments applied to himself. Thus, if I understand the self to be represented most genuinely by spontaneous desire and I see acts of mine that are in conflict with such desires, I might judge them to not be really mine—just as I would judge in the same case with respect to another person that they were not his own.

Thus, the core of what we are doing when we identify some element of the self (whether in our own case or in the case of another) as being or not being really my own or his own, is to make a judgment. But when one reflects upon oneself, one does not merely apply a conception of the self to an individual who happens to be oneself. There is an experiential embodiment of such judgments; an experience of something as being one's own or of coming from one's self. An experience of this sort, which we may call an experience of identification, is an occurrent event. At a certain time, in reflecting upon the different aspects of oneself, one experiences them as one's own.

This use of "identification," understanding it to refer to either judgments that some aspect of oneself is really one's own or to the experiences that embody such judgments, needs to be distinguished from a variety of other uses of the term.

First, within the Freudian tradition, the term "identification" is used to refer to a process whereby an individual takes over the perspective of another person. Thus it might be said that through identification with the parent, the child comes to have the attitudes that the parent has. It is sometimes said that there is a tendency of oppressed parties to identify with their oppressors. This does not mean that they sympathize with their oppressors, but rather, often without realizing it, they take the outlook, even towards themselves, of their oppressors.

A second use of "identification" or "identify" is the more common-sense one in which we say that one person identifies with some other person or collective entity. For instance, I may identify with a certain character in a play, or with an oppressed people half way around the globe.

What does this "identifying" consist in? In a weak sense, this merely involves having some compassion for the object of the identification (e.g., someone we see being beaten on the evening news), but in the strongest sense, to identify with the victim is to have the kind of emotions that one would have if it were happening to oneself. Essentially it is a matter of experiencing things from a certain point of view; in particular, experiencing them from the point of view of the other with whom one identifies. It is experiencing things as if they were happening to oneself.

Films are particularly powerful in this regard because the film maker, through his or her manipulation of the camera, can create a film in which the viewer experiences from the point of view of one of the characters. For instance, the film maker can give the audience the kind of experience that in real life one has only if one is walking down a hall, slowly opening doors. In some really scary murder films we do not witness events from a camera angle directly above the killer and the intended victim. At least some of the time we are allowed to experience things from the point of view of the terrified victim, who does not know what waits around the corner. Coverage on the evening news can also, by selecting camera angles, move an audience into seeing an event from a particular perspective. And when one sees events as if one is someone else, it is a short step to having emotions as if one were someone else.

Neither this ordinary use of "identification" nor the Freudian use, which is built upon it, is involved in the present discussion. It should be seen that this is not a matter of the object of the identification. In the ordinary sense, I might have a strong identification with another party in a conflict in which I have been involved. Thus, looking backwards, I may identify with him and not with myself. But to not identify with oneself, in this sense, does not involve any judgment that it really wasn't me. It just means that in retrospect, I am able to powerfully experience past events from the other's point of view.

There is a third use of "identification," which also needs to be put to one side. It is the sense in which we may ask "What are his identifications?" or "How does he identify himself?" When we ask these questions we are typically seeking information about the groups or collectives with which he feels solidarity, or with whom he will publicly affirm membership. For instance, we may say that he identifies himself as a Jew or as a black person. If we say that someone identifies very strongly as a black person, we are using the term "identification" to call attention to what I have referred to as self-identity. A person's self-identity may be thought of as a system of beliefs about himself or herself that function in a vital manner within his or her emotional life. Although this use of "identification" (e.g., public identification, or the feeling of oneness with members of a particular group) has some important connections with identification as I have been using it, it too is a different usage from identification that involves a judgment that some part of the self is or is not really one's own.

But what is the relationship between having a conception of the self in which the true self, or the core of the self, is taken to reside in a certain segment of the mental geography (e.g., in the emotions, or in moral judgments) and actually experiencing oneself as acting out of oneself when one acts out of this segment of the mental geography? It would seem that part of what it is to have such a conception of the self would be to have a disposition to have certain kinds of identification experiences. One who thinks of *the self* as residing in the moral faculties is likely, when she encounters moral conflict in her own life, to experience *herself* on the side of the moral judgment and not on the side of the forbidden desire. Yet the relationship is somewhat loose. We could imagine someone who thinks of others in terms of a certain conception of the self, but who fails to actually experience her own life in a similar manner. Having a particular conception of the self at most gives rise to a tendency to have certain kinds of identification experiences. It is a reference point in terms of which judgments may be made, but it can also be ignored.

Some writers have used the phrase "an act of identification." This term suggests that the having of identification experiences is something in relationship to which we are not passive. Is identification itself a basic act of the mind, a kind of experience that we directly bring about, similar to the way in which we can at will simply see the diagram ⊠ first as the top of a pyramid and then as an elevator shaft? Is it possible, at will, to simply stop identifying in a certain way, to simply stop experiencing oneself as present in a given action? Or is this, at most, a change in consciousness that one brings about by reflecting on certain things—thus causing it to occur that one experiences in a different way? This is a factual question, the answer to which need not be the same for all people and for all objects of the experience. The truth about how identification experiences occur and how they change is not clear. It is far more complex than is sometimes supposed. In some instances it may fit the pattern of something that is simply under our control; we can simply choose to see ourselves a certain way. In other instances, this experience is something that occurs to us and is something over which we do not have immediate control. In some situations, for instance where there is internal conflict, one can decide for one or another of the elements; one can do something like "embrace" one element rather than another. Frithjof

Bergmann talks about a radical reversal of experience whereby a large chunk of one's life that one resisted, resented, and struggled against is suddenly accepted and embraced as genuinely one's own. This sudden reexperiencing seems to have something of the quality of an action to it—but it remains terribly elusive, and certainly does not characterize the full range of identification experiences.

With respect to any of our aspects—be they emotions, desires, values, personality traits, or specific actions—it is possible to take towards them a perspective in which we view that aspect as truly and deeply one's own, as coming from or expressing who one really is. Alternatively, it is possible to have towards any of these elements just the opposite perspective—that this element is not really one's own. These perspectives may be lasting, or they may shift with respect to the very same object. And someone can be said to have such a perspective dispositionally as well as to have a particular identification experience.

The different aspects of the self that are possible objects of an alienness experience are also possible objects of an identification experience. Indeed, we can understand alienness and identification as contrasting experiences, at least to the extent that someone who is experiencing something as not his or her own is clearly not identifying with it. But as I noted earlier, the alienness experience is both complex and diverse. Some of the time when a person experiences some thing as mine-but-not-really-mine, or as coming from the person that I am but not from my self, these experiences *contain* an identification of the person with some part of the personality or with one side within a conflict. Thus one may say, "That desire is not really mine," thus communicating an estrangement with the desire but an identification with the values with which it conflicts. So the alienation experience may itself embody an identification.

On the other hand, when a person says, "I have beliefs and values, but they are not real; I don't believe what I believe or value that which I value," the person need not be identifying with any element or segment of the self. He or she may simply be experiencing internal discord, which tends to dissolve elements such as beliefs or values.

Like identification experiences, alienness is typically something that happens to us. It can be induced, for instance through reflection, and it may be the result of directly encountering the discord within us. But it is not typically something that we directly impose upon ourselves at will.

It may be thought that experiencing some aspect of oneself as truly one's own bears some very tight relationship to having a specific self-identity (seeing certain properties as capturing who one is). For instance, it may be thought that if a central part of someone's self-identity consists in his having a certain characteristic, then he will identify with those aspects of himself that emerge from that characteristic. For instance, if a major part of someone's self-identity resides in his prowess as a lover, we might expect that he experiences himself as most truly alive, as most totally himself, in his acts of lovemaking.

Yet, nothing of this sort need be true. The self-ascriptions that take on central importance to ourselves (our self-identities) operate quite distinctly from our identification experiences. The person who sees himself as a great lover need not have any special experience of himself in his lovemaking. Similarly, someone for whom being a Catholic may be a vital part of her self-identity, especially in her relations with others, may nonetheless experience her theological beliefs as not really her own.

It might be thought that because both identification with some aspect of one's self and having a certain self-identity involve judgments, it is necessarily the case that one identifies with the components of one's self-identity. It might be thought that this must be the case because the very same judgment is involved in both the identification and the self ascription that figures in self-identity. But this is not quite accurate. Consider someone for whom the fact that he has a particular fear, say a fear of heights, is part of his self-identity. Thus, he sees this as a property of his, and he may experience pride or shame in terms of it, and his belief that he has this property may play a certain role in the dynamics of his life. For instance, he may cite this fact as a way of presenting himself to others. Yet at the same time, when he reflects on this fear he may see it as irrational, and when in the very grip of it he may say to himself, "I am afraid, but I know that there is nothing to fear. This fear does not really reflect me; it is not really mine." Thus, he may be alienated from the very emotion the having of which is part of his self-identity.

This, of course, is itself the mark of a fracture within the personality. And it may be so deep that he comes to experience his entire identity structure as alien. This too is possible. One could reflect upon the fact that one is a person who has a certain self-identity and in pondering this fact about oneself come to experience it as essentially arbitrary or as itself in conflict with something that was more deeply oneself.

Typically one's self-identity is linked to one's identifications. If one has a positive self-identity, then one tends to identify with those aspects of oneself the having of which is part of one's self-identity. If someone has a firm self-identity, and then encounters within herself aspects of herself that conflict with that self-identity, she will have a strong tendency to experience those elements as not really her own. For instance, a person who defines herself as a pacifist and for whom that identity goes very deep, should she encounter emotions that conflict with her own sense of who she is, is not likely to identify with those emotions. It is this question of conflict and self-perception that is the subject of the remainder of this chapter.

INNER STRUGGLE AND SELF-DECEPTION

My primary concern is with the individual's own encounter with his own lack of integrity, with how a still greater sense of his internal disunity may be brought about through self-exploration, with his response to his own incoherence, and with the dynamic import of the alienness experience.

In the West, in the twentieth century, this intense engagement with oneself occurs most often in the formalized psychotherapeutic setting. Traditionally, intensive self-examination has occurred in a religious context. Within the history of Christianity, this self-examination emerges from a focus on the call for purification of the personality. Early Calvinist sects engaged in these efforts to explore and reform the individual psyche, and Perry Miller has written about the extremely fine categories of personal transformation that were developed in this country by the seventeenth- and eighteenth-century New England Congregationalists.[1]

Twelve hundred years earlier, in his *Confessions*, Augustine told of a struggle with himself:

> I was held fast, not in fetters clamped upon me by another, but by my own will, which had the strength of iron chains. The enemy held my will in his power and from it he had made a chain and shackled me. For my will was perverse and lust had grown from it, and when I gave in to lust, habit was born, and when I did not resist the habit it became a necessity. These were the links which formed what I have called my chain, and it held me fast in the duress of servitude. But the new will which had come to life in me and made me wish to serve you freely and enjoy you, my God, who are our only certain joy, was not yet strong enough to overcome the old, hardened as it was by the passage of time. So these two wills

within me, one old, one new, one the servant of the flesh, the other of the spirit, were in conflict and between them they tore my soul apart.

From my own experience I now understood what I had read—that the impulses of nature and the impulses of the spirit are at war with one another. In this warfare I was on both sides, but I took the part of that which I approved in myself rather than the part of that which I disapproved. For my true self was no longer on the side of which I disapproved, since to a great extent I was now its reluctant victim rather than its willing tool. Yet it was by my doing that habit had become so potent an enemy, because it was by my own will that I had reached the state in which I no longer wished to stay. Who can justly complain when just punishment overtakes the sinner? I could no longer claim that I had no clear perception of the truth. . . . But while I wanted to follow the first course and was convinced that it was right, I was still a slave to the pleasures of the second. . . . It was in vain that inwardly I applauded your disposition, when that other disposition in my lower self raised war against the disposition of my conscience and handed me over as a captive to that disposition towards sin, which my lower self contained. For the rule of sin is the force of habit, by which the mind is swept along.[2]

Augustine does not mention any experience of alienness. Yet this is not merely an account of personality change arising out of conflicting desires, but of an individual struggling to change his own personality. The crucial feature is revealed when Augustine says, "In this warfare, I was on both sides, but I took the part of that which I approved. . . . For my true self was no longer on the side of which I disapproved."

It is hard to understand exactly what Augustine is saying here. Does his true self shift from siding with one of these wills to siding with the other? Or is it that one of these wills represents his true self and that he comes to side with it? In either case he arrives at a point where he experiences himself as split into his "true self" and his "lower self," and he finds that the lower self is still in command. Yet he is not merely witnessing a conflict; he *takes the side* that he believes to be right. Nonetheless, this side is still the weaker of the two. While he experiences some of his actions as not coming from his true self, he continues to recognize them as his. He is not involved in a psychotic denial of reality. Nor does his way of formulating the inner discord represent any attempt to flee from responsibility.

Augustine explicitly criticizes the Manichees, who assert that "we have two minds of different natures" and that "they are in conflict because they spring from two opposing substances and two opposing principles."[3] Augustine is at pains to emphasize that both desires are *his own*, even though they are not experienced as equally his own. One set emerges from his true self, the other does not. Rather than being the external spectator of a conflict between two wills that are his equally, he is experientially at one with one of them and "the prisoner" of the other.

An even closer parallel to the current discussion may be found in a sermon by John Donne from 1622. Donne says,

> . . . if upon the earth thou beest in the way to heaven, thou must have a body too, a body of thine own, a body of thy possession; for thy body hath thee, and not thou it, if thy body tyrannize over thee. If thou canst not withdraw thine eye from an object of temptation or withhold thy hand from subscribing against thy conscience nor turn thine ear from a popular and seditious libel, what hast thou towards a man? Thou hast no soul, nay, thou hast no body. There is a body, but thou hast it not; *it is not thine*, it is not in thy power. Thy body will rebel against thee even in a sin; it will not perform a sin when and where thou wouldst have it.[4]

For Donne, if one's body is not in line with one's conscience, "what hast thou towards a man? Thou hast no soul, nay, thou hast no body." If we substitute "self" for "soul" the parallel is clear. One's body did such and such but not one's self (soul). My actions are not my own. I have a body but I do not possess it—it is not mine own.

We should not be misled by Donne's use of the term "body." If we take "body" in a scaled down physiological sense, the inability to control one's body is reminiscent of those cases where the arm goes up even when one wants it to stay down. But Donne addresses himself to a spiritual sickness. His notion of "body" corresponds more fully to what I have called "person." For Donne, the body may have a will and yet that will need not be mine own. If this will subscribes against one's conscience then one has no soul (self). Thus, in Donne's account the soul or self only exists when there is integration between the body and one's conscience. In the absence of this integration there is not a mere conflict between two parts of one's self; it is clear that the conscience part indicates the self, real self, or true self. This is similar to Augustine's taking the side of which he approved and that he knew to be right. And it is also similar to the perspective found earlier in the discussion of Gary Watson's account of freedom.

The discovery that one's actions, will, or emotions are in conflict with one's values is probably the most common source of alienness. The first-person sense of the alienness of actions in conflict with one's values, as well as third-person judgments that such actions are not really actions of the individual (though they are his or hers), implicitly use the moral values of the individual as a guide to the locus of the self. As was pointed out earlier, there is no necessity to this identification. One could have a person/self distinction and not locate the self in this fashion. For instance, a Nietzschean might experience these values as just that which indicates what is not-self. Nietzsche, as was cited earlier, identifies the self with the body and its reasons. Thus Nietzsche and Donne offer radically opposite frameworks for identifying what is really one's own. It is important to remember that this is not merely a matter of alternative identification experiences, but rather alternative theories about the real self that have third-person applicability. That is, both Nietzsche and Donne are operating within a conceptual framework that allows them to make judgments about the real self of other persons, regardless of what that person's own identifications are.

When one does live and experience from within a conception of self that gives one's moral judgments or values a special role in constituting the self, coming to believe that one's actions are motivated contrary to one's values tends to call forth the experience of one's actions happening in spite of oneself. To say that the locus of the self resides with the moral values is not to say that what emerges from desire is viewed as non-self, but rather that its status is uncertain. When it conflicts with the moral judgment it is non-self; however, it will only be so experienced when there is awareness of the conflict.

With Augustine, the inner discord is experienced as a *struggle*; one way of understanding the phenomenology of this struggle is that the identification experience is not stable. On cool reflection, which is to say, when the desire is no longer occurrent, the individual is aware of both the conflict between desire and moral judgment and of the implication that the desire is not of the true self. This awareness expresses itself in his identification with the judgmental component. But it is part of the very power of the desire that when it is occurrent its strength is expressed in its ability to occupy all conscious space or to relegate to a tiny corner of awareness a recognition of the conflict with moral judgment. When the desire is occurrent it is the desired object that occupies consciousness—it is experienced as desirable. When one engages in cool reflection, the desire itself rather than the object of the original desire is now the object of consciousness (e.g., he thinks about the fact that he desires someone sexually, as opposed to sexually desiring that person).

The experiences of Augustine and Donne both involve a question of moral conflict. It is a matter of the individual's experiencing a conflict between values that he affirms and desires that he has or actions that he engages in. As presented in these examples, such conflict may be something that one simply finds within oneself; one encounters it without any necessary inquiry. On the other hand, the experience of moral conflict may result from a sustained inquiry into the moral quality of one's being, an inquiry that reveals to one a variety of unpleasant truths about oneself. And alienness may be the result of this discovery. But inquiry into one's moral standing is only one of a variety of self-explorations that may generate alienness.

I have offered three distinct models for capturing the alienness experience: reduction of aspect, person/self ambiguity, and alternate relation. These correspond to whether the locus of the incoherence is experienced as within the element, within the individual himself or herself, or in the relationship between the element and the individual. I have stressed that alienness is a response to coming to believe certain things that serve as the grounds for concluding that an aspect is not one's own. Alienness-grounding beliefs include:

1. Beliefs that suggest certain elements do not exist in their fullness. "I have no beliefs, values, emotions, actions, desires—they are really something else, something less."

2. Beliefs holding that while there is integration between the element and a larger complex that may be termed a person, that person-complex is not really me (my self).

3. Beliefs suggesting that while these aspects exist they are not properly integrated with oneself in that they do not stand in the proper relation to oneself. "My beliefs are not really mine for I don't know why I have these views."

One particular line of inquiry that may generate alienness is inquiry into how it came to be that one feels, believes, or values in the specific ways in which one does. Thus, one may discover that one has certain attitudes because one was raised in a certain way, or because those were the attitudes of one's parents, or because those were not the attitudes of one's parents and were thus chosen in rebellion in order to achieve a sense of identity in the face of dominant parental pressure.

The nature of this kind of inquiry is to search for deep motivational structures. Thus one does not focus on whatever good reasons one may have for these attitudes, beliefs, values, and so on, but rather on their nonrational (but not nonpurposive) causes. This does not require that the individual have no reasons—no good reasons—for his or her beliefs and judgments and feelings. Even when one has good reasons there is much that needs to be explained. Why was it that certain factors came to appear to one as good reasons? Why was one responsive or sensitive to these factors and not others? Why did one not seek out the counter-arguments?

Where the motivation was strong, the fact that the reasons one had may have been good or adequate grounds may have been causally irrelevant. If they had not been good enough to warrant belief they would have been *seen* as good enough in any event; or alternatively, the motivation to believe certain things may have entered the process not at the point of evaluating evidence but at an earlier point of amassing evidence.

Inquiry of this sort is a quest for an explanation of a certain sort. To demonstrate that a person lacks adequate grounding for his or her attitudes does not in itself refute the correctness of what is believed. Rather it suspends such questions as it pursues a nonrational account of *this particular* person's having certain views.

As was discussed earlier, it is primarily through the rational connectedness of the *cognitive content* of beliefs, values, emotions, and other mental elements that they are capable of cohering with each other. Alternative conceptions of the self may give differing emphases to rational connectedness, but a minimal rationality enters into all conceptions of the self. Because of the centrality of rational connections, the discovery of the nonrational process whereby I came to have the outlook I have has the potential for being alienating in that it suggests the possibility of an inappropriate kind of integration. Thus a belief may be integrated with other aspects of the self in virtue of the fact that my having this belief serves a variety of purposes and needs, but if the belief is integrated in this way it may be integrated in only this way, through the purposes it serves, and not rationally integrated in terms of its cognitive content.

Thus, it should be clear, it is misleading to speak simply about "integration" or "coherence" between the elements; just as with the analogy of the electronic parts that can be wired together to form either a radio, a video recorder, or a telephone, so too it is with human beings. Being a self (attaining selfhood) is something that emerges only when the integration is of a certain sort. It is an integration in virtue of which all the parts are truly one's own, and this integration is subtle (as well as subject to different design specifications depending on the conception of the self).

It is typically the case that our systems of beliefs are lightly integrated in rational terms, but that this lightness is not recognized.

Instead the beliefs are fiercely maintained, and this fierceness, which may in fact result from a need to retain these beliefs, is instead experienced as rationally (i.e., cognitively) warranted. A recognition of either past or present motivation affects our awareness of the lightness of rational connectedness; the element tends to be exposed in its starkness. One sees that one believes things that may not be true; one sees that one has values and attitudes that may lack validity.

Yet even when exposed as strongly motivated but only lightly grounded, the belief-embedded elements have not been eliminated; this is not a process whereby beliefs are necessarily changed or replaced by others. Rather, it is a process whereby their fixedness is shaken; they remain there as one's own but they are unglued. One has them, but they are not fully one's own. In fact they never were, but the inquiry has led one to an awareness of this fact. Thus, *the alienness experience represents a degree of self-knowledge achieved.*

It should also be clear that identification does not suffice to make something one's own. Look at it in the third person. Suppose that we are examining someone else's belief structure and we reach the conclusion that none of these beliefs are tightly integrated in terms of their cognitive content—that they simply float about as handy devices to serve as needed. Yet suppose the individual identifies himself with certain of these beliefs? Does this change anything? Does it substitute for the structural relationship that is missing? I think not. And if the individual at some later point comes to see the loose connectedness that we see, his identification itself might change. Or perhaps it would change if he was able to address more directly the needs and fears he has that underlie the fierceness of his identification.

With respect to these elements that are now seen as essentially "free standing," the situation is quite different than that considered in Augustine's case, where he identifies with one element in a moral conflict. In Augustine's description there is no discussion of grounding, there is the simple conflict between two elements (e.g., a desire that we have and a value judgment that specifies the having of such desires as sinful). In the case at hand, however, the individual is not identifying with a given element as opposed to another. Rather, he is applying an *integration standard* of ownership that is part of a theory or conception of the self, perhaps a conception that strongly locates the self in the rational component and thus demands tight rational integration as a criterion for something's being of the self. In terms of that conception, the elements are not truly his own, and having applied the criteria of that conception, they are now seen (i.e., experienced) as not truly one's own. For Augustine the conflict of values with something else—action, will, emotion—is clear-cut. He is himself aware of the disjunction; he is engaged in a moral struggle with himself in his effort to be good.

Augustine's experience does not have a fully modern ring to it. Since the work of Freud, the major model for the psychic conflicts that arise out of the demands of moral ideals has become more intricate. Instead of the direct absence of integration between our values and our desires or emotions, we have an absence of integration between beliefs or between beliefs and perceptions. The individual does not accurately know herself because she fails to draw proper conclusions about herself from the beliefs she has or should have, given the evidence available to her. This lack of integration between beliefs is itself rooted in a conflict between values and behavior (or wishes, emotions, desires, etc.). However, the individual's struggle is no longer a moral struggle to do or be good, but an unconscious struggle to deceive herself about herself.

In the psychoanalytic approach there is no tendency to identify the person's "real self" in terms of her values. The self is more likely to be conceived of as a composite of conflicting systems (e.g., ego, id, super-ego). Because of this, when the experience of alienness arises out of a conflict between values and something else, there is very little thought given to the possibility that the experience is an accurate perception. Rather, experiencing a part of oneself as not really one's own is seen as an effort to deny reality. In such views, alienness arises from a need to maintain an idealized self-image. The distinction between the person and the self is not seen as a distinction between two real complexes, but between the actual person and her ego-ideal (i.e., the person she aspires to be). Alienness is seen as reflecting an inability to accept the gap between the ideal and the real. It is not seen as part of a healthy dynamic of change, nor as an accurate perception of internal conflict.

In his book, *Self-Deception,* Herbert Fingarette lays great emphasis on this inability to accept oneself as one really is. Fingarette's work is of particular interest because his view that the self is a synthesis, an achievement of the individual that he builds as "he excludes material from the self as well as accepting, incorporating and synthesizing," is quite similar to the view of the self as the integrated personality.[5] Fingarette writes:

I speak of an individual's "engagement in the world". . . . I use it to characterize, in most general terms, what someone does or what he undergoes as a human subject; it is how an individual finds and/or takes the world including himself. It is a matter of the activities he engages in, the projects he takes on, the way the world presents itself to him to be seen, heard, felt, enjoyed, feared or otherwise "experienced" by him. . . .

The immediately crucial point is that we are not in general explicitly conscious of our engagements in the world.[6]

We become explicitly conscious of our engagements through a process of spelling out. We engage in the activity of spelling out only when there is some reason to do so.

The policy of refusing to spell-out one's engagement is merely the most "visible" feature of self-deception. Though highly visible, it is a concomitant of a far more fundamental manoeuvre. The self-deceiver is one who is in some way engaged in the world but who disavows the engagement, who will not acknowledge it even to himself as his. That is, self-deception turns upon the personal identity one accepts rather than the beliefs one has. It is the hallucinator who speaks, but he will not acknowledge the words as his; disowned by him and undetected by others, the voice nevertheless still speaks, and so it is assigned by him to some supernatural being. The paranoid is filled with destructiveness, but he disavows it; since the presence of destructiveness is evident to him, he eventually assigns "ownership" of that destructiveness to others. . . . In general, the self-deceiver is engaged in the world in some way, and yet he refuses to identify himself as one who is so engaged; he refuses to avow the engagement as his.[7]

Thus,

It happens—witness the self-deceiver—that an individual will be provoked into a kind of engagement which in part or in whole, the person cannot avow as his engagement, for to avow it would apparently lead to such intensely disruptive, distressing consequences as to be unmanageably destructive to the person. The individual may be powerfully inclined toward a particular engagement, yet this particular engagement may be utterly incompatible with that currently achieved synthesis of engagements which is the person. . . . The phenomena we classify under such headings as "self-deception," "defense," and "mauvaise foi," are "regressions" to this form of engagement; they manifest our capacity for such isolated engagements even after the emergence of a personal self, and in spite of unacceptability to the person.[8]

The self-deceiver is then someone who is engaged in the world in some particular way, but neglects to spell this out to himself. But this failure to spell out (to become explicitly aware of what he or she is, or how he or she is engaged) is not an oversight nor is it an innocent lapse. It is part of a disavowal of the engagement in circumstances where it would be too distressing to face the implications of that engagement.

The question that Fingarette does not ask is this: If the self is a product created by the individual through the integration of various elements, then wherein is there self-deception (or even error) if elements that are not part of that complex are not seen as part of it? If the self is the fully integrated person, then when there is serious internal conflict, the whole self does not exist. However, it may be represented by some of the fragments. Thus, within the overall collection, it may be possible to distinguish what is self from non-self (or person). This must be distinguished from self-deception. When we are really dealing with self-deception, for instance, someone who denies that she performed some action, her error does not consist in a failure to see the action as coming from her self. Her error of self-deception involves a failure to recognize the existence of the action or the motivating desire at all (e.g., "I wasn't trying to hurt her"; "I'm not jealous"; "There was no nastiness in what I said"). Here then is the difference between alienness and self-deception.

In the case of self-deception the individual is unable to see the engagement for what it is. She says, "I am not angry," "I don't hate him," "I didn't do that." In the case of alienness the person says, "there was this angry feeling of mine, but I was not angry," or "there was this feeling of hatred, but I did not hate him," or even "that was done by me but I didn't really do it." It is because of this actual seeing of the implications or meanings as others would see them that alienness seems so much more bizarre than self-deception. Indeed, alienness is hardly expressible, whereas the self-deceiver's false beliefs are not in themselves odd or paradoxical.

Fingarette speaks of the hallucinator and the paranoid who are in touch with the meanings and existence of elements but attribute them to others: they project and invent fantastic agents to whom they ascribe their actions. But this too is not alienness. The person who experiences alienness does not engage in these neurotic or psychotic distortions. He is able to make the same inferences in his case as he might in the case of others. While the self-deceiver does not experience his own action as having been done at all, and the hallucinatory experiences his own actions as not-his-own, the alienness experience is of actions as both one's-own-but-not-one's-own.

Somehow, despite the fact that Fingarette's view of the self—the self is an integrated complex created by the avowals and disavowals of the individual—suggests that what is not integrated with the complex is not part of the self, Fingarette overlooks alienness entirely. Instead of seeing how his view of self-deception can illuminate *the authentic experience of nonintegration,* he focuses on pathological ways of experiencing such conflicts.

The effect of calling attention to the differences between the various experiences of incoherence and of giving a meaningful interpretation to alienness is to open up a space between neurotic self-deception on the one hand and "self-acceptance" on the other. My thesis is that alienness, far from being an experience that manifests one's self-deception, may be an authentic mode of experiencing the lack of integration within the entire personality. We may think of repression and other neurotic distortions as arising, at least in part, because recognition of what is repressed or distorted would contradict (and thereby imperil) something of immense importance (e.g., one's self-identity as a good, decent, or wise individual). In the alienness experience "unflattering elements" are recognized without being attributed to the self. To the individual himself, this experience of something that is mine-but-not-mine is hardly comprehensible. Insofar as the analysis makes such a mode of experience intelligible, it may make it possible for the conflicted individual to recognize the existence or meaning of certain actions without suffering the loss of self-identity that would be necessitated by simply viewing himself as destructive, vindictive, or cruel.

It may be objected that this experience still remains self-deceptive, that the only fully honest response would be to recognize that one is, or has been, a nasty, cruel, or petty individual. If this view of oneself is at variance with one's explicitly held values or self-image, so much the worse for the self-image. One may either say "he is really cruel," thus dismissing whatever conflicts with this appraisal as not of significance, or one may say, "he is a mixed affair—in part he is cruel, in part he is not."

These two responses are quite different. The first, "he is really cruel, all the rest is mere talk," is implicitly based on a view of how to deal with conflicting fragments. This view may or may not be defensible or shared by others. The second response, "he is a mixed affair," remains correct by remaining on the level of the evidence. It merely restates the fact of fragmentation without committing itself to any position on how to grasp the conflicting aspects. While this may appear to be an acceptable or safe thing to do, it may be criticized on grounds of inauthenticity.

The issue of authenticity is not primarily a matter of taking an objective perspective on oneself; it is a matter of the *dynamic import* of one's perspective. So long as one is alive, the meaning of one's past is not out of the range of one's influence. Insofar as one steps back and adopts a third-person view towards oneself, saying merely, "there is a conflict between my proclaimed values and my actual conduct" or "I am a non-integrated individual," one abandons one's role as a creator of the synthesis. This role is what Augustine assumed when he took the side of what he approved.

I am not putting forward any general claim about what the dynamic import of alienness experiences *must be*. What I am saying is that, at least some of the time, to recognize what is ugly and repellent and to refuse to allow that that is "the real me" is not a way of maintaining a virginal self, in principle untaintable, but a way of committing oneself to the completed construction of a whole self out of the fragments that are not repellent.

On the account I have offered, a person who does not regard as his own an engagement that is inadequately integrated with his self may be correct. Have I then eliminated the possibility of self-deception? Not at all. Self-deception exists in several forms. First, there is the familiar failure to perceive the meaning of actions (e.g., "It was not a hostile act"). Second, there is the case of the person who does not experience alienness, but merely experiences something as alien. That is, instead of recognizing the way in which what is not his is his, he is simply cut off from recognition of any tie to it. He projects the action onto real or imaginary others. Finally, there is the person who experiences alienness when the experience is inappropriate. Not all experiences of something as one's-own-but-not-one's-own are correct. I have never maintained that *any* lack of integration is sufficient for denying that some element is of the self. Just because it is discovered that some action is in conflict with some explicitly affirmed value, it does not follow that it is not integrated in other ways that may be sufficient for it to be of the self. The actual working out of these criteria for the appropriateness of alienness could only be done in terms of a given conception of the self and in terms of that conception's approach to the various instances of fragmentation. Once this is done there would be a range of cases in which an alienness experience verbalized as "I was trying to hurt her but it wasn't really me" would be a variant of self-deception that would fall short of "I wasn't trying to hurt her," which is a more pervasive self-deception. In these cases the honest response would be the admission, "Yes, I was trying to hurt her." In an actual case one would want to know just how securely embedded the value is, and whether the apparent incoherence of the action can be shown to be merely apparent.

The effort to determine the real degree of incoherence of a given element may call for a sustained exploration of the unconscious. This investigation would attempt to show the ways in which what appears to be isolated is in fact part of a larger structure. But we should not assume that this is true in all cases. Indeed, it may turn out that the process of showing how the element is tied to the whole can only be carried out in part. Ultimately, we may be forced to conclude that though a given bit of behavior is part of a larger set of attitudes, desires, and perceptions, this larger complex cannot be identified with the self. One may have to accept the fact that one has no unified self, that there is something closer to a conflict of multiple persons, each of which is incomplete and falls short of selfhood.

Beyond these considerations, as was pointed out earlier, an element is not one's own merely because it is integrated in some fashion with other elements that are part of the self. Our conceptions of the self are extremely subtle and contain specifications as to the kinds of integration that may be acceptable for given elements. Thus, there are some activities that are one's own precisely because they are free from complexity. Insofar as they appear as the direct and spontaneous expression of the self, they are unquestionably part of it. But if we discover that what has appeared light and easy on the surface is in fact highly motivated, its link with the self is shattered. This is the case of the person frolicking in the autumn leaves; in a moment of honesty she recognizes that all this frolicking is done as an object of her own attention. She is trying to give herself an image of herself as carefree, natural, spontaneous, happy. The awareness of the convolutedness of her own self-expression produces a sense of horror at herself. She may be filled with a sense that she doesn't even exist at all, but is possessed—not possessed by some demon that is truly outside herself, but possessed by a grotesque multiplicity of needs and fears that on the one hand is herself and yet is something utterly foreign. This is unlike the previous case in that it need involve no conflict with a value; the motives from which it arises may be acceptable, but not its way of emerging.

As I have stressed, the forms of integration that exist between the self and the activity vary according to the conception of self. But if spontaneous activity is seen as "self-expressive," then the self is conceived as having immediate preferences and direct pleasurings that are reactions to specific features of the immediate present, in particular, a responsiveness to aesthetic contact of all kinds. Thus, in the playing in the leaves example, the problem is not that the individual's actions lacked integration with her wants and beliefs. Nor is the problem that tossing leaves must in itself be done in a carefree manner. Nor even that one cannot for good reason put on a carefree manner in tossing the leaves. But rather the problem is that the complex motivational structure of the action was itself hidden, and that its being hidden was a necessary feature of the successful completion of the project of giving to oneself the image of someone who acts intensely without a complex motivation. It is *the staggering fullness* of this project that is so overwhelming; it suggests the complete infiltration of one's being by such motivations, and the complete absence of anything that is one's own because of simple delight.

The goals of the individual, which are the object of his or her schemes, may themselves be acceptable. But they are expected to operate within a restricted sphere. Insofar as it is discovered that *they penetrate into everything,* we may correctly experience ourselves as inhabited. And this may be so *even if we are inhabited by values or desires of which we approve and with which we identify.* Thus no simple formulation of the criteria of ownership will suffice.

What is this thing that is me, yet inhabits me, this me that is not me? This type of situation may be grasped in terms of person/self ambiguity. And we may even apply this to the cases where we are inhabited by desires and values that we approve of. Still they remain different from the self because they are wired—integrated—in ways that conflict with that of the self.

As inquiry into oneself proceeds, the discovery of *more* integration than one ever imagined, of kinds of integration that one did not suspect, or of integration to elements that clash with one's values, may abolish the experience of the alienness of a *specific* action, only to replace it with the feeling that one's self does not exist at all. When the action is experienced as an isolated occurrence, there is the sense that the self exists over against it. When the same action is shown to be connected to all sorts of things in all sorts of ways, the individual may experience a radical reversal. Instead of being on firm ice and watching a small piece drift off, one comes to realize that one is the small piece and the glacier has slipped away.

Yet, from the position of almost any conception of self, to identify oneself in this manner cannot be correct. An individual who experiences his entire self as alien is someone who cannot accept who he really is. Given the clash between the individual's standards and what he is actually like, we may regard his refusal to recognize himself as understandable, but it cannot be correct. After all, if we have an articulated value on the one side and an entire unified (but perhaps ugly) complex on the other, surely it is the value that is not part of the self. Any concept of self that identified the self with the fragment, the individual's sense of self, or ego-identity, would come close to totally eliminating the possibility of self-deception with respect to what is or isn't part of one's self.

However, in theory building, in constructing a conception of self, the relevant question is: What would be the point of developing a concept of the self that identified the real self in terms of this isolated fragment? The answer may be this: The identification of oneself with the single fragment that is not integrated may itself be *the only healthy or moral act the person is capable of.* If this is true, the moral and therapeutic dimensions of concept formation may outweigh the scientific (predictive), and thus we may attribute to this isolated and weak effort at self-definition the dignity of being correct.

There is a dynamic import to first- and third-person judgments about who or what someone really is. One aspect of this it that in a self-characterization that appears to conflict with an individual's past, she is laying some sort of claim with respect to how she will act and experience in the future. This is not typically a matter of forming an intention to act differently in the future (e.g., an intention to change), but rather the laying of a claim that one is, is presently, such that one would act and feel in the appropriate ways under the relevant circumstances. The issue of whether or not the person is correct cannot be answered except in relation to some criterion for the valid attribution of the relevant character traits. But in choosing between alternative concepts, one of the merits of expanding the extent to which the individual may be correct (i.e., may escape from her past and make semi-authoritative pronouncements about who she is) is that such pronouncements themselves play a significant causal role in bringing about the changes in question. There is a tremendously fine line between self-deception that functions to allow the individual to remain static and self-affirmations that play a role in processes of transformation. Similarly, third-person perspectives on who someone really is can have a powerful impact on whether or not a person remains the same or undergos some degree of change. Thus it is that young people on the way to becoming who they are find it necessary to escape from their family and friends and sometimes even from their culture. To stay at home during a process of rapid reorganization of the self is to be subject to the third-person perception of oneself as "phony." This judgment of phoniness, this discerning look of the other, is the other's most powerful judgment as he arrogates to himself an authoritative stance with respect to one's true being.

Lurking behind the general antipathy to developing concepts that organize the data in such a way as to allow a person to be correct when he retreats to a tiny fragment of his being, is the feeling that this would entail a breakdown of responsibility. If the actions aren't his, then he can't justly be held responsible for them. Indeed, if the entire self may be alien, then when is someone ever implicated by what he does?

If we accept the individual's claim to be who he thinks he is, then how will he ever learn responsibility? Thus, it is felt that acceptance of real guilt may be a necessary stage in the therapeutic process. Fingarette writes:

> The patient in therapy, therefore, must come to see, to experience, to acknowledge with the full vividness of complete and immediate reality his identity with these hitherto unacknowledged, unconscious sub-selves. He must consciously realize the extent to which it is, for example, indeed he who, at least with a part of himself, wants to evade responsibility and to be a child, to be loved as a child, or for example, that it is he who harbors within him murderous impulses toward his father. . . .
>
> There is a relief which the patient may legitimately enjoy subsequently; but it has a different source. Suppose the patient accepts the guilt and follows this by achieving insight into the motives which engender the guilt; then, at last, the patient may be able decisively to influence those motives. Having rejected or transformed those motives, he may feel relieved of his burden of guilt.[9]

This is a significant outlook and worthy of serious attention and inquiry into the actual effects of such processes. However, it must be remembered that when we are dealing with alienness as opposed to self-deception; the individual does recognize the meanings of his conduct, emotions, feelings. What he doesn't do is *identify himself in terms of these meanings*.

Moreover, the responsibility issue should not be pushed too far. Insofar as we are dealing with a sense of the alienness of the entire self, it should not be *assumed* that individual change is a possibility. The individual may at one particular moment have a flash of insight as she perceives and rejects the total complex that she is. She may see that she is dealing with a complete and unified personality and not a mere fragment, and she may see that the person that she is is itself the product of a culture or society that is deeply flawed. For instance, for a brief moment, late in life, she may recognize herself as the totally formed and integrated product of a racist, sexist, and avaricious culture. And in that moment, she may say, "That is not me. I never came into existence. I lived and will die, without even having really existed as myself." It may not be possible for her to change, nor reasonable for her to feel responsible for herself. The alternative to individual responsibility may be *social* responsibility rather than *no* responsibility. Responsibility for oneself may be a historical product to be attained socially and not necessarily available at any point in history; it may be hubris to view oneself otherwise.

This links back to what Parfit said about the question of whether or not a person has survived in certain hard fictionalized cases (e.g., when a person divides). For Parfit the question of survival—of whether or not it is the same person—is an empty question. And so it may be in the case of self-deception, for the question of whether the individual is in self-deception depends upon whether there is anything to deceive himself about. Parfit's answer in the case where there is a lack of continuity is that once we know all of the facts, there is no additional fact to know. So the person we see as a self-deceiver must be seen to be making a decision. What kind of a decision is it? And what kind of a decision are we making when we call him a self-deceiver? These are the interesting questions, and I argue that it all depends on the context. It might be the case that his refusal to view himself as himself is an authentic act of freedom or it might be an effort to deny the implications of what he has been. To know this we would have to know the context. There is no general rule.

Parfit, I noted, argued that in making those choices one was expressing a view about what matters, and that in rationally making those choices one was expressing a rational view about what matters. But matters to whom? Parfit treats it as impersonal. He implicitly assumes that the rationality of what matters does not depend on who is involved. Most of his examples, however, are about personal survival and mostly they involve the first person. But he does not seem to consider that what matters to me about my survival may be different from what matter for another about my survival, and that the issue is not one that can be settled from the first person. If Parfit is correct about the logic of these situations, then there may be two very different descriptions about whether a person has survived and they may both be defensible as expressing for different speakers a rational view of what matters. And it may be that this is exactly analogous to the case of self-deception. Not only are there no additional facts to be known, but the choice of how to characterize the situation may be very different from the first- and third-person points of view—and thus there is a permanent tension about who we really are.

8

Alienness and Authentic Political Engagement

The term "political engagement" is meant to contrast with everyday life. Even in everyday life our own actions may emerge as deeply unintelligible to us, but when this occurs it is something of a shock. The presumption of everyday life is that people know who they are, they know what they are doing, and they know why they are doing it. When we are engaged in the everyday we take it as a given that we are among those people.

Most people go through life without deep political engagement. To be politically engaged is not only to be involved in a project whose centrally motivating consequences typically involve very long time frames and very large numbers of other people; to be politically engaged is to have a significant part of one's self-identity derived from one's engagement in such a project. Not all who carry out acts of political magnitude can be thought of as politically engaged. For instance, the bureaucrat who works in the counter-insurgency division of the war ministry may merely see himself as a civil servant, or as a good family man holding down a secure, well-paying position. Making a revolution is a paradigmatically political project. Revolutionaries are not typically people who are making revolutions in addition to the many other things they do; they are individuals whose self-identity is rooted in their project.

As extreme situations, revolutions throw the individual into contexts devoid of the relative certainties of the everyday. In *Henry IV: Part 2*, Shakespeare tells of revolution, of the problems of action, and of people with very different dispositions to act. Consider the following passage in which the Earl of Northumberland, whose son Hotspur died in insurrection, is told that a new army has arisen to fight against the king:

> The gentle Archbishop of York is up,
> With well-appointed powers: he is a man
> Who with a double surety binds his followers.
> My lord your son had only but the corpse',
> But shadows and shows of men to fight;
> For that same word, rebellion, did divide
> The action of their bodies from their souls
> And they did fight with queasiness, constrain'd,
> As men drink potions, that their weapons only
> Seem'd on our side: but, for their spirits and souls,
> This word, rebellion, it had froze them up,
> As fish are in a pond. But now the bishop
> Turns insurrection to religion:
> Suppos'd sincere and holy in his thoughts,
> He's follow'd both with body and with mind.[1]

Here Shakespeare articulates the problem of alienation in political action: how to prevent the division of "the action of their bodies from their souls." In this case the division is brought about by "that . . . word, rebellion," and the alienation of the soldiers from their own actions is overcome by turning "insurrection to religion." This transformation is said to resolve the internal conflict: no longer do the soldiers hold back; they no longer believe that they are acting wrongly. Thus the great power of revolutionary religious figures.

In *Man's Fate*,[2] his account of the Chinese Revolution, Malraux calls attention to a second problem of alienation within political action.

Kyo could not free himself from that reverberation of machines transmitted by the soil to his muscles—as if those machines for manufacturing truth were encountering, within himself, Vologin's hesitations and affirmations. During his journey up the river he had constantly felt how poorly informed he really was, how difficult it was for him to get a solid basis for his activity if he no longer consented purely and simply to obey the instructions of the international. . . .

"It's not knowing . . ." said the latter, "if it's a question of killing Chiang Kai-shek, I know. As for this fellow Vologin, it's all the same to him I guess; but for him, instead of murder, it's obedience. For people who live as we do there must be a certainty. For him carrying out orders is sure, I suppose, as killing is for me. Something must be sure. Must be.[3]

Here there is no internal moral conflict; Kyo is not someone who turns with revulsion at the prospect of killing another person. His problem is to know that what he is doing makes sense; he seeks certainty in a situation filled with the inevitable ignorance of the actual consequences of actions. Here Kyo struggles with his realization of "how poorly informed he really was" and how he lacked "a solid basis for his activity." Kyo, unable to simply rely upon the Party as a way of bridging this separation of act and consequence, turns toward some other "solution."

In each of these cases there is the threat of some fundamental lack of integrations between the activity and the self. The first is a conflict between the individual's values and the actions he is called upon to undertake. The second is an absence of an adequately known tissue of means–ends connections linking the individual's actions to his ultimate objectives. These disjunctions are not unique to political activity. If political activity on a grand scale has a unique characteristic it is the combination of its structural tendency to produce alienation and the absence of experienced alienness. The question is not so much one of why one might be alienated from one's own activity, but rather "How is it that alienness is not the general experience of the political agent?"

It is interesting to note that the two literary passages we cited, in the very breath that they identify the problem also go on to identify a solution that has been found. The appeal to the bishop as moral authority represents a "solution" to the conflict of values. Where the problem resides in the absence of visible means–ends connections a different authority may be called into play; the Party may emerge as the tactical authority, as the decision maker that knows what needs knowing. Where this is no longer viable, as in the case of Kyo, some other solution is sought. Kyo finds it, paradoxically enough, in killing. Here at least he is in direct contact with a "rationalizing" outcome. There is at least something tangible that is being accomplished.

Of course, these "solutions" do not really achieve integration. Despite the moral sanction of the church, the conflict between means and ends remains. Despite the appeal of "direct action," the problem of eventual consequences has to be faced. They serve as internal expedients, almost like the pontoon bridges that are thrown up so that soldiers can quickly move across the river to engage in the next battle.

In this chapter I will explore the dynamic of alienation within political engagement. It cannot be understood without focusing on political identity, on what is often termed "being political." This is not primarily a matter of action, but of self and self-experience.

ENGAGEMENT AND ALIENATION

Political engagement implies a self-identity that is rooted in political activity. This is not something that is chosen. Rather political activity has a tendency to compel this locus of self-identity upon its participants. There is a process whereby a person becomes politicized, by which I mean much more than merely becoming concerned or involved in social issues. It is a process whereby the individual comes to define himself or herself and others in terms of the political project. Politicization is not something that one does to oneself; it is something that happens to one. How and why it happens is worth considering.

There are different ways in which a person might come to have a certain self-identity. Some of the major features of our identity structures are the result of actions that we take. One might decide to join a particular religious denomination or to attend a particular college or to engage in a certain line of employment. In virtue of that choice one takes on a particular property; one is a Presbyterian or a Cornell student or a nurse. These properties may or may not play a major role in one's identity structure. And it may be that only over time and without one's being aware of it, they do come to play a role such that "being a nurse" or "being a Cornell student" becomes a central part of the individual's self-identity. But there still remains a major element of choice in that one can break that identification by leaving the organization, or by taking a different job.

Moreover, it is often the case that from the third-person point of view we do not view any of these properties as inherently identity giving. Often enough we so totally leave it up to the individual to choose his own identity that the distinction between self-identity and identity is conflated. His identity is merely the self-identity he has.

Yet sometimes it is rather different. Sometimes there is something so important about someone, be it oneself or another, that that feature defines who he is whether he accepts it or not, even whether he knows it or not. As was noted earlier, in literature there is the classic format in which the true identity of the protagonist is known to the reader or audience and the drama involves his coming to discover who he is and the implications of that fact. We find this motif in Oedipus, in the story of Moses, in the tale of King Arthur, and numerous fairy tales of princes and paupers.

In these situations it is never a matter of some incidental fact that is unknown to the individual. Rather it is a fact of such overwhelming import that it imposes itself on the individual. The mere discovery of it is instantaneously transformative or crisis generating. In literature it is the perspective of the author that affirms that these facts are of such overwhelming importance. But this author's perspective emerges from a social life that views certain properties as carrying with them enormous rights and duties and is the basis for a status of inferiority or superiority.

Involvement in deeds of enormous magnitude have this same characteristic. One cannot be the person who flew the plane that dropped the atomic bomb on Japan and merely be that person. One cannot be the man who assassinated President Lincoln and have that be merely one of many characteristics about oneself. Occasionally we find an individual who does treat such a fact about himself or herself as an incidental fact, but this is a matter of his or her self-identity. Our response to such a self-identity is that it is the result of a project of denial. He or she is a person running from themselves, denying their heritage, trying to escape from themself. In short, we sometimes view people as having an objective identity that is imposed by a self-defining reality.

Because political activity involves the individual in action on a grand scale it has a tendency to confer an objective identity. And because the individual herself participates within the social world that views political activity in this way, it also has a tendency to generate the self-identity of the political agent. Thus political activity gives rise to political engagement. The activity comes to construct the self that is expressed through it. It has an inherent power to become self-actualizing. Thus it can have a hypnotizing force on the individual, both calling her into being and expressing that being within the same process. And the more important the role of the individual, the stronger is this power.

While this is a general feature of all action on a political scale, in the modern period this inherent power of political activity—its power to engage the actor, to make an agent out of her—was dramatically raised in intensity through the lens of Hegel and Marx.

MARX, HEGEL, AND HISTORICAL IDENTITY

I shall try to set the stage for discussing various modes of political engagement by considering the relation of self-actualization to political activity that is inherent in Marx's politicization of Hegel. However, not even in Marx's early writings is this matter discussed directly, and one may wonder if Marx himself ever explicitly formulated this aspect of his general outlook. What I am discussing then is not Marx, and not even necessarily Marxism, but rather a certain way of viewing history and politics that emerged most strongly in Marxism. It stands, however, distinct from Marxism and does not rise or fall with beliefs that were specific to Marx.

From our ordinary perspectives, history is about human beings and the conditions of their existence, either individually or in groups. It is about the things that human beings do and the events that happen to human beings. Most early historical writing was political history, accounts of the most momentous acts and calamities that befell the powerful figures around whom history centered. Today much historical writing concerns economic and social conditions, but like political history, the ultimate subject in human life.

Hegel offers a radically different perspective. For Hegel, history is not really about human beings at all. Of course, historical study takes as its object that which happens to human beings, their groups and institutions, but the goings on of humans are not of significance in themselves. They take on significance because they embody something more fundamental: Spirit, Mind or Consciousness. History is reconceived as the study of the self-creation and self-actualization of Spirit as it comes to know itself. The great drama is the evolution of Spirit, and only secondarily and derivatively, the evolution of the finite individuals who are the vehicles through which Spirit is expressed.

This may sound less puzzling in a religious idiom. Accordingly, it would be asserted that history is not about humans but about God. Moreover, the notion of God that is involved is not God as a being that exists for all infinity as an all-knowing creator, but rather a pantheistic presence that is within everything. What occurs in history is the evolution of God; history is the story of God's coming to self-consciousness of the fact that he is God. The way a pantheistic God evolves is through the evolution of the world that is his embodiment; particularly, the evolution of human consciousness.

When Spirit comes to know itself, what it comes to know is that it is Spirit in the process of its own self-creation, which is at the same time the creation of the world. It comes to know itself when it discovers that it is the world. The discovery that Spirit makes of itself externalized as the world is for Hegel an epistemological discovery. The world is neither a given that is just there to be observed, understood, and known, nor is it a hidden reality that lies behind a world of appearances, that can never be known. Rather, the world is the externalization of Mind. Thus, in the end, Spirit comes to self-actualization through an epistemological self-understanding that destroys the subject–object distinction.

To put forward an account of this sort is in some way like writing a piece of literature within which all the characters are defined by their place within the story. The Hegelian perspective, because it presents itself as a perspective that for the first time has penetrated the most fundamental realities of all being—of humans, of God, of existence—is a perspective that cannot merely be accepted and set on the shelf. A Hegelian vision of the nature of existence is not one of many beliefs that one has. It is an overriding story that reveals the true identity of all that occurs within it.

What is the nature of self-experience for the individual who perceives history in Hegelian terms? As individuals we are meaningful as part of a greater Totality—a Totality that is itself moving from potentiality to actuality. If this is our meaning, then our most essential expression of self consists in our participation in this project of the world. Our personal potentials represent highly restricted aspects of human potential. Moreover, as individuals living in a particular stage of the evolution of Spirit, we know that our humanness is itself something undergoing transformation, and that our personal potential will be transcended by the fuller potential of those whose being expresses a more fully developed stage in the life of Spirit.

A particular individual can only achieve self-actualization in virtue of the accident of living at the end of history. This is not the end of physical time, but is the end of the story of Spirit's self-actualization. What self-actualizaton is possible for those of us not embodying the final stage of Spirit is that which comes through an identification of oneself as the embodiment of Spirit, and thus the discovery of oneself in the historical creation of Spirit by Spirit. On Hegel's view, it is he, Hegel, who is the first individual to fully achieve self-actualization, for it is through him that Spirit comes to know itself.

With Marx we have the "existentialization" of Hegel. Human existence is once again placed at the center. History, instead of being the story of Spirit's self-actualization through its embodiment in human culture, is the story of humanity's self-actualization. Alternatively, we may say that history is the story of the self-creation and the self-actualization of the human personality, by human beings, through the discovery that it is the human personality that makes history. The discovery of humankind as the agent of its own creation is a two-pronged discovery. In the first instance it is empirical. It is a theory of culture, and of ideology; it is the recognition of the primacy of changes in the forces of production as the cause of the evolution of human personality or personhood. This social personality is the embodiment of the dominant ideology. In the structures of beliefs, values, self-identities, hopes, perceptions, and needs of human beings, the ideology of any given period is concretely embodied. On the other hand, this discovery of the importance of economic factors is rendered a self-creation of humans by humans through a second insight that parallels Spirit's epistemological discovery that the world is the externalization of Spirit. This is the recognition that the economic relations underlying cultural development are not themselves external forces that act upon humankind, but are themselves the externalization of human reality. To think of history as governed by economic laws that are outside of humanity and act upon it, is what Marx called "the fetishism of commodities."⁴ But whereas in Hegel the discovery that the world is the externalization of Spirit constitutes Spirit's self-actualization, for Marx it merely sets the stage.

One cannot achieve freedom by identifying oneself with the forces that shape one, even if those forces are an expression of the collective nature of humanity. What is necessary is to *actually gain control* over the processes whereby human beings are created. This cannot be achieved by epistemological insight. On the contrary, it is itself an historical outcome that will be brought about through self-conscious *political activity*. This political activity is self-conscious in that it recognizes itself within, and is based upon, an understanding of the historical process. Thus, in Marx as in Hegel, the self-actualization of the individual is only possible at the final stage in the development of the human personality. For Marx, it is political activity based on self-understanding that brings us towards this final stage; for Hegel full self-understanding is the final stage itself.

Of course, any individual can, at any point in history, experience himself or herself as self-actualized. But this feeling is had at the expense of understanding who one is. For Marx, selfhood is achieved only when the full range of human potentialities and needs are developed and expressed. Full self-actualization involves the expression through action of the fully developed personality. The primary locus of one's actions is one's labor within the existing economic relations of one's era. So long as these relations remain unchanged, there exist no forms for the expression through action of humankind's highest potentialities. So long as one suffers from the fetishism of commodities, one fails to understand that the limitation on the range of possible human actions is societally imposed, and one may erroneously imagine that expressing what is highest in humanity can be done merely through right conduct, personal choice, and virtue.

Those who have a sense of self-actualization during transitional historical phases are blind in a second respect. In our terms, these individuals have mistaken their persons (the person they find themselves to be) for their selves. They have identified with what is accidental and arbitrary and will be overcome in the course of historical development. They are out of touch with that which is most essentially themselves. Even if we restrict ourselves to the private sphere, what is actualized is not the human self but the historically given person. In terms of our earlier discussion of the self as the integrated personality, we can say that in a Marxist view of the self, integration of the personality is only a necessary condition of selfhood. Selfhood, or the fully human self, is an historical product that can be understood as an integrated personality with certain specific component values, beliefs, perceptions, and notions of self-identity. These components, in general, are historical products. The existing personality types at any given point in time are a function of the forms of activity (i.e., the economic structures) of the particular age and the place of the individual within that structure. Thus, our personality, including the existing level of needs that govern our subjective sense of self-actualization, is itself a social product, and most typically a deficient one.

The person that we are, with our particular self-identity, is what is to be overcome. Thus, it is from the concrete minutia of what we are like that *we should be alienated*. For instance, our conceptions of worth, or of beauty, our values and desires that determine the things that give us pleasure, or a sense of triumph, pride or achievement—all these are corrupt. They all partake in the ideological structure of an oppressive social order. For instance, one takes pleasure and pride in those aspects of oneself that allow one to dominate others in various competitions: the competition for wealth, for status, for the better forms of work, for the most sought after members of the opposite sex. When seen properly, these aspects of one's personality are seen to be expressions of the total social order with its inherent class structures, its necessary scarcities (e.g., the means of life) and its artificial scarcities (e.g., scarcity of self-esteem and social recognition). In terms of our earlier discussion, the analyses of Marxism may be treated as alienness-causing beliefs that give us reasons to reperceive much that constitutes our self-identity. On a psychological level, moreover, they reveal that for many individuals there is a conflict between their moral views and self-image on the one hand and the specific realities of their personalities on the other. Thus, even the prima facie integration of the personality is shown to be erroneous. Typically, within even highly integrated personalities there are hidden contradictions—hidden, because only social analyses can reveal the nature of the elements.

Given this, one cannot throw oneself into projects that might be satisfying because one cannot identify with those aspects of one's personality that would thereby be satisfied. For instance, one cannot simply join the competitive dynamic of contemporary life; neither the qualities that allow one to succeed nor the pleasure one takes in the fruits of success is truly one's own. Thus, there is engendered an experience of the alienness of most of what we might have otherwise taken as reflecting our truest self: our desires, our tastes, our views and values. In ordinary terms, the Marxist is not at one with himself or herself. If he or she is fully aware of this inner discord, this inner contradiction, then central aspects of the person are experienced as non-self.

This experience of aspects of oneself as alien is not uncommon amongst thorough-going critics of any cultural order. However, the reaction to the political critique of personality is often a form of individual omnipotence-fantasy in which the individual believes that *he* is capable of radically transforming himself as an individual *irrespective* of the social order. In part, this split with a Marxist perspective arises from non-Marxist beliefs about the possibilities of personality change. But beyond this there is a non-Marxist perception of personality. Personality is viewed as something to be found in and only in localized interpersonal relations. But Marx's basic point is that interpersonal relations are not localized. One's personality or nature is historically fixed in the main because one's relations with others are fixed and *expressed* through economic relations. This is not primarily a matter of a causal relation between the economic forms and the nature of human beings in a given historic period. The economic form *is* the form of humanity in disguise.

The tendency to see the economic realm as a neutral universe within which the issues of character, of personality, of virtue, vice, identity, and spirituality are not revealed is itself an historical product that emerged only in the eighteenth century. Marx thus reaffirms in secular-historical terms an orientation towards the economic sphere that was present both in the Middle Ages and the Reformation.

Non-Marxist self-experience emerges in various forms. Those who experience themselves as existing in opposition to the present totality tend to experience themselves as outside of that totality. Thus, most social critics tend to be alienated from the society, experiencing *estrangement* rather than *shame* for a totality of which one is a part. But from a Marxist perspective, the identification of self as magically outside the totality represents a flight of romanticism, a fantasy of individual transcendence that cannot be achieved. Thus, while we are all fated to not be self-actualized within the existing social world, one who sees history as Marx did knows this is her fate, and that she cannot get beyond this realization. No leap to a different social order, to a utopia, personal or social, is possible.

Thus, the politicization of Hegel brings a new form of loss. It is the loss of one who discovers that he or she is not to be. It is the discovery that not only will one always remain in potential, but that one will be in conflict with one's potential, always tending to be something incompatible with it. This is so because one is inevitably a part of one's historical epoch. The concrete meaning of this is (a) one is one's social activity, (b) one's social activity is given to one, and (c) one can't find in any given historical period the social activity that belongs to another period. In short, there is nothing to do that would count as self-actualizing activity. Yet one has a self-identity that recognizes one's true self in one's necessarily unexpressed and undeveloped potentialities.

Insofar as there is any role that escapes from this, it is that of the revolutionary who knows herself. She lives in opposition to a world that is inside of her as well as outside. She is one whose self-identity consists in part in the fact that she knows that she is and must be alien to herself. More generally, the only life that to some extent escapes from this trap is that of the individual whose social activity participates in the process of the conscious creation of the human self on a social scale. Only through such activity does one gain an objective identity that is unified with those aspects of the historic person that remain as it becomes the human self. That is, only through such activity does subjective self-identity merge with objective identity. Marxism thus gives rise to a self-identity that understands itself in terms of the role it will actually play in the process of the creation of the human self, and Marxism offers itself as the guiding vehicle through which one attains the complementary objective identity.

Thus, the overwhelming psychological power of Marxism emerges because it stands as the revelatory story of the world, through which one can understand and become oneself. It retains the Hegelian conception of history as a movement towards self-actualization, but it is the self-actualization of human beings, not Spirit. In relation to this ideal and account of the human past, the meaning of individual and social reality may be discerned. That is, the relationship of events, persons, and structures to this process is experienced as their "real meaning." Thus, at one and the same time, Marxism lifts political activity to the level of vehicle for individual and historical self-actualization, and destroys all alternative conceptions of self-actualization.

The politicization of Hegel results then in not only giving to political activity unique powers as a realm of self-actualization, but it gives to *political analysis* a unique power of *revealing true identity*, and it strips away from the self many of the elements of the personality that might otherwise constitute the features of self-identity around which an active life would coalesce. Thus political activity emerges as political engagement and this engagement becomes total, subsuming all else within it.

The outcome then is an incredible tension. On the one hand, political activity becomes the locus of all that is meaningful. On the other hand, political activity is not an ideal locus for self-expression. More often than not, people are apt to feel out of touch with themselves and in danger of losing themselves in such activity. As we noted at the outset, the great problems are those of moral conflict and the unintelligibility of one's own action. Only if action is integrated with our values and beliefs can action be expressive of the self; yet because of the realities with which one deals, this contact is difficult to establish. Appeals to moral and/or tactical authorities represent attempted solutions. Where these are seen as inadequate, "direct action," whether of a violent or a humanitarian sort, has its appeal. Yet, this too is inadequate.

THREE MODES OF POLITICAL ENGAGEMENT

It is possible to distinguish three distinct modes of political engagement. They represent more than three different styles of action; each of them represents a different way of dealing with the problem of self-identity and potential alienation. The three types are (1) objectivist engagement, (2) integral engagement, and (3) rationalist engagement. I have identified each of these forms of political engagement with an historic figure, respectively, Trotsky, Gandhi, and Bentham.

Let me begin with objectivist engagement. The core of the objectivist outlook is that one's identity is determined by the actual role that one plays, not by the consequences one intends or the values one holds dear.

Leon Trotsky, maker of the Russian Revolution, is history's most dramatic and outspoken objectivist. I will use Trotsky as the exemplar of this mode of engagement, but it should be understood that this perspective is not unique to either Trotsky or Marxism.

For Trotsky the most important facts about a person bear on his or her role in the processes of historical development and class struggle. In terms of our notion of identity, the Trotskyite would say that "being bourgeois" or "being counter-revolutionary" or "being revolutionary" are part of the objective identity of those who are bourgeois, counter-revolutionary, or revolutionary. These are designations that do not depend on the individual's own view of himself (i.e., his self-identity). They are a matter of objective identity, of who someone really is irrespective of who he thinks he is or how he identifies himself. The criteria for their application specify a particular social role. Merely having certain views, intentions, and attitudes does not suffice to determine which of these identity-defining designations applies.

Thus, one is always in danger of not knowing who one is, not in the sense of lacking a self-identity, but in that one may be attributing to oneself an identity (social role) that one does not have. One may fancy oneself a revolutionary and actually be a counter-revolutionary. To be in this kind of error, where one's subjective self-identity does not accord with one's objective identity, because of political ignorance, is indeed a pathetic fate. The most damaging criticism one can make of someone or some group that regards itself as revolutionary is to maintain that it is *really* counter-revolutionary, or an unwitting lackey of the bourgeoisie, or an oppressor of the proletariat. Such "insights" are supposed to come from objective social analysis. What should be recognized is that the familiar judgments of an agent's character are suspended, because from within an objectivist engagement, character traits are not themselves central aspects of an individual's identity.

This stress on actual consequences is reflected in how the objectivist deals with the issue of justifying abhorrent means. Consider the following passage from Trotsky's essay, "Their Morals and Ours."

A means can be justified only by its end. But the end in turn needs to be justified. From the Marxist point of view, which expresses the historical interests of the proletariat, the end is justified if it leads to increasing the power of man over nature, and to the abolition of the power of man over man.

"We are to understand then that in achieving this end anything is permissible?" sarcastically demands the Philistine, demonstrating that he understands nothing. That is permissible, we answer, which *really* leads to the liberation of mankind. . . . It deduces a rule for conduct from the laws of the development of society, thus primarily from the class struggle, this law of all laws.

"Just the same," the moralist continues to insist, "does it mean that in the class struggle against capitalists all means are permissible: lying, frame-up, betrayal, murder and so on?" Permissible and obligatory are those and only those means, we answer, which unite the revolutionary proletariat. . . . Precisely from this it follows that *not* all means are permissible. When we say that the end justifies the means, then for us the conclusion follows that the great revolutionary end spurns those base means and ways which set one part of the working class against other parts. . . .

These criteria do not, of course, give a ready answer to the question as to what is permissible and what is not permissible in each separate case. There can be no such automatic answers. . . .

Is individual terror, for example, permissible or impermissible from the point of view of "pure morals"? In this abstract form the question does not exist at all for us. . . . Our relation to the assassin remains neutral only because we know not what motives guided him. If it became known that Nikolayev acted as a conscious avenger for workers' rights . . . our sympathies would be fully on the side of the assassin. However, not the question of subjective motives, but that of *objective* expediency has for us the decisive significance. Are the means really capable of leading to the goal?[5]

When one performs an act that one views as abhorrent, one is in some degree of conflict with one's values. For Trotsky this conflict can be overcome if the means are justified in terms of overriding ends. Such a predisposition to conflict elimination may seem a necessary feature for any programmatic politics. To insist upon more integration than this is to allow historical realities to render one impotent. Given the nature of the world, one cannot be politically significant and at the same time more coherent than this. To seek a greater degree of unity is a matter of self-indulgence.

This view seems to have been held quite self-consciously by Trotsky.

In his "Moralists and Sycophants Against Marxism," he lashes out at those who would propose a code of conduct for the revolution.

> However, so long as this code remains unaccepted as a rule of conduct by all the oppressors and the oppressed, the warring classes will seek to gain victory *by every means*, while petty-bourgeois moralists will continue as heretofore to wander in confusion between the two camps. Subjectively, they sympathize with the oppressed—no one doubts that. Objectively, they remain captives of the morality of the ruling class and seek to impose it upon the oppressed instead of helping them to elaborate the morality of insurrection. . . .
>
> They openly demanded a *return* to Kant . . . if their ideas are plumbed to the bottom, it appears that they have joined an old cause, long since discredited: to subdue Marxism by means of Kantianism; to paralyze the socialist revolution by means of "absolute" norms which represent in reality the philosophical generalizations of the bourgeoisie. . . .
>
> Civilization can be saved only by the socialist revolution. To accomplish the overturn, the proletariat needs all its strength, all it resolution, all its audacity, passion and ruthlessness. Above all it must be completely free from the fictions of religion, "democracy" and transcendental morality— the spiritual chains forged by the enemy to tame and enslave it. Only that which prepares the complete and final overthrow of imperialist bestiality is moral, and nothing else. The welfare of the revolution—that is the supreme law!
>
> A clear understanding of the interrelation between the two basic classes—the bourgeoisie and the proletariat in the epoch of their mortal combat—discloses to us the objective meaning of the role of petty-bourgeois moralists. Their chief trait is impotence.[6]

In this remarkable passage, Trotsky has not only argued the necessity of ignoring moral strictures, he has provided the individual with a way of perceiving herself that will minimize the sense of moral conflict caused by her actions. One's moral inhibitions, and the sense that to act contrary to one's moral strictures is to act contrary to one's self, are the inroads that the defenders of the social order have made into one's person. The very notion of oneself that identifies self in terms of these moral values is a factor in the class struggle. The proletariat must free itself from "the spiritual chains forged by the enemy to enslave it." Thus, the inner conflict and the potentially paralyzing alienness that lies behind the "means and ends" debate are subjected to a political analysis. From the perspective of the imperative towards a positive social and historical identity, these moral strictures are themselves subjected to an alienation, an expulsion, from the self-identity.

They are relegated to a bracketed position, a realm where they are mine-but-not-really-mine. They continue to exist, but now they are disconnected elements, not fully belonging to the self. Thus, the potential for experiencing one's actions as alien is avoided through a political analysis that establishes a new alienness, not now of the actions but of the moral strictures. By means of this form of analysis there is a relocation of one's sense of what is self and not-self. The therapy for paralysis is the objective understanding of its causes and functions.

What is involved here are second-order value judgments, value judgments about the values one holds. Trotsky subjects morality itself to the utilitarian standard. Through the adoption of the second-order value perspective, the Trotskian agent reestablishes his linkage with his activity. He does this by essentially estranging himself from those value judgments that tend to "divorce the actions of the body from the soul." For this to be successful, it is not necessary that the individual fully eliminate the inhibiting judgments. Rather, in judging them the individual estranges himself from them; puts them in a bracketed category in which even if they continue to have some emotional force that emotional force is seen as foreign, as not really one's own.

In functioning in this way the objectivist is not urging identification with second-order rather than first-order value judgments. She is not taking a position on where the self resides in a hierarchy of self-reflection. (See the debate between Watson and Frankfurt considered earlier.) Rather what she says is that you are your social or political role. If you make incorrect second-order value judgments, and thus incorrectly judge your first-order values to be supportive of the move-ment to a classless society (or whatever fundamental desiderata the objectivist seeks) and if you act accordingly, the fact that you identify with such objectives even in your second-order value judgments is totally irrelevant. You are determined by the consequences of your actions, not by your identifications, even on the secondary level.

Central to Trotsky's analysis is the empirical claim that by and only by means contrary to moral strictures can the liberation of humanity be achieved. Conceptions of the self and in particular criteria of identity are evaluated in terms of their role in furthering or retarding this historical process.

Trotsky's analysis of the effect of the internalization of moral prin-ciples (i.e., they lead to impotence and retard the liberation of human-ity) serves as an alienating belief. That is, in virtue of coming to hold this belief about one's own values, one comes to view them as not really one's own, but as implants, as subtle means of control that have been foisted upon one as a gigantic trick designed to support the power structure.

Yet this outcome, that the individual who makes such a second-order judgment about his own values will feel alienated from them, is itself not a necessity. It is theoretically possible to reach such a conclusion about the import of one's own values and still embrace them as one's own. In saying this, I am not talking about the situation in which one simply does not care about the liberation of humanity and so is unmoved by having reached such a conclusion about one's values. Rather, it is possible to see one's values as in fact being problematic, and yet to still not feel at a distance from them. The alienation that Trotsky is able to bring off in virtue of his analysis occurs only when there is a prior internalization of the objectivist criterion for identity—that you are your social role.

The rejection of abhorrent means, even when one believes that they are the only way of attaining valuable ends, is at the core of integral engagement. It is well represented by Kierkegaard, though in his case it is not yet *integral politics*, but rather a more general integral engagement with the world. In *Purity of Heart is to Will One Thing*, he writes:

> What means do you use in order to carry out your occupation? Are the means as important to you as the end, wholly as important? Otherwise it is impossible for you to will only one thing, for in that case the irresponsible, the self-seeking, and the heterogeneous means would flow in between in confusing and corrupting fashion. . . . In time and on earth one distinguishes between the two and considers that the end is more important than the means. One thinks that the end is the main thing and demands of one who is striving that he reach the end . . . to gain an end in this fashion is an unholy act of impatience. . . .
>
> If a man sets himself a goal for his endeavor here in this life, and he fails to reach it, then, in the judgment of eternity, it is quite possible that he may be blameless. Yes, he may even be worthy of praise. . . . He might even have been prevented from reaching the goal just by being unwilling to use any other means than those which the judgment of eternity permits. In which case by his very renunciation of the impatience of passion and the inventions of cleverness, he is even worthy of praise. *He is not, therefore, eternally responsible for whether he reaches his goal within this world of time.* . . . To the temporal and earthly passion the end is unconditionally more important than the means. On that very account, it is the passionate one's torment, which if carried to its height must

indeed make him sleepless and then insane, namely, that he has no control over time, and that he continually arrives too late, even if it was by merely half an hour. And what is still worse, since earthly passion is the rule, it can truthfully be said, that it is not wisdom which saves the worst ones from going insane, but indolence. On the other hand, the blessed comfort of the Eternal is like a refreshing sleep, is like "the cold of snow in the time of harvest" to the one who wills the Eternal. He whose means are invariably just as important as the end, never comes too late. Eternity is not curious and impatient as to what the outcome in this world of time will be. It is just because of this that the means are without exception as important as the end. To earthly and worldly passion, this observation must seem shocking and paralyzing. To it conscience must seem the most paralyzing thing of all. For conscience is indeed "a blushing innocent spirit that sets up a tumult in a man's breast and fills him with difficulties."[7] (emphasis mine)

Of course, Kierkegaard would be subjected to a ruthless class analysis and shown to be objectively promoting the interests of the status quo—and such a turning of one's back on "the world of time" would be seen to be in keeping with the general political function of the religious outlook. However, integralism is not restricted to the nonpolitical. As integral *politics*, it seeks the same degree of integration that Kierkegaard does, and situates moral strictures in a central position in the self complex. This integral politics is most closely associated with the name of Gandhi. While we may doubt that the historical Gandhi "lived up to" the Gandhian style, the identification of him with the integral mode is well established.

In understanding integral engagements in political activity, it is important to not deny the conflicts. Thus it is possible to hold the view that only by using tactics that involve no violation of the dignity of the other is it possible to achieve the political objective. But then the conflict with the objectivist is really over who is accurate in his means–ends assessments. The objectivist himself would embrace nonviolence if he were convinced that this was the way to accomplish the end. The sharpest contrast between alternative engagements arises when there is agreement on the consequences. Needless to say, in the real world the waters are often muddied.

Thus, the crucial aspect of integral engagement is not the tactic of nonviolence; rather, it is that nonviolence is not primarily a tactical feature. As a distinctive mode of being political integral engagement is distinguished by the fact that *the factual connections between means and ends simply do not occupy crucial importance*. For a given means to be justified it is not sufficient that it produces the greatest good. Indeed it may not even be necessary that it leads to any worthy end outside itself. Instead *political activity is a necessary vehicle for the emergence and expression of selfhood.* Change may result, but then it may not. The overriding problem is that of how to be oneself in the face of social reality.

Integralism responds to the fact that the social world calls into question one's integrity. "Integrity" is meant quite literally. The wholeness that is constitutive of the self is imperiled by actions one is called upon to perform, or it may be compromised in virtue of one's past actions, or just in virtue of being alive within an unjust social order.

The paradigm of resistance to an action one is called upon to perform is conscientious objection. Luther's phrase, "I can do no other" occupies a central place in the social and legal perception of the conscientious objector. Rather than seeing this as a denial of freedom, or a bowing to external moral forces, the emphasis should be placed upon the "I"—if I did other, I would not be "I." The action in question violates the wholeness of the self; the self could not be the agent of such actions.

Similarly, acts of civil disobedience sometimes serve primarily as public declarations that define the self and limit the extent to which one is implicated by the facts of the world. As such they are direct efforts to preserve wholeness. Of course, Gandhi's activities were not mere matters of testament, but were intended to achieve specific political goals. In *Gandhi's Truth*, Erik Erikson writes:

> Truthful action, for Gandhi, was governed by the readiness to get hurt and yet not to hurt—action governed by the principle of ahimsa. . . . I think Gandhi implied in it, besides a refusal to do physical harm, a determination not to violate another person's essence. . . . Gandhi reminds us that, since we cannot possibly know the absolute truth, we are "therefore not competent to punish. . . ."
>
> And in all this, the resister must be consistently *willing to persuade* and to enlighten, even as he remains ready *to be persuaded and enlightened. He will, then, not insist on obsolete precedent or rigid principle, but will be guided by what under changing conditions will continue or come to feel true to him and his comrades, that is, will become truer through action.* . . .
>
> Gandhi, at one time, urged any individual or authority that was "fasted against" and which considered the fast to be blackmail "to refuse to yield to it even though the refusal may result in the death of the fasting person."[8]

It is clear that the "truth" that Gandhi is concerned with is not the same as that of Trotsky. For Trotsky it is a matter of actually knowing what will occur, as opposed to mere belief without certainty. For Gandhi, "truth" is a matter of "being in the truth"; it describes a state of being of the agent. This includes thoughtfulness, but does not center on factual knowledge. Rather, truth is unity, what we have called integration. Action that is true is action that is fully integrated with all the values and belief of the self. One is the true agent of it.

We must not lose sight of the centrality of personal integration to this mode of political activity. In his autobiography, *The Story of My Experiments With Truth*, Gandhi relates how his endeavor to attain full personal integration led him to vow to observe brahmacharya (sexual abstention) for life. He explains that the "Brahmacharya means control of the senses in thought, word and deed."[9] When it is fully achieved, this control is the peaceful, fluid control of unity rather than effort. In a passage reminiscent of Augustine, he writes, "I have yet to achieve complete mastery over thought, which is so essential. Not that the will or effort is lacking, but it is yet a problem to me wherefrom undesirable thoughts spring their insidious invasions."[10]

He sees his mode of political activity, Satyagraha, as arising out of this renunciation. "I can now see that all the principle events of my life, culminating in the vow of brahmacharya, were secretly preparing me for it."[11]

The integralist mode, then, aims at achieving full integration within political activity. There is to be no pretense in manner, no ideological deception, no false certainty and no conflict between one's values and the means one employs.

Does the integralist escape from the dilemma of political activity: self-actualization is obtainable only through a political life but political life is inherently self-alienating? Consider Trotsky's reflections on Gandhi:

> The Indian bourgeois is incapable of leading a revolutionary struggle. They are closely bound up with and dependent upon British capitalism. They tremble for their own property. They stand in fear of the masses. They seek compromises with the British imperialism no matter what the price; and they lull the Indian masses with hopes of reform from above. The leader and prophet of this bourgeoisie is Gandhi. A fake leader and a false prophet![12]

Putting the ad hominem abuse aside, this critique of Gandhian methods amounts to the claim that regardless of his subjective intentions, the social role of his approach did not promote the interests of the oppressed. Put in a larger perspective, an objectivist might regard the integralist as having suffered the horrifying fate of having acquired, in virtue of his objective role, an identity in direct opposition to that which would have been self-fulfilling. Instead, his real identity, as revealed in his objective social role, is in total conflict with his motives, intentions, and self-identity.

From the objectivist perspective this pathetic outcome is what happens when one insists on full personal integration in the face of historic conditions that do not permit it. It is not that political activity is inherently fractured, but that the degree and kind of unity it can have is dictated by the particular conditions of the historic period.

Moreover, the objectivist can point to fundamental fractures that prevent the integralist from achieving the unity he seeks. This issue does not arise if the means–ends connections are known by the integralist to support his specific behavior. But if they are believed, by the integralist himself, to not do so, then he himself has a higher order assessment of his own behavior and values, and according to this assessment he is either irrelevant to the cause that he is committed to or detrimental to its actual fulfillment. Can the integralist proceed if he reaches this kind of judgment about himself?

One option is to simply bracket these higher order judgments; to do this the integralist might, like Kierkegaard, adopt a skeptical stance towards his own ability to make such judgments. He might say that these are things than mere mortals can never know. But what if the evidence is rather persuasive? The integralist is forced to either deny the persuasive power that his own beliefs lead him to accept, or he must face up to and accept the objectivist's conclusion that (in the most difficult case) he is actually harming the values to which he is committed. And if he accepts this conclusion about his own activity, then that very activity that in one respect emerges from his deepest convictions in another respect must be viewed as alien. But this outcome defeats the entire integralist project. Thus the integralist is under enormous pressure to in fact deny or not think about the empirical claims that the objectivist puts forward.

From this perspective an ironic shift occurs: it is Trotsky, the extremist, who emerges as the political expression of the "well-adjusted" individual, emerging from a political psychotherapy or analysis able to accept his limitations and yet function in the world. (The ability to function being a formal property, equally compatible both with "functioning in accord with the social system" and with "functioning as a revolutionary in opposition to that social system.")

What Trotsky seems to have been able to accept are the limitations that his historicity placed upon him. Thus, he was able to avoid alienness because alienness, as we have seen, is not a simple function of the perceived lack of integration but is also a function of the degree and type of integration demanded by a conception of the self. From a Marxist perspective one might historicize these criteria of self and agency so that a healthy concept of the self and agency does not center on a degree of integration that is historically impossible. In particular, a healthy conception of the self would allow that the self is present in an activity even when the activity was in conflict with the individual's moral outlook, so long as the activity maximized the amount of integration permitted by the historical context and the demands of effective action. Thus, while one would always live with some degree of incompleteness and disunity, one would not experience activities that were integrated to the historically possible maximum as alien. Therefore, feelings of alienness arising from moral conflict inherent in political activity might be grasped as the expressions of regressions to bourgeois and ahistorical conceptions of self, agency, and unity. This, at any rate, is an articulation of an outlook that we find implicit within Trotsky's outlook. And it is a perspective of considerable power and sophistication.

However, even if we accept this way of understanding how to experience conflicts between one's values and one's methods, once one has reached the conclusion that such methods are necessary and that to reject them is itself to play the role of one's own enemy, the objectivist still faces the second incoherence that is inherent in political activity. Can she be reasonably sure of those means–ends connections? Or at some point is she not threatened with the terrifying realization that in fact she really does not know? Why does the objectivist have no sense of her activity as alien, as unintelligible because of the wide gap that separates what she can know from what she must know in order to act at all?

After Trotsky wrote "Their Morals and Ours," the editors of *New International* invited John Dewey to respond. The choice of Dewey was particularly appropriate, as he had just served as chairman of the Commission of Inquiry that had traveled to Mexico to hear Trotsky give testimony in his own defense against the charges of Stalin. These issues of means and ends and foresight took on worldwide significance as not only the Moscow Trials but the murder of Trotsky himself were soon to be defended as necessary means.

In his article "Means and Ends," Dewey agrees with Trotsky that "the end in the sense of consequences provides the only basis for moral ideas and action, and therefore provides the only justification that can be found for means employed."[13] He then goes on to say:

> One would expect, then, that with the idea of the liberation of mankind as the end-in-view, there would be an examination of *all* means that are likely to attain this end, and that every suggested means would be weighed and judged on the express ground of the consequences it is likely to produce.
> But this is *not* the course adopted in Mr. Trotsky's further discussion.[14]

And finally:

> The only conclusion I am able to reach is that in avoiding one kind of absolutism Mr. Trotsky has plunged into another kind of absolutism. There appears to be a curious transfer among orthodox Marxists of allegiance from the ideals of socialism and scientific methods of attaining them (scientific in the sense of being based on the objective relations of means and consequences) to the class struggle as the law of historical change.[15]

The "curious transfer" that Dewey notes, the "shift from one kind of absolutism to another" is what concerns us here. Of course it is possible for Trotsky to maintain that *he* does have adequate knowledge of what the future holds, and thus his actions and manner are appropriate. But surely we must reject this suggestion.

Even in everyday life, it is hard enough to have a good sense of the consequences. In discussing the experience of alienness in its everyday context, this difficulty was seen to yield a bewildering sense of openness. How much more this must be the case when we extend the horizon, when the actions in question affect thousands or millions of people.

Consider for example, the well-worn example of British appeasement of the Nazis at Munich. The effort to avoid war by allowing the Germans to take Czechoslovakia clearly failed. And it has been argued that if the Western powers had intervened militarily that the Germans were prepared to retreat. And on this basis supposedly is erected "an historical lesson." But what lesson is to be found here? What do we really know about what would have happened otherwise? Can we say with any degree of confidence that had there been an allied stand that in the long run it would have been for the better? Is it not equally likely that a stand at that point would have only postponed the German aggression, that the retreat would have only been tactical and that Germany would have continued to expand its strength. Or perhaps that under such conditions, Hitler might have ultimately been less likely to have opened a second front by attacking the Soviet Union before finishing off the Western nations? And if these are open questions, then clearly it is open as to whether or not, even in retrospect, we can do anything but guess at whether it was better or worse from a consequentialist point of view that Hitler was appeased.

So if the knowledge claims of the objectivist cannot be accepted, then there is a different question. Are the practitioners of this mode of political activity not only in error about the extent of their knowledge, but also deluding themselves? And if so, why are they engaged in a manner that is at its core committed to self-deception?

What makes the continued presence of self-deception and coarse ideology in politics so curious, is the seeming availability of an alternative. After all, why not be a well-balanced rationalist?

If objective political engagement is personified by Trotsky, rationalist political engagement is well represented by Bentham. Interestingly, Trotsky himself realized that his focus on objective consequences had a formal similarity to Bentham's principle of utility. Typical of Trotsky, he dismissed these formal similarities with a derisive comment about the bourgeoisie and the irrelevance of formal similarities.

Consider then two alternative versions of a principle of utility:

1. Do that act which has the greatest *expected* utility

2. Do that act which will produce the greatest utility

As similar as these principles may appear, they represent fundamentally different orientations towards political agency. As far as explicit content is concerned, principle (1) identifies the act to be done in terms of available evidence and probable consequences. The decision-making criterion is greatest *expected* utility; the act to be done is the act whose consequences when weighted by the probability of their occurrence emerges as better than any other alternative. Which act satisfies the principle in a given choice situation depends on the evidence that is available to that particular decision maker. Principle (2) focuses only on the actual consequences of the acts. It is concerned with the objective nature of the outcomes rather than with a reasonable assessment of future outcomes.

As I have noted, Trotsky's orientation is more adequately captured by (2). He is concerned with the actual outcomes. Means are justified in terms of their effects. He does not talk about choosing the means that *appear* as if they will have the most desirable effects. Bentham, on the other hand, said, "By the principle of utility is meant that principle which approves or disapproves of every action whatsoever, according to the tendency which it *appears* to have to augment or diminish the happiness of the party whose interest is in question" (emphasis mine).[16]

One might maintain that the only way one could be said to be *trying* to act in accord with (2) is by choosing the act that appears to satisfy it. And thus, one might argue, a devotion to the objectivist principle implies a devotion to the rationalist principle and thus, for the decision maker, it comes down to the same problem—trying to identify that act most likely to produce the greatest good.

But this response errs in two respects. First, the claim that the best way to satisfy the objectivist principle is to satisfy the rationalist principle is an empirical claim that when taken as a generalization applicable to all persons is surely false. For many people, simply following well-established rules or obeying the orders of some particular authority, without making any effort to establish probable utilities, would be the best strategy for actually achieving the most good.

More importantly from the point of view of the dynamics of self-identity/alienation, the two principles are part of a much more fundamental difference. It is a difference with respect to identity; in particular a difference with respect to which characteristics of a person serve to establish who he or she really is.

The rationalist engagement involves a self that is displayed in its reasonableness, balance, and above all else, in *doing one's best*. When one has done one's best one acquits oneself of one's responsibility. The objectivist outlook calls for correctness, period. The emphasis is on the objective outcome rather than upon the decision maker's rationality, responsibility, or intention. This is not to say that the rationalist approach must necessarily be less concerned with what the actual consequences are. It is possible to view the individual as having in addition to an obligation to do that act that has the greatest expected utility a second obligation to pursue with enormous diligence his effort to determine what the likely consequences will be. Yet a deep difference remains. It has to do with how the agent views his or her own identity as determined by having in fact rather than in intent acted in ways that promote the political good to which he or she is devoted.

From the point of view of one's own feelings of agency and alienness, the world is very different for a Bentham than it is for a Trotsky. The rationalist agent, who thinks of himself in terms of what he regards as identity-defining properties (e.g., motives, personality characteristics) has the validity of his self-identity largely in his control. That is, he can be something of the person he sees himself to be, merely by doing his best. He is defined by his motives, his beliefs, his propensity to forethought, his efforts, his character. Under normal circumstances these aspects of the self involve matters with which the agent is well acquainted; thus his identity is something that is known to him, and as is natural, his identity is to a large extent created and maintained by his self-identity. That is, the agent's own understanding of who he is plays a central role in shaping the self in such a way that he is in fact exactly who he thinks he is.

The objectivist, on the other hand, finds her identity always in danger of slipping out of her control. Since her self-identity is composed of the objective social roles she believes herself to play, its validity is maintained only insofar as her politics plays the historical role she imagines it to play. Psychologically this results in a far greater need to know, to actually know, what the consequences will be. Sometimes this need is met by actual knowledge and sometimes by ideologically held beliefs, that is, beliefs that are held with an unwarranted degree of certitude.

Trotsky expressed this vast confidence in his own knowledge and the possibilities of learning when he wrote:

> The "Trotskyists" learned the rhythm of history, that is, the dialectics of the class struggle. They also learned, it seems, and to a certain degree successfully, how to subordinate their subjective plans and programs to this objective rhythm.[17]

Without this certainty there is not enough sense of integration to carry on effective political action, but with it revolutionary political activity can provide whatever self-fulfillment transitional people are capable of. Thus, Trotsky writes:

> They know how to swim against the stream in the deep conviction that the new historic flood will carry them to the other shore. Not all will reach that shore, many will drown. But to participate in this movement

with open eyes and with an intense will—only this can give the highest moral satisfaction to a thinking being![18]

One might point out that the Trotskyite and the Benthamite use very similar criteria in making decisions, but from the Trotskyite standpoint there is a triviality to "formal or psychological similitudes."[19] What is important is being right in fact. "Compared to revolutionary Marxists, the social-democrats and centrists appear like morons, or like quacks beside physicians: they do not think one problem through to the end."[20]

So part of the answer to the question of self-deception within the objectivist engagement is that an objectivist perspective on identity places the individual under enormous strains to believe that he knows the facts. If he accepts the rationalist perspective, if he accepts that all he has are probabilities and maybe weak ones at that, then his own self-identity becomes unglued. To say this is to say that the very fabric of his personality is in danger of being unraveled. Yet if one is driven towards self-deception in virtue of an objectivist orientation, can one instead embrace a rationalist engagement?

First, it should be remembered that the objectivist perspective on identity is not something the objectivist chooses. It is something that is carried implicit in a certain vision of history. It is a world that conforms to the tale of King Arthur: until he withdraws the sword from the stone, young Arthur is not known to himself or to others. But he is always that person who will be king, and once it is known to himself that that is who he is, that is his self-identity. The objectivist perspective on identity, which says that one's role within the story determines who one is, emerges from the power of the story itself.

Second, the rationalist outlook has problems sustaining itself in the context of political activity, however well it may be suited for the terms of everyday life. There is something self-defeating about being merely hopeful yet well aware of the way things may fail. It gives rise to a mode of nonengagement. Out of integration with one's beliefs about the limitations of what one really knows, one holds oneself back. Every action has a tentative quality. It has been chosen only because it seems more likely to lead to desired outcomes than other alternatives. This lack of engagement is itself a factor that enters into the process. Doubts and concerns may themselves prevent success.

This arises most acutely with respect to leadership. If one is only partially committed to a specific line of action, how does one get others to commit themselves? Could one, for instance, raise an army of volunteers on the grounds that *probably* the war will be won and if so, *probably* great good will come of it? The contexts of political activity demand a different manner of engagement.

Furthermore, the psychological viability of Benthamist reasonableness is limited to certain specific contexts. There is a world of difference between the relatively genteel application of Bentham's calculus to questions of legislation and welfare economics and its application to revolution. We should remember what Kierkegaard said, "It is not wisdom which saves the worst ones from going insane, but indolence."[21] Most likely no one ever was an act-utilitarian. If one is consistently and scrupulously act-utilitarian, then one strips away the familiar habitual limits to possible actions, and one breaks through the moral restraints embedded in the perceptions and conducts that govern the everyday world of interpersonal contacts. To do this is to have an explosion of imagination far greater than that of the immoralist of existential literature who announces, "Everything is lawful!" or "Everything is possible!" At least if one is outside the moral order, one is free to indulge desire, and this is limiting, stabilizing, and habitual. The act-utilitarian is inside the moral order and thus outside the realm of desire, and yet outside the realm of moral rules—that is truly dizzying. For him anything is possible and there are no other principles to limit possibility. Each possible action must be appraised individually, according to the specific consequences of performing that particular token. Existential literature notwithstanding, it is utilitarianism, adherence to a decision rule that contains a specific description of the act to be done, which results in a terrifying freedom. Anything may be required! We ward off the impact of this openness to possibility by restricting the range of actions we will consider and the range of consequences we will notice, to those of the everyday. But to do this is to abandon the political.

To apply utilitarianism to the political is to extend one's time span indefinitely, and to extend to the billions the number of persons affected. The range of possible outcomes moves towards the infinite: on the one hand there is the possible destruction of all life, and on the other the final evolution of the human spirit. Applied as best one can, in a world where a given political and economic order means millions of deaths and stunted lives, consequentialism bursts the bounds of decorum. Could it be that Trotsky, who prided himself on thinking things through to the end, was the first serious act-utilitarian?

Consider Trotsky again. His context is not that of the hypothetical introductory-ethics classroom. Yet the problems that he faced are exactly those extreme situations cited in classroom discussion to test the viability of conflicting theories. In the classroom it is possible to finally throw one's hands in the air and say, "I don't know what I would do" or to dismiss the idea that we need an ethics that can handle the most wildly imaginable situations—"What if you are in a strange country and you and your family are taken captive and you are told that unless you kill one of your children, you and all of your children will be tortured and then killed?"

For Trotsky, this is the context he operates in. And perhaps just because he was a political agent and not merely a bureaucrat with the power of a general, he was intensely aware of it. He wrote, "Stalin arrests and shoots the children of his opponents after these opponents have been themselves executed under false accusations."[22] Suddenly he faces the charge, "The detention of innocent relatives by Stalin is disgusting barbarism. But it remains a barbarism as well when it was dictated by Trotsky (1919)."[23] And it is true, Trotsky did order hostages to be taken. How then is he to distinguish himself from Stalin? He writes:

> If the revolution had displayed less superfluous generosity from the beginning, *hundreds of thousands of lives would have been saved.* Thus or otherwise I carry full responsibility for the Decree of 1919. It was a necessary measure in the struggle against oppressors. Only in the historical context of the struggle lies the justification of the decree as in general the justification of the whole civil war which too, can be called, not without foundation "disgusting barbarism."[24]

So the difference between his execution of hostages and that ordered by Stalin is that in his case they were *in fact* justified acts. We must try to experience the magnitudes of the consequences involved. He says, if there had been less "generosity" it would have resulted in the saving of *hundreds of thousands of lives.*

The context created by open-minded act-utilitarianism on the political landscape is not pretty. It was not paranoia that turned many socialists and trade unionists away from the Communists in disgust. Trotsky himself relates,

> . . . an episode which in spite of its modest dimensions, does not badly illustrate the difference between *their* morals and *ours.* In 1935, through a letter to my Belgian friends, I developed the conception that the attempt of a young revolutionary party to organize "its own" trade unions is equivalent to suicide. It is necessary to find the workers where they are.

But this means paying dues in order to sustain an opportunist apparatus? "Of course," I replied, "for the right to undermine the reformists it is necessary temporarily to pay them a contribution." But reformists will not permit us to undermine them? "True," I answered, "undermining demands conspirative measures. Reformists are the political police of the bourgeoisie within the working class. We must act without their permission and against their interdiction."[25]

If following a utilitarian principle leads to such actions, even if we have gotten to the point of being able to accept odious means because they lead to future good, we need to at least be sure that they do lead to the justifying ends. Once one has killed the hostages, their deaths define one in spite of one's intentions. One can no longer merely be one who thought their deaths were necessary; one is either one who killed when it was necessary or when it was not necessary. Either Trotsky was the same as Stalin or he was not.

Something happens to utilitarianism when it is political. The space within which "reasonable people may disagree" expands in the direction of including everything. No longer does utilitarianism circumscribe a friendly club within which all are good, reasonable, and well-intentioned people. All forms of monsters may enter that club. Once one seriously breaks with the unity that Kierkegaard demands and Gandhi seeks, once one is willing to let one's actions be determined by expected utility, one has let one's nature rest upon the adequacy of one's foresight. Under these circumstances, where one is willing to kill innocent hostages if this seems likely to produce the best consequences, one had best be right. In short, when fully acted out in political activity, the psychological space of the Benthamist mode drives itself into the very different space of the Trotskyist mode. The actions dictated by the rule of expected utility are such that they defeat the rationalist perspective on identity; they force one towards an objectivist position on identity.

Even outside the pressures generated by morally odious means, the objectivist perspective on identity generates pressures to believe one knows the facts. If one lives in terms of one's historical role, if one's self-identity is of a consequentialist sort because one's concept of identity is consequentialist, then it is one's highest level acts that are self-defining (i.e., the act of producing the distant consequence). When this is so, one has no actual experience of oneself as performing the acts that are self-defining. The meaning of one's present activity is not only not within one's immediate control, it is instead in the hands of others. These others exist in the historical future. One is bound to them because they will determine who you have been. Seen from the other direction, we bear the burden of determining the meaning of the actions of those long dead (e.g., the Jew who loses all Jewish self-identity renders futile the acts of those that chose to suffer rather than convert). What this means is that we cannot know the objective meaning of who we are unless we know the long-term consequences of our present activity. Without this knowledge one looks at one's present activity and knows only that it is giving one one's identity. But what that identity is, we do not know. If we have a self-identity generated out of our ideals and intentions and yet a consequentialist concept of identity, we do not know if we are really ourselves. Identity slips through our fingers. Political activity loses its capacity as a felt source of self-actualization. It becomes the realm within which our identity is established but no experienced self-actualization is ever warranted. The self we would have ourselves become may always be precisely what we are ruling out through our actions. It may not be psychologically possible to function with this awareness. Under such conditions, one must believe that one knows what one is doing; one must reject the rationalist's honesty with respect to how little he or she really knows.

This does not mean that rationalists are not to be found engaged in grand-scale political activity. What it suggests is that they have to avoid the rigorous application of the principle of expected utility. For then one enters realms of action where only a positive consequentialist self-identity can sustain one. And one will have to avoid a political view of the world and history, for this generates a political notion of identity. And finally one must act only when one knows a great deal, otherwise one's honest manner will undermine one's actions. In sum, rationalist engagement yields a self-imposed blindness and limitation. Thus, it too emerges as a mode of engagement necessarily rooted in self-deception.

POLITICAL SELF-DECEPTION

When a political agent is led to self-deception about how much he knows, he may find in extreme situations that he has to constantly maintain himself in a stance of not facing his limitations. He may have to actively screen himself from conflicting evidence. With this comes a particular form of separation of the self from activity. It is a separation that is visible in the manner with which the agent carries out his activity. It is a separation that manifests itself as the appearance of *more* engagement in the activity than one really has. This is fanaticism.

Fanaticism is not a matter of *what* is being done. An extreme act is not an act of fanaticism because of its content. If it is fanatical it is because of how it is done, in relation to the agent's beliefs and evidence. One can do an extreme act on slim grounds and not be a fanatic if one does it in a way that does not deny one's lack of knowledge. However, the extreme act often has a false manner because one feels a need for a fidelity of commitment that does not betray to oneself one's lack of confidence. One blinds oneself to one's misgivings. In this way the activity or series of activities lose their flexibility. They become stiff and mechanical; there no longer is a constant adjustment of behavior to awareness, to knowledge of new conditions. One "steels oneself up" because rigidity is required. One does not throw a bomb because one is a fanatic, nor is one a fanatic simply because one has thrown a bomb. Rather, we have to make ourselves fanatical in order to throw the bomb. Though the act itself might be justified in terms of maximum expected utility, most Benthamists cannot throw bombs.

It is not that a given activity type must be done in a specific manner. But rather that just as there are manners that reflect the degree of internal integration of the activity token, the degree to which the complex is an activity, so too different manners reflect different degrees of agency, different degrees to which the self is in the activity, to which it is self-activity. When there is a false manner, not only is much of the self not in the activity, but its falseness—by denying entry to one's beliefs and attitudes, to one's doubts and misgivings—denies entry to the self at all. In its extreme we call this madness.

It would be grossly unfair to the objectivist spirit to paint a picture in which the enormous pressure to actually know the consequences of actions leads only to coarse ideology, self-deception, and fanaticism. The most obvious response to the need to know is in fact to seek true knowledge, and Marx, for one, stands out for his understanding of the importance of social science to political activity. It is not surprising that Marx's major work falls largely within economics. The transition from what he called "utopian socialism" to "scientific socialism" is captured by the recognition of the importance of understanding the processes of social development. The abandonment of the spirit of utopianism is the abandonment of a belief in the power of individuals to create a radically different social order merely on the basis of a description of that order and the will to do so. Instead, the emphasis shifts to the necessity of understanding the nature of historical evolution, and situating political activity within the realm of possibilities revealed by an understanding of social change.

As understood by Marx, "scientific socialism" involved more than a reliance on knowledge. It involved a conception of a *method* of attaining that knowledge that is scientific. Broadly speaking we could talk of a method of experimentation, but when applied to social transformation this is not a matter of experimentation in one sphere and application in another. Rather, the actual attempt, the political process itself, is to become the method whereby one learns how to transform society. Thus in part Marxism faced the problem of the absence of knowledge by answering that the process of political change will be carried out in a manner that generates knowledge.

But beyond this, the process of transformation is seen as a way of solving the utopian's dilemma: "Who will teach the teachers?" Through the process of political activity not only does one gain necessary propositional knowledge that may be applied, but one brings into existence the kind of agents that are required to carry out the transformations. Thus the critical notion in the Marxist process is the creation of the revolutionary. This takes the explicit form of the proletariat's becoming a class that knows itself, not just in the sense of class identity but in terms of its fuller identity, which it comes to understand when it understands the nature of history and capitalism and its role in the transition to communism. Because the process involves transformations that are themselves grounded in economic development, the process is not voluntaristic. As such, it is not subject to the various forms of corruption and failure that have befallen experiments grounded solely in a moral ideal and will, most notably, the religious/utopian communities of the past, to which one might add twentieth-century Soviet Union.

All this is contained in Marx's notion of *praxis*. This notion significantly lifts the burden off the objectivist agent. She can accept the fact that it is possible that she may be in error on specifics because she sees herself as part of an extended piece of political activity carried out by an historical community of political actors who are engaged in a *method* of political activity and reflection that in the end will generate the knowledge that they need for their success. And when this is seen as the only way in which the needed transformations can come about, then even if one is wrong one is still part of a larger group of actors that will in the end have played the role one sees oneself as playing.

But what if there is no such praxis? Or what if we are unable to specify or to actually carry out political activity through which such learning occurs? Or what if we have no way of knowing whether it is we or others who are in fact carrying out such an activity? If this is the case, then having the idea of such a praxis is insufficient; it still remains the case that our identity is unknown and that our self-identity is subject to dissolution.

The sorry truth is that no such actual praxis has been discovered. If one is a possibility then it remains elusive. But if no such praxis has in fact been found, then how has alienness been avoided? First there is what we have discussed, false certainty and self-deception. But beyond this there is a deeper answer that does not lie in false belief. It lies in a different direction—the abandonment of the objectivist perspective on identity. For all the hardheaded analysis *of others* in terms of a consequentialist identity, for all the dismissal of intentions in favor of objective consequences, political activity has typically been made possible in the face of ignorance by a final reversal—good intentions are everything! Identity is defined ultimately in terms of intentions and thus political activity is not felt to be separated from the self because it arises from these intentions. So long as one knows what one is intending, one feels at one with oneself. This is the internal definition of voluntarism.

This retreat to intentions rather than knowledge of consequences as the source of the subjective self-identity of the political agent must be disguised from himself, for his political orientation insists that the only valid self-identity is that which is grounded in knowledge of true identity (i.e., objective consequences). And with this self-deception as to where his sense of identity is coming from, comes this as well: a turning away from a concern with truth.

Its worst manifestation within the Marxist tradition was the abandonment, by those that actually held state power through leadership in the Party, of a concern with whether what they lead is really the Party in any other sense than that they have given this name to the organization they dominate. Is it a party that will successfully lead the transformation of humanity and society? This is a question not solved but for a time resolved by silencing all voices that might question its actual identity.

In sum then, I have maintain that objectivism, especially Marxism, on the one hand deepens the sense of the alienness of aspects of self and drives one towards political activity as the one sphere in which one can truly be the agent of one's activity. Yet paradoxically, political activity is not an ideal vehicle for self-expression, and the Marxist orientation towards objective social consequences deepens the sense of alienness. On the other hand, a Marxist analysis of morality in terms of its social role helps to limit the sense of alienness that arises from moral conflict by locating one's moral strictures in a bracketed area of self (i.e., the person one finds oneself to be). But because of this freedom from moral restraint, even greater emphasis is placed on knowledge of the objective consequences. And here there are two roads to take. One tends to achieve integration of subjective self-identity with objective social identity through activity guided by knowledge of long-term consequences. The other focus is less on knowledge than on method. However, once we reject a belief in the proletariat as the transformed and transforming agent, we are left without any actual method or knowledge. Thus, the actual attainment of knowledge or the actual attainment of a self-correcting praxis becomes the only alternative to alienness, self-deception, or quietism for political beings.

It is because no actual praxis has been found, and because reality so often disconfirms the most confident expectations, that political identity and agency is unstable. Because of its comprehensive social and historical notion of identity it offers the promise of the only true self-actualization we can attain. Yet because of our finitude that same notion of identity generates contradictions too powerful to be long sustained by most people.

9

Alienated Labor

I conclude this study with a short discussion of Marx's discussion of alienation and human activity. I will not pursue this in depth, but some consideration of Marx's early writings is in order. These writings contain, from an historical point of view, the most important discussion of alienation, and the reader may be interested in how my discussion links to his. Specifically, I wish to show that my understanding of agency in terms of alienation finds its parallel in Marx's thought, particularly in his notion of *self-activity*. This concept has not received much attention from Marx's many commentators, and it is only through having reached an analogous formulation through a very different route that I have been able to appreciate Marx's formulation. I believe that it is these early writings of Marx that will in the future remain of most interest, and indeed, may become of more interest now that twentieth-century communism has been generally discredited.

AGENCY AND MARX'S NOTION OF SELF-ACTIVITY

Let me recall the distinctive features of the account of agency presented in the previous chapters. The question "Is he an agent?" has been treated as a distinct question from "Is it an action?" Agency is the presence of the self in its actions; and the sense of agency is the sense of the presence of the self in actions. To say that a person is alienated from some element of his or her self is to affirm the absence of integration between the self and that element; alienated activity is activity without agency. Alienness is the experienced awareness of alienation.

Activities are understood as internally integrated complexes. Both agency and activity are matters of degree. Some activity types (forms) lend themselves to greater degrees of activity in their performance; two tokens of a given type may differ in their degree of activity.

This account fits well with Marx's outlook. For him the dominant forms of activity are *historically* given. Only in a given historical period will doing an activity of a given type be a means for sustaining life. As activities are complexes that include things external to the body and mind of the individual, the shift in these externals throughout history produces a shift in the available forms of activity. In different periods people work on different raw materials, with different tools and machines, with different perceptual faculties, and for different purposes. These differences do not primarily reflect differences between individuals, but rather differences between historical eras. The individual is faced with the given limitations of his particular historical period, each of which is typified by the dominance of certain activity types. Economic change at its essence is change in the specific kinds of activities human beings engage in.

Not only are the available activity types different for different historical periods, they also differ in the extent to which they are expressions of the individual who is doing the work. In part this is a reflection of the internal structures of the dominant activity types. In the language of the preceding chapters, there is more activity to the dominant types in a period of production via individual craftspeople than there is in a period of industrialization with its standardization and mechanization of the productive process. The fact that in one period workers are interchangeable, with little or no necessary training or apprenticeship, reflects the internal structure of the dominant activity types. In *Wage Labour and Capital* Marx writes,

> as the *division of labour* increases, labour is *simplified*. The special skill of the worker becomes worthless. He becomes transformed into a simple, monotonous productive force that does not have to use intense bodily or intellectual faculties. His labour becomes a labour that anyone can perform.[1]

Activity expresses the individual differently in different eras for another reason: it may be chosen for reasons that are themselves more or less expressive of the individual. In the era of wage labour, the worker works merely to stay alive. This is the constriction of the relationship of the person to his or her actions to a single means–ends connection. Using the concept of agency in the way I have explicated it, one could say that each historical era offers different degrees to which the individual may actually be an agent with respect to his or her own activity.

It is hard to overemphasize the importance of these factors for Marx. Insofar as we may talk of a Marxian ideal, it is best described as the full self-expression of the developed individual through activity. The drama of historical development is a matter of the changes in the extent, manner, and general possibility of self-expression through activity; history is a process through which an evolving and developing human personality is brought into being through these very changes. For Marx the degree and nature of the possible self-expression of the individual through his or her labor is not merely an effect of historical change. It is the driving force of that change.

It is in *The German Ideology*[2] that he develops his view of the full historical significance of blocked self-expression. These passages offer an understanding of the way the condition of alienated labor functions *within* the materialist view of history.

In reading Marx's account of historical change, it is important to recognize that when he lays stress on the significance of changes in the forces of production, this is not at the expense of human beings as historical agents. He emphasizes that "revolution is the driving force of history,"[3] and that "circumstances make men just as much as men make circumstances."[4] Thus, in his view an adequate historical explanation will tell us both why people act (e.g., make a revolution) in their own terms *and* why their terms *are* as they *are* (as well as when they will be successful).

Marx employs a set of concepts that are used in explaining historical events in the agent's terms. Without defining them, he introduces concepts such as "self-activity" and "what belongs to an individual as a person." As we shall see, these concepts play a basic role in his description of history. Time and time again, Marx draws attention to the workers' *experience of their own activity*. He writes, "only the proletarians of the present day, who are completely shut off from all self-activity, are in a position to achieve a complete and no longer restricted self-activity."[5]

The proletarian revolution differs in that it can achieve *unrestricted* self-activity but not in its achieving self-activity per se. Indeed, history itself can be described in terms of what is or is not a condition that permits self-activity.

> The conditions under which individuals have intercourse with each other, so long as the above-mentioned contradiction is absent, are conditions appertaining to their individuality, in no way external to them; conditions under which these definite individuals, living under definite relationships, can alone produce their material life, and what is connected with it; are thus the *conditions of their self-activity* and are produced by this self-activity. (my emphasis)[6]

But conditions that may at one point in time be conditions of self-activity may subsequently be conditions within which self-activity is stifled.

> These various conditions which appear first as conditions of self-activity, later as fetters upon it, form in the whole evolution of history a coherent series of forms of intercourse, the coherence of which consists in this: that in the place of an earlier form of intercourse which has become a fetter, a new one is put, corresponding to the more developed productive forces, and hence, to the *more advanced mode of the self-activity of* individuals—a form which in its turn becomes a fetter and is then replaced by another. (my emphasis)[7]

Marx is careful to warn against mistakenly imputing to earlier ages an experience of their conditions that is had only by later ages.

> The definite condition under which they produce, thus *corresponds,* as long as the contradiction has not yet appeared, to the *reality* of their conditioned nature, their one-sided existence, the one-sideness of which only becomes evident when the contradiction enters on the scene and thus *only exists for the later individuals.* Then this condition appears as an accidental fetter, and the consciousness that it is a fetter is imputed to the earlier age as well. (my emphasis)[8]

Marx seems to be saying that at a certain stage people do not experience themselves as fettered (unfree, restricted, unexpressed) in their activity, even though they are. At some later point they have a different and more accurate experience of their conditions.

If the term "agency" is substituted for the term "self-activity," then Marx is making an historical point similar to what I suggested earlier: that the individual's experience of agency (or freedom) depends upon how the individual identifies himself or herself. For Marx this is not merely true of specific individuals but of classes of individuals.

In the era of industrialization, the division of labor is carried to its furthest point. It is extended to all phases of activity and into the activity itself. There is a "division of the conditions of labour, tools, and materials."[9] These do not belong to the worker, for she works for the industrialist for money. This unrestricted division of labor produces a change in the worker's relationship to her work. It may be contrasted with a period in which the division of labor was still "natural" (i.e., based on natural dispositions, needs, accidents). Describing the earlier, more restricted division of labor, Marx writes:

> In the town, the division of labour between the individual guilds was as yet quite natural, and, in the guilds themselves, not at all developed between the individual workers. Every workman had to be versed in a whole round of tasks, had to be able to make everything that was to be made with his tools. The limited commerce and the scanty communication between the individual towns, the lack of population and the narrow needs did not allow of a higher division of labour, and therefore every man who wished to become a master had to be proficient in the whole of his craft. Thus, there is to be found with the medieval craftsmen an interest in their special work and a proficiency in it, which was capable of rising to a narrow artistic sense. For this very reason, however, every medieval craftsman was completely absorbed in his work, to which he had a contented, slavish relationship, and to which he was subjected to a far greater extent than the modern worker, whose work is a matter of indifference to him.[10]

With the unrestricted division of labor, the condition of the worker worsens specifically in the internal features of work activity.

> Never, in any earlier period, have the productive forces taken on a form so indifferent to the intercourse of individuals *as* individuals, . . .
> The only connection which still links them with the productive forces and with their own existence—labour—*has lost all semblance of self-activity* and only sustains their life by stunting it. While in the earlier periods self-activity and the production of material life were separated, in that they devolved on different persons, and while, *on account of the narrowness of the individuals themselves,* the production of material life was considered as a subordinate mode of self-activity, they now diverge to such an extent that finally material life appears as an end, and what produces this material life, labour (which is now the only possible, but as we see, negative form of self-activity) as the means.[11]

When Marx says that "finally material life appears as an end . . . and labour as a means" he is calling attention to the fact that the way in which we tend to think of economic life is itself an historical product. In earlier eras, economic activity was not viewed as a means to an end (e.g., consumption) but was viewed as having an inherent significance as a realm within which the self was expressed. It is only when the possibility of agency or self-activity within the economic sphere diminishes to almost nothing that we lose sight altogether of the economic sphere as a sphere of direct self-actualization.

As a result of this process there develops "a class which forms the majority of all members of the society, and from which emanates *the consciousness of the necessity* of a fundamental revolution."[12] This revolution is different from preceding revolutions, and this difference is based on what is now necessary to attain self-activity.

> All earlier revolutionary appropriations were restricted; individuals, whose self-activity was restricted by a crude instrument of production and a limited intercourse, appropriated this crude instrument of production, and hence merely achieved a new state of limitation.[13]

In this revolution, conditions are such that self-activity can only be obtained by altering the very nature of production itself. *The dominant activity types of the age must be transformed.*

> In all revolutions up to now the mode of activity always remained unscathed and it was only a question of different distribution of this activity, a new distribution of labour to other persons, whilst the communist revolution is directed against the preceding *mode* of activity, does away with *labour*, and abolishes the rule of all classes with the classes themselves.[14]

It is important to recognize that the denial of self-activity is something that emerges in the experience of the class that revolts. Otherwise the concept of "self-activity" would have no place in an historical explanation that proceeds from specific historical individuals who make a revolution, having come to a consciousness of its necessity. If the consciousness of the individual was not a crucial intervening variable, the historical account would degenerate into the deduction of revolution from the concept of the self-estrangement of humanity. Thus, Marx writes:

> The difference between *the individual as a person* and what is *accidental to him*, is not a conceptual difference but an historical fact. This distinc-

tion has a different significance at different times—e.g. the estate as something accidental to the individual in the eighteenth century, the family more or less too. It is not a distinction we have to make for each age, but one which each age makes itself. (my emphasis)[15]

In this crucial passage Marx is explaining the logic of his concept of self-activity. What he seems to be saying is that what is or is not self-activity differs in different ages. To determine what is self-activity one does not apply some ideal of the self to history, rather one reads it off from history. And the way one reads it off is not by measuring history against some conception of the self (which need not be ideal) but by attending to the distinction made by the age itself. If this is transformed into the terms I have been using, it appears to say that agency (which is what Marx means by self-activity) is a function of the specific individual's self-identity. Depending on how one understands one's own identity, one will experience oneself as free or unfree within a productive process. And further, the self-identity of individuals is itself a social product. Thus, the distinction between what is and is not self-activity is not made by the application of a theory but is brought about by material conditions. This accounts for its being a distinction made by the *age*, and not one made differently by each individual living in that age. Thus, in developing "self-activity" as a concept to be used in historical explanation, Marx endeavors to steer a course between a metaphysical view of the self and a subjective view of the self.

In the proletarian revolution the workers' self-identity will be expressed in their efforts to abolish wage labor and will itself be transformed by that revolution:

The transformation of labour into self-activity corresponds to the transformation of the earlier limited intercourse into the intercourse of individuals as such. . . . Whilst previously in history a particular condition always appeared as accidental, now the isolation of individuals and the particular private gain of each man have themselves become accidental.[16]

Here he is asserting that workers will come to see their very separation from each other as inconsistent with their fulfillment—they will experience themselves in such a way that they will not be able to experience themselves as free so long as they remain isolated individuals. Their very fulfillment requires their overcoming their isolation.

To put this in the vocabulary I offered in previous chapters, Marx is saying that through the process of social change, the self-identity of workers will change so that they come to understand themselves as part of a collectivity. And in terms of that changed self-identity they will only be able to experience activity as self-expressive when it is part of a cooperative rather than competitive effort, when each is acting for the good of all, rather than for his own isolated good. But this is not merely a matter of motivation; for it to be real it must be reflected in changed structures of ownership; in particular, in the abolition of private property.

Thus, Marx's account of historical change rests upon not only the consciousness of individuals that produce revolutions, but very specific kinds of consciousness. At the center is the individual's *experience* of his or her activity as not-being-self-activity. This in turn rests upon the individual's self-identity, which has undergone, in the final stage, a transformation such that separation from other individuals is experienced as separation from oneself.

WORKERS AND ALIENATED WORK

Within this general framework of how self-identity and thus the experience of self-activity (agency) is transformed by economic change and is itself a central factor in producing political transformation, the *Economic and Philosophic Manuscripts of 1844* can be read as an in-depth analysis of the situation of self-activity in the industrial period. To speak of alienated labor is to speak of the absence of self-activity (agency). First I will consider the nature of the worker's *experience*; then in the final section I will deal with the state of alienation and its relation to this experience.

Marx asks, "What then, constitutes the alienation of labour?" He answers:

First, the fact that labour is *external* to the worker, i.e., it does not belong to his essential being; that in his work, therefore, he does not affirm himself but denies himself, does not feel content but unhappy, does not develop freely his physical and mental energy but mortifies his body and ruins his mind. The worker therefore only feels himself outside his work, and in his work feels outside himself. He is at home when he is not working, and when he is working he is not at home. His labour is therefore not voluntary, but coerced; it is *forced labour*. It is therefore not the satisfaction of a need; it is merely a *means* to satisfy needs external to it. Its alien character emerges clearly in the fact that as soon as no physical or other compulsion exists, labour is shunned like the plague. External labour, labour in which man alienated himself, is a labour of self-sacrifice, or mortification. Lastly, the external character of labour for the worker appears in the fact that it is not his own, but someone else's, that it does not belong to him, that in it he belongs, not to himself, but to another. Just as in religion the spontaneous activity of the human imagination, of the human brain and the human heart, operates independently of the individual—that is, operated on him as an alien, divine or diabolical activity—in the same way the worker's activity is to his spontaneous activity. It belongs to another; it is the loss of his self.[17]

This multidimensional characterization can be sorted into conceptually distinct elements:

Phenomenological
1. The worker does not feel content; he is unhappy
2. He only feels himself outside his work; in his work he feels outside himself

Behavioral dispositions
3. If no physical or other compulsion exists, labor is shunned like the plague

Motivation
4. His labor is not voluntary but coerced; it is forced labor
5. It is not the satisfaction of a need, but merely a means to satisfy needs external to it

Relation to his identity
6. The labor is external to the worker, i.e., it does not belong to his essential being
7. In his work he does not affirm himself but denies himself

Effects
8. He does not develop freely his physical and mental energy but mortifies his body and ruins his mind
9. It is a labor of self-sacrifice, or mortification

External relations
10. It is not his own, but someone else's; it does not belong to him
11. In it he belongs, not to himself, but to another

The catalogue he provides is in many respects the same as those factors considered in my discussion of the structural web that links self and activity when there is agency. And it is tempting to say rather simply that the alienated laborer is not the agent of his activity and that he experiences alienness in the performance of his work. We are told that in his work he feels "outside himself" and that the activity "does not belong to him." But this would not be accurate.

The worker Marx describes does not have the depth of inner incoherence I have been considering. The key point about the alienated worker is that *he knows why he is doing what he is doing.* He acts out of a desire and objective that is genuinely his own. In *Wage Labour and Capital* Marx writes:

> Labour power is, therefore, a commodity which its possessor, the wage-worker, sells to capital. Why does he sell it? *In order to* live.
>
> But the exercise of labour power, labour, is the worker's own life-activity, the manifestation of his own life. And this *life-activity* he sells to another person in order to secure the necessary means of subsistence. Thus his life-activity is for him only a means to enable him to exist. He works in order to live. He does not even reckon labour as part of his life, it is rather a sacrifice of his life. It is a commodity which he has made over to another. Hence, also, the product of his activity is not the object of his activity. What he produces for himself is not the silk that he weaves, not the gold that he draws from the mine, not the palace that he builds. What he produces for himself is wages, and silk, gold, palace resolve themselves for him into a definite quantity of the means of subsistence, perhaps into a cotton jacket, some copper coins and a lodging in a cellar. And the worker, who for twelve hours weaves, spins, turns, builds, shovels, breaks stones, carries loads, etc.—does he consider this twelve hours' weaving, spinning, drilling, turning, building, shoveling, stone breaking as a manifestation of his life, as life? On the contrary, life begins for him where this activity ceases, at table, in the public house, in bed. The twelve hours' labour, on the other hand, has no meaning for him as weaving, spinning, drilling etc., but as earnings, which bring him to the table, to the public house, into bed.[18]

What Marx describes is the complete absence of any agency or self-activity *in* the work. All the activities—spinning, drilling, turning, building—are themselves no longer manifestations of life. The worker has sold his life in order to live. And yet, as extreme as this situation is, the worker *does* have one of the most important forms of integration between himself and his activity. He knows why the activity is done. He does it for a reason and he is aware of that reason.

Moreover, the act of selling his life-activity is something that itself emerges from a self that is reasonably well integrated. The ends he believes he will attain are consistent with his values (he keeps himself alive, he prevents his family from dying). His beliefs are well founded. The higher level acts that are generated by the work activity are an expression of his self.

It is the work itself, the physical activity, which fails, in-itself, to be self-expressive, and may be self-destructive. The product, as ongoing outcome, does not express his values, his aesthetic, his personality. He lacks the most *intimate* connections with his activity. In part, this occurs because the form of the activity does not permit a great deal of perceptual modifiability. The production process has been redesigned so as to limit the amount of individuality that *can* enter the product. The worker has no opportunity of producing anything that is a distinct expression of himself; and those aspects of himself that are central do not enter the product.

Given this situation we may say that the worker is aware of herself as in a minimal yet powerful state of connectedness with her activity. She experiences the labor as not expressing the core of her being, but she also knows that in doing it she does express something of herself: her need for money, her understanding of the marketplace, her determination to support her family, her commitment to her children, and so on. This is a powerful, yet purely instrumental connection. It comes from her, but she is not active in it. While her sense of agency is partial, it is sufficient to yield an experience of the action as her own; the alienated worker is not having alienness experiences when she feels alienated from her work.

To grasp Marx's perception of the worker's experience, here as elsewhere, it is important to know his view of the long-term level of wages. Since Marx believed that these must decline, we may assume that he believed that in the long run the worker would not experience his work as part of the project of achieving "freedom" or self-activity for himself or his family.

The fact that the worker as described by Marx does not experience alienness makes sense given the absolute necessity of the work in order to keep himself and his family alive. But when we shift to the contemporary period, we find that Marx was totally wrong about wage levels. Compared to what Marx envisioned, the worker of today does not have to do what he does. The income level necessary for physical survival in the industrialized countries is only a tiny fraction of what most people today earn. And for much of the population in a country such as the United States, there is the well-confirmed belief that it is possible through focused schooling, hard work, savings, and good luck to achieve movement out of any particular class position, if not in a single lifetime, then at least for one's children.

For the modern individual, work can and does become part of a complex individual and familial project. Not only is there some degree of economic opportunity for almost all members of the society, but for those with considerable opportunity, managing that opportunity becomes the central life project. And it is this individual with opportunity and options, not Marx's alienated workers, for whom alienness is a possibility. The contemporary economic agent cannot explain to himself what he does in terms of the necessity of survival. Rather he has to explain it to himself in terms of social and economic objectives that he holds for himself and his family. But these objectives and calculations are ones that he may come to see as not really his own. And if he reaches that turn, a point at which his own objectives—be they the objectives expected of him by his culture or background—appear to him to be foreign and unintelligible, it is then that he will experience his life as having not been his own.

And in this I think Marx was correct, that it is this perception that our life is not our own that can prove to be a powerful political force seeking thoroughgoing political and social change—in particular change that seeks to transform our sense of self in such a way that we do not experience ourselves as confirmed when we have outstripped the other in competitions that by definition can only have a few winners.

Put in these terms, alienness may be the wave of the future. The present moment (Fall 1990), which the apostles of competitive markets and economic individualism regard as a decisive historical triumph, is likely to pass, and rather quickly. It is a great irony, but I believe that after we have passed through the flush of self-congratulations now so present in the market economies, the demise of communism as a system will be a major cause of our turning inward and discovering that much of our own economic and social life renders us unintelligible to ourselves. The alienness that emerges from this realization is one that can play a constructive role in shaping and solidifying a sense of self in terms of which many of the most basic structures of contemporary economic and social life will be experienced as fetters that block self-activity. And if this occurs, there will be new energy and renewed interest in radically different economic and social alternatives that give rise to and confirm radically different self-identities.

We have not reached the end of our socioeconomic evolution. The next phase will be one in which the economic sphere is once again perceived as a realm of inherent significance, one in which we seek to become full agents of our activity.

References

Chapter 1

1. Ludwig Wittgenstein, *Philosophical Investigations,* trans. G.E.M. Anscombe (New York: Macmillan, 1953), sec. 621.

2. See H. L. A. Hart, "The Ascription of Rights and Responsibilities," in *Logic and Language,* ed. Anthony Flew (Garden City: Anchor Books, 1965).

3. Parfit uses these terms to categorize two different views of what a person is. They serve well to grasp two different accounts of what agency is, and it would seem that they are related. If one had a reductionist view of what a person was it would be hard to understand what a nonreductionist view of agency would be. But it might be possible to have a nonreductionist view of the self (as a Cartesian ego) and still have a reductionist view of agency.

4. Roderick Chisholm, "The Agent as Cause," in *Action Theory,* ed. Myles Brand and Douglas Walton (Dordrecht, Holland: D. Reidel, 1976), 199.

5. Richard Taylor, *Action and Purpose* (Englewood Cliffs: Prentice-Hall, 1970), 134.

6. Roderick Chisholm, "Freedom and Action," in *Freedom and Determinism,* ed., Keith Lehrer (New York: Random House, 1966), 20.

7. Chisholm, "The Agent as Cause," 210.

8. See, for instance, Irving Thalberg, "How Does Agent Causality Work?" in *Action Theory,* ed. Myles Brand and Douglas Walton (Dordrecht, Holland: D. Reidel, 1976).

9. Lawrence Davis, *Theory of Action* (Engelwood Cliffs: Prentice-Hall, 1979).

10. See Lawrence Davis, "Wayward Causal Chains," in *Action and Respon-*

253

sibility, ed. Michael Bradie and Myles Brand (Bowling Green: The Applied Philosophy Program, Bowling Green State University, 1980), 55.

11. It might be maintained that if we had a complete account of what occurs physiologically when we act that this would in fact shed some light on the philosophic problem of actions. With this I do not disagree, but it does not lend support to Goldman's specific analysis. My belief is that detailed physiological analyses will tend to support the very different analysis I provide in Chapter 2.

12. A. I. Meldon, *Free Action* (London: Routledge and Kegan Paul, 1961), 7–9.

Chapter 2

1. The examples are to be taken narrowly. Taken broadly they signify compound rather than molecular activities.

2. I regard the claim that activities are always caused by wants and beliefs as a sort of psychosocio myth. The tendency to so conceive human behavior is furthered by analyses of actions as events or bodily movements caused by volitions, intentions, or wants. These mental states play no necessary role in an account of activity, and I regard them as often having the status of mythic entities introduced to make behavior, which would otherwise have to be explained along other lines, seem rational. This fictional world is not the creation of philosophers; it is participated in quite generally. It is part of a general human self-perception that no doubt predates systematic philosophizing. From this self-perception there flows, in everyday life, the earnest yet erroneous attribution of wants and beliefs to oneself. Indeed, this is more than mere attribution, for such attributions play a role in the creation and wants and beliefs, though they come into being at a point subsequent to the behavior they are often thought to have prompted. This elimination of certain forms of alienness through the postulation of relevant wants and beliefs functions to make one seem less strange to oneself. It thus reduces the sense of conflict and fragmentation, and thus, drawing attention away from the causes of our alienness, it becomes morally and politically significant.

Chapter 3

1. Patanjali, *Yogi Sutras* (Allahabad: The Liverpool Press, 1924), 29.

2. Patanjali, *Yogi Sutras,* 31.

3. Ibid., 32.

4. Ibid., 96.

5. Ibid., xii.

6. Plato, *The Republic,* trans. Cornford (New York: Oxford University Press, 1945), 140.

7. Plato, *The Republic,* 142.

8. Plotinus, *The Enneads,* trans. S. MacKenna (London: Farber and Farber, 1969), 159.

9. Friedrich Nietzsche, *Thus Spoke Zarathustra* in *The Portable Nietzsche,* ed. Walter Kaufman (New York: Doubleday, 1956), 147.

10. Nietzsche, *Zarathustra,* 137–39.

11. D. H. Lawrence, *Psychoanalysis and the Unconscious* (New York: The Viking Press, 1960), 11.

12. Lawrence, *Psychoanalysis,* 15.

13. Ibid., 16.

14. Villiers de l'Isle-Adam, "The Desire to be a Man," in *The Existential Imagination,* ed. Karl and Hamalian (New York: Fawcett Publications, 1967), 92.

15. Frithjof Bergmann, *On Being Free* (Notre Dame: University of Notre Dame Press, 1977).

16. Bergmann, *On Being Free,* 64.

17. Ibid., 65.

18. Ibid., 82.

19. Ibid., 84.

20. William McDougall, "Organization of the Affective Life," *Acta Psychologia* 2, no. 3 (1937):469.

21. Marcus Aurelius, *Meditations,* in *The Perfectibility of Man,* trans. John Passmore (Scribner: New York, 1970), 56.

22. Anthony Storr, *The Integrity of the Personality* (Baltimore: Penguin Books, 1963).

23. Carl Jung, *The Integration of the Personality,* trans. Dell (New York: Farrar and Rinehart, 1939).

24. Harold Searles, *Collected Papers on Schizophrenia and Related Subjects* (New York: International Universities Press, 1965).

25. Searles, *Collected Papers,* 468.

26. Ibid., 469.

27. Ibid., 470.

28. Ibid., 471.

29. Ibid., 403.

30. Ibid., 405.

31. See Schactel, "On Alienated Concepts of Identity," in *Man Alone,* ed. Eric and Mary Josephson (New York: Dell, 1962).

32. Heinz Kohut, *The Restoration of the Self* (New York: International Universities Press, 1977), 57.

Chapter 4

1. Harry Frankfurt, "Freedom of the Will and the Concept of a Person," in *Free Will,* ed. Gary Watson (New York: Oxford University Press, 1982), 92.

2. Frankfurt, "Freedom," 86.

3. Ibid., 91.

4. John M. Fisher, ed. *Moral Responsibility* (Ithaca: Cornell University Press, 1986), 48.

5. Gary Watson, "Free Agency," in *Free Will,* ed. Gary Watson (New York: Oxford University Press, 1982), 97.

6. Watson, "Free Agency," 104.

7. Ibid., 105.

8. Ibid., 106.

9. Ibid., 107.

10. Ibid., 109.

11. Clark Moustakis, *The Self* (New York: Harper, 1956), 3.

12. Norman O. Brown, *Psychology Today,* Aug. 1970, 44.

13. Heinz Kohut, *The Restoration of the Self* (New York: International Universities Press, 1977), 5.

Chapter 5

1. Karl Jaspers, *General Psychopathology* (Chicago: University of Chicago, 1963), 121.

2. H. J. Shorvon, in *Proceedings of the Royal Society of Medicine* 39 (1946):779, as quoted in Brian Ackner, "Depersonalization," *Journal of Medical Science* 100 (October 1954):844.

3. Edith Jacobson, "Depersonalization," paper presented to the New York Psychoanalytic Society," February 1, 1958.

4. M. N. Searl, "A Note on Depersonalization," *International Journal of Psycho-analysis* 13 (1932):329.

5. R. D. Laing, *The Divided Self* (Baltimore: Penguin, 1965), 73.

6. Laing, *The Divided Self,* 80.

7. Ibid., 87.

Chapter 6

1. Friedrich Nietzsche, *Twilight of the Idols,* in *The Portable Nietzsche,* ed. Walter Kaufman (New York: Doubleday, 1956), 501.

2. Nietzsche, *Zarathustra,* 171.

3. Ibid., 148.

4. Hans Reichenbach, *The Rise of Scientific Philosophy* (Berkeley: University of California Press, 1959), 302.

5. Reichenbach, *Rise,* 292.

6. Friedrich Nietzsche, *The Genealogy of Morals,* in *The Birth of Tragedy and the Genealogy of Morals,* trans. F. Golfing (New York: Doubleday, 1956), 178.

7. Nietzsche, *Zarathustra,* 146.

8. David Hume, *A Treatise of Human Nature,* Book I (Cleveland: World, 1962), 328.

9. Derek Parfit, *Reasons and Persons* (Oxford: Clarendon Press, 1984), 281.

10. Parfit, *Reasons and Persons,* 281.

11. Ibid., 279.

12. Ibid., 254.

13. Ibid., 63.

14. Ibid., 274.

15. Ibid., 307.

16. Ibid., 305.

17. Nietzsche or Lawrence might warn of the danger that in so viewing one's life one might lose touch with the present, not just for a moment but throughout one's life. And thus, one would have lost touch completely with one's real self.

18. This possibility also opens wide the potential for self-deception.

19. Jean-Paul Sartre, *Being and Nothingness* (New York: Philosophical Library, 1956).

20. Sartre, *Being and Nothingness,* 55.

21. Ibid.

22. Ibid., 56,

23. Ibid.

24. Ibid.

25. Ibid., 57–58.

26. Ibid., 58.

27. Ibid.

28. Ibid.

29. Ibid., 59.

30. Ibid., 60.

31. Ibid.

32. Ibid., 62.

33. Ibid., 63.

34. Ibid.

35. Ibid., 64.

36. Ibid., 59.

37. Parfit, *Reasons and Persons,* 280.

Chapter 7

1. Perry Miller, *The New England Mind* (Boston: Beacon Press, 1968).

2. Augustine, *Confessions* (Middlesex: Penguin, 1961), 164–65.

3. Augustine, *Confessions,* 174.

4. John Donne, *Sermon XV,* folio of 1690, in *Seventeenth Century Prose and Poetry,* ed. Witherspoon and Warnke (New York: Harcourt, Brace and World, 1963), 71.

5. Herbert Fingarette, *Self-Deception* (London: Routledge and Kegan Paul, 1969), 82.

6. Fingarette, *Self-Deception,* 40.

7. Ibid., 67.

8. Ibid., 87.

9. Herbert Fingarette, *On Responsibility* (New York: Basic Books, 1967), 87.

Chapter 8

1. William Shakespeare, The Second Part of King Henry IV, I.i. 189.

2. Andre Malraux, *Man's Fate,* trans. H. Chevalier (New York: Random House, 1961).

3. Malraux, *Man's Fate,* 145.

4. Karl Marx, *Captial,* trans. S. Moore and E. Aveling (New York: Random House, 1906), 81.

5. Leon Trotsky, "Their Morals and Ours," *New International* (June 1938):172.

6. Leon Trotsky, "Moralists and Sycophants Against Marxism," *New International* (August 1939):231–33.

7. Soren Kierkegaard, *Purity of Heart is to Will One Thing,* trans. D. Steere (New York: Harper and Row, 1956), 201–03.

8. Erik Erikson, *Gandhi's Truth* (New York: Norton, 1969), 412–17.

9. M. K. Gandhi, *An Autobiography or the Story of My Experiments With Truth* (Ahmedabad: Navajivan, 1948), 259.

10. Gandhi, *Autobiography,* 388.

11. Ibid., 384.

12. Leon Trotsky, "An Open Letter to the Workers of India," in *The Age of Permanent Revolution: A Trotsky Anthology,* ed. Isaac Deutscher (New York: Dell, 1964), 248.

13. John Dewey, "Means and Ends," *New International* (August 1938):232.

14. Dewey, *Means,* 232.

15. Ibid., 232.

16. Jeremy Bentham, *Principles of Morals and Legislation* in *The Utilitarians* (Garden City: Doubleday, 1961), 17.

17. Leon Trotsky, "Ends and Means in Morality," in *The Age of Permanent Revolution,* ed. Isaac Deutscher (New York: Dell, 1964), 340.

18. Trotsky, "Ends," 340–41.

19. Ibid., 334.

20. Ibid.

21. Kierkegaard, "Purity of Heart," 203.

22. Trotsky, "Their Morals," 169.

23. Ibid.

24. Ibid.

25. Ibid., 171.

Chapter 9

1. Karl Marx, *Wage Labor and Capital, Selected Works* (New York: International Publishers, 1968), 92.
2. Karl Marx and Friedrich Engels, *The German Ideology,* Parts 1 and 3, ed. R. Pascal (New York: International Publishers, 1947).
3. Marx and Engels, *German Ideology,* 29.
4. Ibid.
5. Ibid., 67.
6. Ibid., 71.
7. Ibid., 71–72.
8. Ibid., 71.
9. Ibid., 65.
10. Ibid., 46–47.
11. Ibid., 65–66.
12. Ibid., 69.
13. Ibid., 67.
14. Ibid., 69.
15. Ibid., 70–71.
16. Ibid., 68.
17. Karl Marx, *The Economic and Philosophical Manuscripts of 1844,* trans. Martin Milligan (Moscow: Foreign Languages Publishing House, 1961), 72–73.
18. Marx, "Wage Labor and Capital," 74–75.

About the Author

Jerome M. Segal is a research scholar at the Institute for Philosophy and Public Policy at the University of Maryland, College Park. He is the author of *Creating the Palestinian State: A Strategy for Peace* (Lawrence Hill, 1989).